Praise for Robert K. Fitts's *Mashi: The Unfulfilled Baseball Dreams of Masanori Murakami, the First Japanese Major Leaguer*

"This is an excellent baseball story, a story of cultural adaptation and conflict, and above all the story of one man's opportunity and the obstacles he overcame to make the most of that opportunity."
—**Duncan Jamieson**, *Journal of Sport Literature*

"Mashi Murakami's impact can still be felt in baseball stadiums on both sides of the Pacific. He is a pioneer in every sense of the word—a true ambassador for the game of baseball."
—**Allan H. "Bud" Selig**, the ninth commissioner of baseball

"Fitts, coupled with Murakami's voice and experiences, tells the proud tale of a young man who was whisked into the spotlight and became a shining example of the equality that could be reached between the Japanese and Americans on the baseball diamond. Reading *Mashi* brings us all a few steps closer to what it was like to be there on this landmark journey."
—*San Francisco Examiner*

"Rob Fitts has fabulously transported us back to Mashi's family roots, childhood passion for the grand game, and his trajectory to become the first Major Leaguer from Japan. It is a discovery and rediscovery of culture, baseball dynamics/politics, and the man who transcended the sport as a gigantic touchstone 'pioneer' for future players from Asia."
—**Kerry Yo Nakagawa**, author of *Through a Diamond: 100 Years of Japanese American Baseball*

"Sometimes historical analysis can't compete with a good personal story, as Robert K. Fitts—a baseball expert and former archaeologist—proves with his newest book, *Mashi*."
—*Japan Times*

Praise for Robert K. Fitts's *Issei Baseball: The Story of the First Japanese American Ballplayer*

2021 SABR Baseball Research Award

"Long before Ichiro Suzuki and Shohei Ohtani, Japanese Issei were trying to prove they were the best immigrant baseball players in America. During the Jim Crow era of Major League Baseball, a handshake and a victory on the field were their just reward. Rob Fitts majestically re-creates the mood of the era and sheds light on a glorious period of this epic American odyssey."
—**Kerry Yo Nakagawa**, author, filmmaker, and historian

"Rob Fitts is not only an esteemed baseball historian; he's also one of the top writers in the game today. He excels at painting pictures with words and taking the reader on a journey back in time with his prose. *Issei Baseball* is an enjoyable read for true baseball fans."
—**Bill Staples Jr.**, coauthor of *Gentle Black Giants: A History of Negro Leaguers in Japan*

"Robert K. Fitts's *Issei Baseball* meticulously tells the important story about the Japanese's essential role in the history of baseball in a way that not only will inform its readers but will also ensure that Issei's story is never forgotten."
—**R. Zachary Sanzone**, *NINE: A Journal of Baseball History and Culture*

"Fitts provides a historical account that illustrates the work happening within the Japanese American community to organize, promote, and cover Issei baseball."
—**Katherine Walden**, *Western Historical Quarterly*

"A book rich in detail, Robert K. Fitts's *Issei Baseball* adds a valuable piece to the story of the Japanese people in America and is a noteworthy contribution to the legacy of the Issei and the game they loved."
—**Samuel O. Regalado**, author of *Nikkei Baseball: Japanese American Players from Immigration and Internment to the Major Leagues*

Praise for Robert K. Fitts's *Banzai Babe Ruth: Baseball, Espionage, and Assassination during the 1934 Tour of Japan*

"How did two nations that shared the values of the same national pastime go from baseballs to bullets? Historian Rob Fitts tells a dark tale of baseball caught between democracy and fascism in prewar Japan. Banzai Babe Ruth is a sayonara home run!"
—**John Thorn**, official historian for Major League Baseball

"This is a well-researched, fascinatingly told tale of two superpowers whose shared passion for baseball wasn't enough to maintain the peace, though it did help to restore it in the years following World War II."
—**James Bailey**, *Baseball America*

"This dramatic story, equal parts baseball and history, should appeal to anyone interested in Japanese cultural and political history and the sports-politics nexus."
—*Library Journal*

"Admirable and deeply researched."
—**T. Rees Shapiro**, *Washington Post*

"*Banzai Babe Ruth* is far more than just a sports story. . . . No one could have told this incredible story better than Robert K. Fitts."
—*ForeWord magazine*

"If I could have taken one road trip with anyone in the history of American sport, I think I would have traveled with Babe Ruth and the All American All-Stars on their eighteen-game tour of Japan in November 1934. With the drumbeat growing louder and louder as World War II approached, with the Babe suddenly at loose ends near the end of his baseball career, and with home runs and innocence dwarfed by political machinations and suspicions, the trip played out like a B-movie potboiler. Luckily for us, Robert K. Fitts invites us along in Banzai Babe Ruth, his well-written chronicle of all that happened."
—**Leigh Montville**, author of *The Big Bam: The Life and Times of Babe Ruth*

"Fitts is excellent at capturing occasional bouts of dissension among the American players, describing the respectable quality of play by their Japanese opponents, and especially at capturing the ominous atmosphere that surrounded the tour. Fans will love the stats and player photos, too!"

—**Tom Lavoie**, *Shelf Awareness*

In the Japanese Ballpark

Best Wishes and Banzai!

Rob Fitts

In the Japanese Ballpark

Behind the Scenes of Nippon Professional Baseball

ROBERT K. FITTS

University of Nebraska Press | Lincoln

© 2025 by Robert K. Fitts

All rights reserved
Manufactured in the United States of America

The University of Nebraska Press is part of a land-grant institution with campuses and programs on the past, present, and future homelands of the Pawnee, Ponca, Otoe-Missouria, Omaha, Dakota, Lakota, Kaw, Cheyenne, and Arapaho Peoples, as well as those of the relocated Ho-Chunk, Sac and Fox, and Iowa Peoples.

∞

For customers in the EU with safety/GPSR concerns, contact:
gpsr@mare-nostrum.co.uk
Mare Nostrum Group BV
Mauritskade 21D
1091 GC Amsterdam
The Netherlands

Library of Congress Control Number: 2025017524

Set in Chaparral Pro by A. Shahan.

To the memory of Wayne Graczyk and Marty Kuehnert

I am forever grateful for the guidance and encouragement they gave me and so many others over the years

Contents

List of Illustrations	ix
Introduction	xi
Japanese Baseball Timeline	xvii
Nippon Professional Baseball (NPB) Teams	xxiii
Glossary	xxv

PART 1. SETTING THE STAGE

1. Robert Whiting, Journalist	3

PART 2. ON THE DIAMOND

2. Matt Murton, Player	15
3. Shungo Fukunaga, Minor League Player	25
4. Natsuo Yamazaki, Umpire	33
5. Trey Hillman, Manager	43

PART 3. IN THE BALLPARK

6. Jim Allen, Sportswriter	53
7. Jennie Roloff Rothman, Superfan	64
8. Yasuro Karibe, Oendan Leader	73
9. Taylor Foote, Mascot Team	81
10. Saori Ogure, Cheerleader	90
11. Keiko Suzuki, Uriko (Beer Girl)	98
12. Kenjiro Kajita, Ballpark Security and Intern	105

PART 4. IN THE CLUBHOUSE

13. Toshihiro Nagata, Data Analyst	117
14. Ichiro Kitano, Trainer	125
15. Ken Iwamoto, Interpreter	135

PART 5. THE FRONT OFFICE

16. Marty Kuehnert, General Manager	141
17. Tomoko Namba, Team Owner	153
18. Shun Kakazu, Assistant General Manager	161
19. Jonathan Fine, Assistant General Manager	169

PART 6. THE BUSINESS OF BASEBALL

20. Shigeo Araki, Marketing Director	181
21. Tomoki Negishi, Marketing and Business Development	188
22. Noamichi Yokota, Marketing and Merchandising	197
23. Ryozo Kato, NPB Commissioner	205
24. Edwin Dominguez Alvarez, Agent	213
25. Tatsuo Shinke, Sport Cards	221

PART 7. CONCLUSION

26. Bobby Valentine, Manager	235
Appendix A: Tips on Following NPB from Outside of Japan	247
Appendix B: Tips on Collecting Japanese Baseball Cards and Memorabilia	251
Appendix C: Tips on Attending Games in Japan	256
Appendix D: Recommended English-Language Books on NPB	260
Notes	263
Acknowledgments	265
Index	267

Illustrations

Robert Whiting	8
Matt Murton	19
Shungo Fukunaga	30
Natsuo Yamazaki	37
Trey Hillman	46
Jim Allen	57
Jennie Roloff Rothman and Gerome Rothman	67
Yasuro Karibe	76
Taylor Foote and Slyly	85
Saori Ogure	94
Kenji Kajita	109
Toshihiro Nagata	120
Ichiro Kitano	128
Ken Iwamoto	135
Trevor Raichura, Randy Bass, and Marty Kuehnert	147
Tomoko Namba	157
Shun Kakazu	165
Jonathan Fine	172
Shigeo Araki	184
Tomoki Negishi	192
Noamichi Yokota	200
Ryozo Kato with Robert Fitts	209
Edwin Dominguez Alvarez	217
Tatsuo Shinke	226
Bobby Valentine with former MLB pitcher Masato Yoshii	239

Following page 114

The Hanshin Tigers cheering section at Tokyo Dome

The Hiroshima Toyo Carp oendan at Mazda Zoom-Zoom Stadium.

Carp fans during the Lucky 7 festivities at Mazda Zoom-Zoom Stadium.

Takero Okajima of the Tohoku Rakuten Golden Eagles slides into home.

A close play at third base at Seibu's Belluna Dome.

The Hiroshima Carp cheering section at Tokyo Dome.

Concession stand at Mazda Zoom-Zoom Stadium.

Stadium food at Es Con Field in Hokkaido

Wataru Karashima of the Tohoku Rakuten Golden Eagles lays down a sacrifice bunt

Celebrating a "sayonara home run" at Rakuten Mobile Park Miyagi

Munetaka Murakami of the Tokyo Yakult Swallows at Meiji Jingu Stadium

Introduction

It was 90 degrees with stifling humidity in Yokohama Stadium. Sweat poured off my brow, my shirt was soaked, and it was only the second inning. I needed a cold beer. I caught the attention of a *uriko*, also known as a beer girl. Clad in her distinctive short, yellow dress, the young woman jogged up the stadium stairs with a hefty beer keg strapped to her back. With a smile and a quick bow, she expertly filled a plastic cup with ice-cold draft beer. Flush from the heat and exercise, she gave me change for my ¥1,000 bill, turned quickly, and trotted up the steep steps to the next customer.

For the next two hours, I enjoyed the raucous atmosphere of Japanese baseball. Fans chanted in unison, horns blew, drums beat, and flags waved at every at bat. The rhythms were infectious. I swayed with the beat, clapping along. During the seventh inning, everyone stood and sang the home team's fight song. A regular-season Japanese game has the atmosphere of a seventh game in the MLB World Series.

All the time, the uriko continued to jog up and down the stadium's steps, serving draft beer at a rapid pace. I marveled at her stamina. Certainly, her nightly job was more demanding than most CrossFit workouts. I began to wonder, *How heavy was that beer keg? How many beers did she sell? How much did she get paid? Did she have to contend with lewd customers?* I realized how little I knew about what happened off the diamond at a baseball game.

Baseball is the Japanese national pastime, the country's most popular sport for 125 years and a 1.3-billion-dollar industry. Japan has a distinctive style of baseball both on and off the field. On the diamond, the players favor small ball, dominated by contact hitting and the running game, over the MLB power game with its gargantuan home runs. They play precise defense, rarely making a mistake. Pitchers tend to nibble at the corners with breaking balls rather than challenging hitters with blazing fastballs down the middle of the plate. Off the diamond, clubs are owned by large corporations that have used the teams as marketing tools rather than entities designed to make a profit. These large parent companies control many aspects of the game, including how the media reports the game, labor relations, and marketing strategies. With the organized cheering sections, beer girls, dancing cheerleaders on the field, blaring horns and beating drums, team songs, seventh-inning balloon releases, and yakisoba and curry at the concession stands instead of popcorn and hotdogs, the ballpark experience in Japan is unique. Foreign fans often have dozens of questions.

To answer these questions and help American fans gain a greater appreciation for Nippon Professional Baseball (NPB), I decided to turn to the true experts, the people who play, oversee, promote, and watch the game. *In the Japanese Ballpark* features edited interviews with twenty-six individuals to provide a behind-the-scenes look at the game.

I spoke with participants in the games, such as players, managers, and an umpire; support staff, including an interpreter, trainer, and data analyst; front office personnel, such as an owner, general and assistant managers, and marketing directors; ballpark workers, including cheerleaders, a mascot, beer girl, and usher; and professionals who surround the sport, such as baseball writers, a player agent, a league commissioner, and a sports-card dealer. Through their personal experiences, these individuals reveal the inner workings of the professional game in Japan and explain the cultural aspects that make NPB different from MLB. For example, why are many Japanese clubs content with losing money? Why do managers in Japan have more authority than they do in MLB? Why are many teams' mascots as popular as their star players? Why are Japanese fans more engaged than American fans? How does baseball contribute to Japanese society? How will Japanese professional baseball react to MLB's aggressive entry into the Asian market and the loss of its top players?

To gain various perspectives on the Japanese game, I interviewed people who held a wide variety of jobs in Nippon Professional Baseball. I also tried to get roughly half foreigners and half Japanese. Foreigners with knowledge of both NPB and MLB are often better able to recognize differences and make comparisons between the two leagues. Furthermore, foreigners who have adapted to living in Japan are often conscious about cultural differences and practices that native Japanese would just take for granted. This trait is especially important, as this book is written to help foreigners better understand Japanese baseball. On the downside, foreigners often miss the nuances of Japanese behaviors, and they tend to view Japan through their own cultural lenses, making them prone to pass judgement and rely on stereotypes. Japanese, on the other hand, have a greater understanding of the subtleties of their own culture and often offer different explanations for behavior that perplex foreigners. As cultural insiders, however, they can have difficulty explaining behavior that they view as just common sense.

I conducted most of the interviews over Zoom between November 2023 and June 2024. For interviews with Japanese speakers, I used interpreter Trevor Raichura. Most of the conversations lasted between 90 and 120 minutes. I began the interviews with prepared questions to direct the conversations, but I encouraged the subjects to discuss any topic they felt was important to understanding Japanese baseball. These exchanges often led to unexpected insights.

I then edited the transcripts into narratives by removing my questions, editing the responses, fixing grammatical errors, and rearranging the topics. The goal was to create chapters that seem as if the interviewee is speaking directly to the reader. Whenever possible, the statements in the interviews were fact-checked. Incorrect dates and statistics were updated, and tall tales that had grown with time were corrected or deleted. Nonetheless, these narratives are the statements and opinions of the interviewees and should not necessarily be taken as solid fact without verification. The first drafts of the narratives were returned to the interviewees for them to check for accuracy.

This process revealed a difference between American and Japanese baseball. In the United States, writers can interview players or staff by reaching out directly to the individual. The interviewee's team is rarely involved in the process. In Japan, however, many teams control access to their players and employees. One team forbade its employees from speaking to me, while the public relations departments of several other teams required a list of all questions before the interviews as well as the right to review and edit the final narrative. Although most of the teams were very helpful and courteous, this was a time-consuming process that often resulted in substantial changes to the narratives as teams removed any statement that could possibly be seen as controversial.

In the Japanese Ballpark has seven sections. In Part I, Robert Whiting, the best-selling author of several books on Japanese baseball, sets the stage by explaining what the game was like when he first arrived in Japan in 1962 and how it has changed since then.

The second section, "On the Diamond," focuses on the participants of a baseball game: the players, umpires, and managers. Former Hanshin Tiger star Matt Murton discusses life as a foreign player; Shungo Fukunaga talks about his experience in the Japanese minor leagues; Natsuo Yamazaki talks about umpiring in NPB; and Trey Hillman discusses managing in Japan.

Part III, "In the Ballpark," provides an insider's perspective on what happens during a game. Jim Allen discusses the media; Jennie Roloff Rothman explains fan behavior; Taylor Foote talks about the Hiroshima Toyo Carp's mascot Slyly; Saori Ogure discusses life as a Fighters' cheerleader; Keiko Suzuki talks about being a uriko; Yasuro Karibe explains what it's like to be in the Carp's *oendan*; and Kenjiro Kajita talks about serving as a stadium usher and security guard, as well as about high school baseball and analytics.

"In the Clubhouse," the fourth section, focuses on a team's support staff. Toshihiro Nagata of the Yakult Swallows discusses analytics; Ichiro Kitano of the Chunichi Dragons talks about being a trainer; and Ken Iwamoto of the Hokkaido Nippon Ham Fighters chats about interpreting, the Fighters' front-office strategy, and Shohei Ohtani.

Part V, "In the Front Office," features former Rakuten Eagles general manager Marty Kuehnert, Yokohama DeNA BayStars owner Tomoko Namba, SoftBank Fukuoka Hawks assistant general manager Shun Kakazu, and Hiroshima Toyo Carp foreign assistant manager and attorney Jonathan Fine. Each discusses the strategies for building a team both on and off the field.

The sixth section focuses on the business of baseball. Shigeo Araki discusses the business strategy used to turn around the Chiba Lotte Marines in 2005–2006 and the business strategy of Samurai Japan; Tom Negishi focuses on the marketing of the Rakuten Eagles and the company Pacific League Marketing; Noamichi Yokota talks about ticket and merchandise sales for the Yomiuri Giants as well as using baseball to promote social change; Ambassador Ryozo Kato discusses the role of the commissioner in NPB; Edwin Dominguez Alvarez explains the economics of player contracts and the role of an agent in NPB; and Tatsuo Shinke talks about the sports-card industry in Japan.

Former Chiba Lotte Marine manager Bobby Valentine concludes the narratives by reflecting on how Japanese baseball has changed since he first managed in 1995 and the future of NPB.

Four appendixes provide practical information for fans who want to dive deeper into Japanese professional baseball. Appendix A, "Tips on Following NPB from Outside of Japan," suggests resources for following NPB in English. Appendix B, "Tips on Collecting Japanese Baseball Cards and Memorabilia," presents a short history of Japanese baseball cards and provides information of where to buy cards and memorabilia. Appendix C, "Tips on Attending Games in Japan," provides information on how to get tickets and watch games in Japan. Appendix D, "Recommended English-Language Books on NPB," recommends books on Japanese baseball.

For readers just learning about Japanese baseball, some background may help understand references in the chapters. Horace Wilson is credited with introducing baseball to Japan in 1872. The game flourished in Tokyo and spread across the county after a team of Japanese schoolboys defeated an adult American team from the Yokohama Country and Athletic Club in 1896. By 1905, most of the high schools in Japan fielded baseball teams. The National High School Baseball Championship, often known as Koshien, began in 1915. Baseball remained an amateur game until the 1930s (except for two short-lived professional teams in the 1920s). Following on the success of a barnstorming tour by Babe Ruth and a team of American League All-Stars, Matsutaro Shoriki formed the professional Tokyo Yomiuri Giants in late 1934, and other clubs soon followed. The Japanese Baseball League held two professional tournaments in 1935, and league play began in 1936. After a break in 1944 and 1945 due to World War II, the Japanese Baseball League continued through the end of the 1949 season. In 1950 the league was reorganized as Nippon Professional Baseball with two leagues: the Central and the Pacific. Currently, six teams are in each league, with the league champions meeting in the Japan Series each October. In 2004 the Pacific League created a playoff in which the second- and third-place teams play a three-game series, with the winner moving on to play the first-place team in a six-game series to determine the league champion. In this second playoff, the first-place team is given the home-field advantage for the entire series in addition to an automatic one-game lead. Now known as the Climax Series, the Central League adopted the same playoff format in 2007.

Spring training in NPB, known as spring camp, starts each year in early February. The regular season begins around April 1 and scheduled games conclude near the end of September but are usually followed by a week or two of make-up games to accommodate the league's many rainouts. After the season ends, teams have fall camps in November where players from both the major league squad (called *ichi-gun* in Japanese) and the minor league squad (called *ni-gun* in Japanese) prepare for the following season.

NPB schedules have several differences from MLB. Mondays are usually off days for all teams. As a result, most teams use a six-man starting rotation so that pitchers start just once a week. For three weeks starting in late May, all teams play several series of interleague games. Games in Pacific League stadiums use the designated hitter, which the league adopted in 1975, while pitchers bat in games held in Central League ballparks. This interleague series is currently sponsored by Nippon Life, which crowns the team with the best interleague record and presents an Interleague Most Valuable Player Award each season. NPB also has two All-Star Games, played on consecutive days in mid-July.

NPB has a limit on the number of foreigners a team may have on its roster. This number has changed over time, but currently teams are limited to five foreign players on the ichi-gun roster. There are no limits on the number of foreign players on the ni-gun roster.

In Japan, games can end in ties. The rules determining when a game ends in a draw have fluctuated throughout the years. Currently, a game is declared a tie if the score is even after twelve innings. This rule has been in place since 2001, except during the 2011 and 2012 seasons and during COVID-19 pandemic seasons. During the 2011 and 2012 seasons, to save electricity, no inning was allowed to start after three-and-a-half hours from the first pitch. In 2020, games were limited to ten innings, and in 2021, games were limited to only nine innings.

A timeline of the history of Japanese professional baseball is located at the end of this introduction. Those wanting a more detailed account of Japan's rich baseball history should see the recommended reading in appendix D.

Japanese Baseball Timeline

1869 Baseball is played in Kobe Foreign Settlement.
1871 Crew of USS Colorado plays first documented games on Japanese soil.
1872 Horace Wilson introduces baseball to Japan.
1876 First documented game occurs between Japanese students and Americans.
1878 Hiroshi Hiraoka organizes Shimbashi Athletic Club.
1886 Ichiko (First High School) forms baseball team.
1896 Ichiko defeats American team from Yokohama Country Club.
1905 Waseda University tours United States.
1906 Waseda vs. Keio University games suspended for twenty years after riot.
1907 Hawaiian St. Louis becomes first foreign team to tour Japan.
1908 Reach All-Americans become first professionals to tour Japan.
1913 New York Giants and Chicago White Sox tour Japan.
1914 Tokyo-area university league established.
1915 National High School Baseball Championship established.
1920 First professional team Nihon Undo Kyokai is formed.
1923 Nihon Undo Kyokai renamed Takarazuka Kyokai.
1924 Koshien Stadium opens.
1925 Tokyo Six University League established.
     Waseda vs. Keio games resume.
1926 Meiji Jingu Stadium opens.
1927 Philadelphia Royal Giants, a Negro League All-Star team, tour Japan.
1929 Takarazuka Kyokai disbands.
1931 Major League All-Stars with Lou Gehrig tour Japan.
1934 American League All-Stars with Babe Ruth tour Japan.
     All Nippon team remains together as professional team named Dai Nippon Tokyo Yakyu Club.

1935	Dai Nippon Tokyo Yakyu Club tours United States and becomes the Tokyo Yomiuri Giants.
1935	Osaka Tigers (later Hanshin Tigers) formed.
1936	Japanese Professional Baseball League established.
1937	First full season of Japanese pro baseball occurs.
1944	Professional league disbanded due to Allied air raids.
1946	Professional league resumes play.
1947	The Sawamura Award to honor the top pitcher in the Central League is created.
1948	First professional night game held on August 17 at Yokohama Stadium.
1949	San Francisco Seals tour Japan.
1950	Central and Pacific Leagues created to form the Nippon Professional Baseball League.
1951	Wally Yonamine becomes first American player in post-War Japan.
	First Central vs. Pacific League All-Star Game takes place.
	Giants win first of three-straight Japan Series titles.
1952	Eleven foreigners join leagues, including Jyun Hirota, John Britton, and Jimmie Newberry.
1955	Giants win first of five-straight pennants.
	New York Yankees tour Japan.
1956	Brooklyn Dodgers tour Japan.
1958	Shigeo Nagashima wins Rookie of the Year award.
1959	Shigeo Nagashima hits a sayonara home run in first baseball game attended by Emperor Hirohito.
	Sadaharu Oh has his rookie season.
	Japanese Baseball Hall of Fame founded.
1960	Tetsuharu Kawakami becomes Giants manager and begins creating an all-Japanese championship team.
1961	Shigeo Nagashima wins first of five Central League MVP Awards.
1962	Hanshin Tigers win first pennant.
	Sadaharu Oh wins first of thirteen-straight Central League home run crowns and first of thirteen RBI titles.
1964	Hanshin Tigers win second pennant, as Gene Bacque becomes first American to win the Sawamura Award.

	Masanori Murakami becomes first Japanese to play in Major Leagues.
	Sadaharu Oh sets single-season home run record of 55.
1965	Yomiuri Giants win first of nine-straight championships.
	Amateur draft established.
1966	Los Angeles Dodgers tour Japan.
1972	Yutaka Fukumoto sets single-season stolen-base record of 106.
1973	The Giants complete the last of nine-straight Japan Series titles.
	Sadaharu Oh wins Triple Crown.
1974	Sadaharu Oh wins second Triple Crown.
	Shigeo Nagashima retires.
	Tetsuharu Kawakami resigns as Giants manager.
1975	Pacific League adopts designated hitter.
	Hiroshima Carp signs Joe Lutz as the first non-Asian manager but Lutz is replaced after one month. Under direction of Takeshi Koba, the Carp go on to win its first pennant.
	Hankyu Braves win first of three-straight Japan Series titles.
1977	Sadaharu Oh breaks Hank Aaron's career home run record on September 3.
	Robert Whiting publishes *The Chrysanthemum and the Bat*.
1978	Yakult Swallows win their first pennant and Japan Series.
1979	Don Blasingame takes over as manager of the Hanshin Tigers.
1982	Seibu Lions win first of three pennants in four years under manager Tatsuro Hirooka.
1983	Yutaka Fukumoto breaks Lou Brock's career stolen-base record.
1985	Hanshin Tigers win Japan Series for first time.
	Randy Bass wins first Triple Crown.
1986	Randy Bass wins second Triple Crown.
1988	Natsuo Yamazaki becomes a professional umpire in NPB.
1989	Robert Whiting publishes *You Gotta Have Wa*.
1990	Pacific League pitchers become eligible to win the Sawamura Award.
	Hideo Nomo wins Rookie of the Year, MVP, and Sawamura Awards.
1992	*Mr. Baseball*, starring Tom Selleck, released.
1993	Hideki Matsui and Ichiro Suzuki's rookie seasons happen.

	Free agency established.
1994	Ichiro Suzuki sets record for most hits in single season.
	Ichiro Suzuki wins first of seven-straight batting titles and first of three-consecutive MVP Awards.
1995	Hideo Nomo joins Los Angeles Dodgers and wins National League Rookie of the Year Award.
	Bobby Valentine manages Chiba Lotte Marines.
	Slyly becomes the mascot of the Hiroshima Toyo Carp.
1998	Yokohama BayStars win Japan Series.
2000	Giants, managed by Shigeo Nagashima, beat Hawks, managed by Sadaharu Oh, in so-called ON Japan Series.
	Kazuhiro Sasaki joins Seattle Mariners and wins Rookie of the Year.
	New York Mets and Chicago Cubs open MLB season in Tokyo.
2001	Games are limited to twelve innings.
	Ichiro Suzuki joins Seattle Mariners and wins American League Rookie of the Year and Most Valuable Player Awards.
	Tuffy Rhodes hits 55 home runs to tie Sadaharu Oh's single-season record.
2002	Alex Cabrera hits 55 home runs to tie single-season home run record.
2003	Hanshin Tigers win first pennant since 1985 but lose to Hawks in exciting Japan Series.
	Hideki Matsui joins New York Yankees.
	Trey Hillman manages Nippon Ham Fighters.
2004	New York Yankees and Tampa Bay Devil Rays open MLB season in Tokyo.
	Nippon Ham Fighters move from Tokyo to Sapporo, Hokkaido.
	Bobby Valentine returns to manage Chiba Lotte Marines.
	Pacific League institutes a three-team playoff.
	NPB players strike for two days in September for first time in history.
	After the season, the Orix BlueWave and Kintetsu Buffaloes merge to become the Orix Buffaloes.
	Marty Kuehnert becomes first foreign GM in NPB history.
2005	The Tohoku Rakuten Golden Eagles have their inaugural season.
	Valentine's Chiba Lotte Marines win Japan Series.

JAPANESE BASEBALL TIMELINE / xxi

	Interleague play begins.
	Yu Darvish has his rookie season.
2006	Japan wins inaugural World Baseball Classic.
	Trey Hillman's Nippon Ham Fighters win Japan Series.
2007	Central League institutes a three-team playoff. The playoffs are renamed the Climax Series.
	Yu Darvish wins Pacific League MVP and Sawamura Awards.
2008	Ryozo Kato becomes NPB commissioner.
2009	Japan wins second World Baseball Classic.
	Yu Darvish wins his second Pacific League MVP.
2010	Matt Murton joins Hanshin Tigers and breaks Ichiro Suzuki's record for most hits in one season.
	Natsuo Yamazaki retires as an NPB umpire.
2011	Opening Day postponed due to the Tohoku earthquake.
	Masahiro Tanaka wins Sawamura Award.
2012	Yokohama BayStars become Yokohama DeNA BayStars.
	Yu Darvish debuts in MLB.
	NPB players threaten to boycott World Baseball Classic.
2013	Japan finishes third at World Baseball Classic.
	Tohoku Rakuten Golden Eagles win Japan Series.
	Wladmir Balentien hits 60 HRs to set Japan record.
	Masahiro Tanaka wins Sawamura Award and Pacific League MVP with 24–0 record.
	Shohei Ohtani has his rookie season.
	Lively ball scandal happens. Ryozo Kato resigns as NPB commissioner.
2014	Matt Murton wins Central League batting crown.
2016	Shohei Ohtani wins Pacific League MVP.
	Matt Murton retires from NPB.
2017	Japan finishes third at World Baseball Classic.
	Shungo Fukunaga has his rookie season.
2018	Shohei Ohtani enters MLB.
2020	Season is shortened to 120 games due to COVID-19 pandemic.
	Games are limited to ten innings.
	Shungo Fukunaga has his last NPB season.
2021	No extra-inning games are allowed.

	Yoshinobu Yamamoto wins his first of three-consecutive Pacific League MVP and Sawamura Awards.
	Shohei Ohtani wins American League MVP.
	No vocal cheering, horns, or whistles allowed in the stands.
2022	Munetaka Murakami wins Triple Crown with 56 HRs, the most by a Japanese player.
	Ban on vocal cheering, horns, or whistles in the stands continues.
2023	Japan wins World Baseball Classic.
	Vocal cheering and all instruments reinstated.
	Shohei Ohtani wins American League MVP.
2024	Shohei Ohtani signs largest contract in sports history to play for the Los Angeles Dodgers.
	Yoshinobu Yamamoto joins the Dodgers.
	Shohei Ohtani becomes first player in MLB history to hit 50 home runs and steal 50 bases in the same season.

Nippon Professional Baseball (NPB) Teams

Table 1. Central League Teams

TEAM	STADIUM	LOCATION
Chunichi Dragons	Vantelin Dome	Nagoya
Hanshin Tigers	Hanshin Koshien Stadium	Nishinomiya, Kobe
Hiroshima Toyo Carp	Mazda Zoom-Zoom Stadium	Hiroshima
Tokyo Yakult Swallows	Meiji Jingu Stadium	Tokyo
Yokohama DeNA BayStars	Yokohama Stadium	Yokohama
Yomiuri Giants	Tokyo Dome	Tokyo

Table 2. Pacific League Teams

TEAM	STADIUM	LOCATION
Chiba Lotte Marines	ZOZO Marine Stadium	Chiba
Fukuoka SoftBank Hawks	Fukuoka PayPay Dome	Fukuoka
Hokkaido Nippon-Ham Fighters	Es Con Field Hokkaido	Kitahiroshima, Hokkaidō
Orix Buffaloes	Kyocera Dome	Osaka
Saitama Seibu Lions	Belluna Dome	Tokorozawa, Saitama
Tohoku Rakuten Golden Eagles	Rakuten Mobile Park Miyagi	Sendai

Glossary

Best Nine	Annual award for the best player at each position in each league.
Chuhai	Short for *shochu highball*, a canned cocktail made with *shochu*, seltzer, and lemon.
Gaijin	Japanese term for foreigner.
Gaiya	Outfield, also the cheering section that sits in the outfield.
Ichi-gun	A club's top, major league team.
Kansei	The region in central Japan that includes Osaka, Kobe, and Kyoto.
Kanto	The greater Tokyo area, including Yokohama, Chiba, and Saitama.
Kawaii	Very cute or adorable.
Naiya	Infield.
Ni-gun	A club's minor league team, also called the farm team.
Oendan	The official cheering group for each team.
Otaku	A person with all-consuming interests, particularly in anime, manga, video games, collectibles, or computers.
Sawamura Award	Annual award given to best pitcher.
Sayonara home run	A home run that ends a game.
Shochu	A traditional Japanese distilled alcohol.
Uriko	Salesgirl
Wa	Harmony, especially within a social group
WBC	World Baseball Classic
Yakyu	Japanese name for baseball

In the Japanese Ballpark

Part 1 / **Setting the Stage**

1 / Robert Whiting, Journalist

Journalist Robert Whiting is the best-selling author of *The Chrysanthemum and the Bat* and *You've Gotta Have Wa*, along with other books on Japanese baseball and life in Japan. In 2023 he received the Society of American Baseball Research's Henry Chadwick Award for lifetime contributions to the study of baseball.

◆

Baseball was introduced to Japan in 1872 by an American professor named Horace Wilson, who was invited, along with a number of teachers, engineers, and other professionals, to help Japan modernize after 250 years of feudal isolation. Wilson introduced baseball to his students, and the Ministry of Education declared that baseball was good for the development of the national character. It was Japan's first group sport. Soon, Meiji Gakuin and a few other universities in Tokyo created baseball teams and started playing each other. But baseball really became popular in 1896 when a prep school called the First Higher School of Tokyo, or Ichiko, played a team of diplomats, missionaries, and traders from the Yokohama Country and Athletic Club in the first formal baseball game played between Japanese and Americans in twenty years.[1] The Yokohama team hadn't wanted to play, as Ichiko was a prep school for boys who wanted to go to Imperial University and the students were just eighteen to twenty-two years old. At that time, Japanese were not even allowed on the Yokohama Country and Athletic Club fields. But the principal of the school complained to the foreign ministry about Yokohama's refusal to play, so the ministry put pressure on the U.S. embassy, which put pressure on Yokohama. In the end, they scheduled a game for May 1896.

What wasn't commonly known at the time was how hard Ichiko practiced. For those players, baseball wasn't just a spring and summer sport; they practiced year-round. Practice started after the New Year's holidays and went to the end of the year. They practiced before school and after school, and during the spring, summer, and winter vacations they held special baseball camps. The majority of the students at the First Higher School of Tokyo came from samurai families, so they adopted the samurai ethic about hard training. For example, it was forbidden to use the word *ouch* because that was considered a sign of weakness. If you got smacked in the face with a fastball, you were allowed to use the word *kayui*, which means "it itches," and that was it! The captain of their team was famous for swinging the bat one thousand times a night in the team dormitory. I don't know if you have ever swung a bat one thousand times, but it's not easy to do. I can barely make it to one hundred before I collapse. The team's motto was "bloody urine." If you didn't practice so hard as to urinate blood at the end of the day, then you hadn't practiced enough, or you weren't serious enough.

When they played, the Japanese won, 29–4. This was big news. The daily newspaper reporters had come down to cover the game, and it was reported on the front page of the broadsheet newspapers like *Asahi Shimbun*. Afterward, the Americans said, "Well, we didn't practice as much as we should have. We'd like a rematch." They played a rematch on June 6 and the Japanese won, 32–9, and then they won a third time, 22–6. It wasn't until the Americans recruited the best players from several U.S. naval ships docked at Yokohama that they actually won a game. The historian Kyushi Yamato wrote that foreigners could not appreciate the impact of these Japanese victories. The Japanese felt if they could beat the Americans at their national sport of baseball then they could surpass them in other fields, like industry and commerce. Japan was trying to modernize and catch up with the rest of the world after this long period of isolation, so the victories became inspirational. This was how baseball became the national sport of Japan.

The national high school baseball tournament, which is held for two weeks every summer at Koshien Stadium in Osaka, started in 1915. It is now the most popular sporting event in the land, and one of the most popular events in the world. After that, Babe Ruth and Lou Gehrig and some American League All-Stars came in 1934 and that helped start the professional baseball league in Japan. At the beginning, some people didn't think it would succeed because playing baseball for money was considered impure. That's the samurai ethic again. But that turned out not to be the case. The Yomiuri Giants drew standing-room-only crowds when they played and became quite popular.

You can still see the influence of Ichiko and the samurai ethic in Japanese baseball. Suishu Tobita, a baseball commentator who coached the Waseda University team to victory over American teams in international play, declared that the practices of Ichiko should be the model for all of Japanese baseball, and he copied them when coaching at Waseda. His practice was nicknamed "death practice," *shi no renshu*, and he was famous for saying things like, "It's only when a player is on the ground with froth coming out of his mouth that you can say he's practiced as hard as he can." That became the model when the professional league started. They picked up on the endless practice to develop a player's fighting spirit.

I first came to Japan with the U.S. Air Force in 1962, and they sent me to this facility in Fuchu just outside Tokyo. I liked Japan so much that I decided to stay after my discharge. I enrolled at Sophia University and got a small apartment. The only thing I could really understand on TV was baseball. Half of the commentary was in English anyway, or English-derived words, like *homu ran* (home run), *auto* (out), and *sutoraiku* (strike). If a player got injured and came out of the game, it was called a *dokutastoppu* (doctor stop). At that time, Giants games were on the TV every single night nationwide. Everybody loved the Giants. They were by far the most popular entertainment in the country. Any night during the baseball season, you could walk into a bar or restaurant, and their game would be on TV, or you'd climb into a cab and the driver would have the Giants game on the radio. So, you could start conversations with people you didn't know just by asking what the score was and if Sadaharu Oh had hit any home runs.

I learned to read Japanese by buying the sports papers. There were six nationwide sports dailies with circulations up to a million. The front-page stories were always on the Giants. So, I used to go to a coffee shop, buy a newspaper, and sit there with my dictionary and try to read the game reports and feature articles.

I went down to Korakuen Stadium to watch Sadaharu Oh and Shigeo Nagashima, the two big stars of the Yomiuri Giants. Old Korakuen Stadium, which was torn down and replaced by the Tokyo Dome, was modeled after Briggs Stadium in Detroit. It was a double-decker stadium with narrow seats. It wasn't very noisy. In American ballparks there was always the guy next to you who stood up and yelled insults and threw things. But not in Japan, where it was all very polite. The only noise was made by the cheering groups in the outfield called *oendan*. Back then, the oendan were not as organized and not as big as they are now. You'd have several rows of people sitting there, and the cheerleader would be telling them to raise their arms or wave their hands over their head. They had set cheers for each player. Their favorite one was *kattobase*, which means "knock it out of the park." So, Nagashima would come up, and they would chant, "*Kattobase* Nagashima! *Kattobase* Nagashima!" If you wanted to join them, they would give you a yelling test to see the quality of your voice and figure out where to place you in the group.

The ballpark food was not as good as it is today. They had what they called hot dogs, but they were made out of fish meal. You had to smother them with mustard to hide the taste. But the problem with the mustard was that it was really spicy, painfully hot! Which I didn't know the first time. I just covered the hot dog with mustard and had to run to the bathroom to wash my mouth out. Even back in the 1960s, Japanese stadiums had these really good-looking girls running around in shorts carrying huge containers of draft beer. You'd see some tiny little girl, who looked like she weighed about 92 pounds, carrying this huge container of beer. They're running up and down the steps of Korakuen Stadium, and the steps were so steep that you needed to be a mountain goat to navigate them.

Korakuen was quite pleasant. You could sit in what they called the jumbo stand. It was out above left field between the third baseline and left field. You could sit up there on a summer night with a cool breeze coming in and see the lights of Tokyo, the neon signs, and the trains going by, and then in this pool of light down below on the field, Sadaharu Oh would step in with this one-legged stance and hit a home run. It was great!

Oh was the most striking player. He had this aikido teacher named Hiroshi Arakawa, who was also his batting sensei. Oh had a hitch in his swing, so Arakawa taught Oh to correct it by standing on one leg. You see a lot of guys lift their legs in Japan as the ball comes in and they move into their swing, but Oh would stand on his left leg within his right leg raised to his knee even before the pitcher went into his windup. He looked like a flamingo. He just had perfect balance, and a ninety-mile-an-hour fastball would come in, and he'd hit it over the fence or hit a wicked line drive. It was great to watch him.

Oh batted third and Shigeo Nagashima hit fourth. Nagashima was the Golden Boy who had hit a home run at the only regular professional game the emperor ever attended. He had movie-star good looks, and he had these mannerisms: the way he stood, cocked his head, or shook his shoulders. He was always doing something that attracted attention. Oh would be at bat, and Nagashima would be in the on-deck circle, but everybody was watching Nagashima to see what kind of quirky movement he would make. And he was a showboat at third base. There would be a ground ball to shortstop, and the shortstop would come in, and then all of a sudden Nagashima would cut in front of him, grab the ball and throw it to first. So, he had this reputation as a hot dog.

In 1973 I left Japan and moved to New York. People would ask me about Japan, and I would tell them about baseball—what the baseball games were like and how it was really different from the United States. I explained how the Japanese used the sacrifice bunt anytime the first batter got on base, how the managers and coaches were always running out on the field to give advice to the players, and about the constant practices. Baseball is a year-round sport in Japan. In America spring training starts in the middle of February, and the players are on the field for two or three hours before they head off to the nearest swimming pool or golf course. The Japanese were out there from the break of dawn. Back in the hotel, they had a training room so that players could go in and take one thousand swings before they went to sleep. It was just constant dedication.

I told them about Sadaharu Oh and his nightly practice with a samurai sword. He'd suspend a piece of paper from the ceiling and tried to slice it in half with the sword, which is very difficult because the force of the air from the swing would move the paper around. And that they had things like the one thousand fungo drill for players, where they had to field ground balls until they dropped from exhaustion. It's not really a fielding or conditioning drill, but a drill to build fighting spirit, to make you reach your limits and then try to surpass them. I saw players do this drill. At the end they would be lying on the field, froth coming out of their mouths, and the coaches would be hitting line drives at the prone player, yelling, "Get up! Get up, you lazy SOB!"

Robert Whiting. Courtesy of Robert Whiting.

During the games, pitchers followed a routine where the first two pitches would be strikes and then the next three pitches would be outside of the strike zone. It seemed like every count went to 3–2, or 2–3, as the Japanese used to say before 2010 when they listed the strikes before the balls, because managers would fine pitchers who gave up hits while ahead in the count. So, you got two quick strikes and then an automatic three balls and then you had several fouls before something would finally happen. It was a very slow, tedious game.

Later on, I found out that they had pregame meetings in the clubhouse to review video of the opponents, and after the game they had something called a *hanseikai*, which was a "self-reflection conference" where they would go over the mistakes the players made and guys who really screwed up were called out for special practice the next morning. The idea in America was that you were responsible for your job. You were supposed to know what to do, and if you couldn't do it, they would get somebody else who could do it. In Japan, the attitude was that the players were stupid. They had to be told what to do all the time, so there was this constant browbeating, plus some physical violence too. If a player screwed up, made an error, a manager or coach might whack him over his head. That kind of thing happened quite a bit.

It was a really structured environment. They had a name for it: "controlled or managed baseball." Off the field it was even worse because there were all these rules and regulations and constant meetings. Some players used to say that playing baseball in Japan was like working for a Japanese corporation, like being a salary man. I had worked for a Japanese company, so I could see the similarities between the Japanese approach to baseball and to corporate life. I realized that baseball was a useful tool to look at Japanese culture. It provided a window into the culture, their values and assumptions.

As I told these stories about Japanese baseball, people said, "Oh, that's really interesting! You should write a book." I went to Barnes and Noble and bought a book on how to write nonfiction because I had no idea how to go about it. Then, I sat down and wrote *Chrysanthemum and the Bat*. It got turned down by twelve publishers in a row before I found one. It was published in 1977, and the translated version became a best seller in Japan. So that launched me on my career.

Japanese baseball has changed a lot since then. They still do their meetings every day—pregame meetings and the *hanseikai* after the game. Those will never stop, I guess, but they're not as fanatical about training as they used to be. The one thousand fungo drill used to be an integral part of spring camp for every team. It was quite popular for a long time, but it's not done so much anymore. But in the 1970s, every player had to do it at least once during spring camp, just to prove how tough they were.

It used to be that a starting-rotation pitcher in Japan would throw every three or four days, and then pitch in relief between starts. For example, if there was a three-game series between the Giants and the Hanshin Tigers in the early 1970s, Yutaka Enatsu, the Tigers ace, would start the first game and the third game, and relieve in the second. Starting pitchers would also throw one hundred practice pitches a day between starts. That was considered the norm. But you don't see that anymore. They are more careful about pacing themselves and taking care of their arms. That started to change when Choji Murata, a big star on Lotte, went to see Dr. Frank Jobe in Los Angeles in 1982 and became the first Japanese player to have Tommy John surgery.

It's an interesting story. Murata tore a ligament in his elbow, and he thought that the only way to cure a sore arm was to throw more, which was a common belief in Japanese baseball at the time. So, Murata kept throwing. It just made it worse and worse. He stood under icy cold waterfalls to strengthen his fighting spirit. And that didn't work. Then a Japanese American fan sent him a letter telling him about Dr. Jobe and Tommy John surgery. Murata was skeptical but his wife talked him into going to L.A. to have the surgery. When Murata came back, he only pitched once a week, and he had a hundred pitch limit. He was very vocal about taking care of his arm. There were a lot of interviews on TV, where he would talk about pitchers pacing themselves and say that the human arm is not a piece of rubber—it needs some rest. Some people criticized Murata for being lazy. That's how it started, and now a lot of Japanese have had Tommy John surgery. So that helped change the attitude toward pitching and saving the arm. The idea that fighting spirit can overcome any physical limitation has sort of receded into the background. They're a lot savvier now.

Murata had a big impact, and so did Hideo Nomo. I interviewed Nomo, and he said that the real reason that he went to the States was not because he wanted to play in America but because he wanted to get away from his manager Keishi Suzuki, who was ruining his arm through overuse. Once Nomo went to the Majors, the Japanese press and fans started covering the Major Leagues, and people saw how the big-league pitchers were treated. Nomo would come back to Japan and say things like the Japanese way of training and pitching is really crazy.

A lot has changed since Nomo and other Japanese pitchers started playing in the Major Leagues. For example, Masato Yoshii pitched for the New York Mets, and he manages the Chiba Lotte Marines now. He has this outstanding pitcher, Roki Sasaki, who will probably be posted to the Major Leagues. The Marines are very careful about how they treat him. He pitched a perfect game and then the next game that he started, five days later, he pitched eight perfect innings and Yoshii took him out. Yoshii didn't let him start the ninth, because he thought Sasaki was getting tired, and he didn't want him to hurt his arm. You wouldn't have seen that twenty or thirty years ago!

I think the quality of Japanese baseball has really improved. The players are bigger and stronger. They used to have this phobia about weight training. They thought it would screw up their flexibility, so they weren't allowed to lift weights, but that taboo has disappeared. Now they're all in the weight room. They have learned a lot from the American way. Japanese are more internationally minded than they used to be.

When Matsutaro Shoriki was running the Giants in the 1950s and 1960s, he kept pushing for a real World Series, and he always wanted his Giants to play the world champions. But I don't think that Shoriki's dream of a real World Series will ever come true. There's no money in it, so the Americans won't do it. I was told that the president of SoftBank offered the Major Leagues millions of dollars to play a real World Series if SoftBank won the Japan Series. But MLB just said that's nothing to us. "Who's going to come and watch the champions play the SoftBank Hawks?"

Instead, the World Baseball Classic (WBC) has taken the place of a real World Series in the minds of the Japanese. And they think, "Well, we won the WBC, so we've proven that we're the best in the world." To me the WBC is meaningless because the Americans aren't really serious about it. They see it as just an exhibition game, and they don't send their best pitchers. Justin Verlander and Max Scherzer, the stud American pitchers, don't play. Their teams don't want them to play because they're afraid they might get injured and hurt their teams' chances in the regular season. For once, I'd like to see the Americans take it seriously. I know that just sounds like sour grapes. What I would say if I were listening to me is, "Whiting, you're so full of shit. Admit that the Japanese are better than the Americans!"

But I did notice how exciting the Samurai Japan team was during the WBC. You saw a lot of three-pitch strikeouts, and the Japanese used the hit and run more often and better than the Americans did. They had a really dynamic approach to the game, and I think that was because of Shohei Ohtani's influence. Because he would go after batters, he pitched the Major League way.

You could make the argument that Ohtani is the best player in the history of the Major Leagues. You could argue that. Just look at the past few seasons. There's no other player who has ever done what he did—46 home runs one season, and then 34 home runs and 15 wins as a pitcher the next year, and 44 home runs the following year. It was just an incredible feat.

I'll probably get in trouble for saying this, but the Japanese have always had a complex about the United States. A Japanese succeeding in the United States shows that the Japanese are equal to Americans. Back in the era of the ON (Oh-Nagashima) Giants, they would play these postgame series against Major League teams, and they would invariably lose pretty badly. Tetsuharu Kawakami, their manager, would say that there's no difference between the baseball skills of the Americans and Japanese—the Americans are just bigger and stronger. Now they have Ohtani, who is 6'4" and 225 lbs. He's built like an NFL tight end, and he's bigger than most American players. He throws the ball one hundred miles an hour and hits the ball five hundred feet. He's also a really good-looking guy. I'm just waiting for him to appear in a Hollywood movie. So, he's done a lot for the self-image of the Japanese. Just turn on the TV or pick up a sports paper here; half the time, what Ohtani does is the lead story in sports.

Especially in light of the WBC and Ohtani, I don't think that the Japanese feel inferior to the Major Leagues anymore. I think they feel that they're on par with the Americans. After all, Nomo, Daisuke Matsuzaka, Hideki Matsui, and Ichiro have all performed well in the Majors. Ichiro even set the all-time hits record for a single season. It's quite clear to me that you could take several teams of Japanese All-Stars and enter them in the Major Leagues, and there's a good chance they would win their division over the course of the season.

But, if you're really cynical and you wanted to be critical of the Japanese game, you could say, as some people do, "Well, you know, Nomo wasn't that great. He just had this really screwy wind up, and that's all. He wasn't really a stud pitcher." Or you could say, "All Ichiro did was hit ground balls, and he just beat them out." And, "Hideki Matsui was a 50–home run hitter in Japan, but the best he could do in the States was 31. So not that great." But there's nothing negative you can say about Ohtani. The Japanese have always wanted parity with American baseball, and now they can say, "We have finally arrived. We're not second class anymore." I think that has done a lot for the national confidence.

Part 2 / **On the Diamond**

2 / Matt Murton, Player

Outfielder Matt Murton played for the Chicago Cubs, Oakland Athletics, and Colorado Rockies before joining the Hanshin Tigers in 2010. In his first season, he broke Ichiro Suzuki's record for the most hits in an NPB season. During his six seasons in Japan, he was a four-time All-Star and won the 2014 Central League batting crown.

◆

As soon as I landed in Osaka in late January 2010 to play for the Hanshin Tigers, I was ushered straight into a press conference. There was a ton of media. I sat at a table with a backdrop behind me and tried to speak as much Japanese as I could. I had been practicing all the way over on the airplane. I can't remember what I said, but it was broken at best. I was just hoping that they understood. My uncle, who had done a good bit of travel overseas, told me that one of the biggest mistakes Americans make when going to a new country is we don't drop our American ways. You should never forget who you are, but you should embrace their culture. Go in with open arms and make sure people understand that you are going to do what you can, although it's not going to be perfect. So, trying to speak Japanese was just one way, like a tip of the hat if you will, to say, "I'm going to do the best I can to assimilate into the culture here."

A few days later, I arrived in Okinawa for what is known as Spring Camp. On day one, after breakfast, we loaded into a van and rode over to camp. All kinds of people were waiting to welcome us. We went out on the field and began with a ceremonial team run. We then clapped together and started stretching. And we stretched, and we stretched, and we stretched. It was like thirty to forty minutes. I've never been a part of a stretch so long in my life. Typically, in the United States after you finish stretching, you play catch with your teammates to get loose. I got ready to play catch, but all of a sudden there was this pause in the action on the field. I'm looking around. *Where are all my teammates? Am I missing something? Am I supposed to be somewhere?* They had all gone into the dugout because, very common in Japanese culture at that time, the guys were taking a smoke break! Five minutes later, they start popping back out, and we began playing catch.

There were a few more surprises on that first day. During batting practice in the United States, they use one batting cage. In Japan, there are three cages, or turtles as we call them, on the field. They have a right-handed BP (batting practice) pitcher, they have a curveball machine in the middle, and they have a left-handed BP pitcher. There were safety nets all over the field, and the batters took rep after rep. There was a morning session, a lunch, and an afternoon session. I'll never forget lunch on my first day in Okinawa. It was udon, and to me as an American, it looked like a bowl of soup. So, I grabbed my spoon and start sipping the broth and pulling the noodles out. Everybody in my general vicinity paused and was staring at me. I looked up, and I'm like, "What in the world is going on?"

And my translator was kind enough to say, "Hey, you know, that is udon. We eat it with chopsticks." They were just baffled that I was eating it with a spoon.

Spring camp lasted about four weeks. It started off with skill development, team practicing, and a lot of repetitions. After a handful of weeks, once the pitchers were built up a little bit, we hit live BP off those guys for a few days, and then we played some games. The point was skill development. Even on game days, we'd spend the mornings working on our craft before we went out and played in the afternoon. After the four weeks, we went to our home in Kobe, and we played games in local stadiums. Most people think that Japanese baseball typically has smaller stadiums. In other words, the distances from home plate to the fence are shorter. That's changed over the years. A lot of the new ballparks have gotten closer to Major League ballparks in their sizes.

Spring camp was certainly more than I'd ever experienced in the United States, but it was not as intense as what was depicted in *Mr. Baseball* or *You Gotta Have Wa*. Every generation is going to tell a different story about what it was like for them. I think there was a gradual shift driven by Ichiro Suzuki having been over in the United States and the exposure that Japan had to Major League Baseball. Those who were thirty and older had a different regimen than the kids who were under thirty. For those who were under thirty, it was very much like what I read about. Those who were over thirty were starting to ease off a little bit, but they still worked really hard. Even though I wasn't over thirty, the U.S. players were automatically dumped into that thirty-and-over bucket. But I was crazy enough to say, "No, no, I'm just going to be like everybody else." And I paid the price because I was sore, and it was hard to get up in the morning!

My family came over a few days after I got back to Kobe. The team took care of the apartment and all those transition things, like getting a doctor, setting up our TV, and things like that. The support was incredible. The director of the international department gave us a tour of the area. He showed us everything: where the dry cleaners and the grocery store were, how to buy milk, what the proper thing was to get for whatever the circumstance. He was walking us through all that stuff, and I leaned over to him and said, "Man, I can't tell you enough how grateful I am for all you are doing to help and making my family feel welcome."

And he leans in, smiles, and goes, "I'm glad that you feel that way. We worked overtime to make sure that's the case. We do that because there's absolutely no excuse now for you not to perform on the field."

I'll never forget opening day at Koshien Stadium. It was a packed stadium, and you could feel the energy that the fans were bringing and their passion and their love for the game. I remember just having this overwhelming feeling, and I started thinking about all that had happened for me to be there at that moment: the good and the hard things that happened along the way from when I was a little boy to being in Major League Baseball. I'll never forget that.

Japanese fans are incredible. You know those moments in the United States when the fans get really passionate and you can just feel the emotion in the stadium? That emotion, and this is not an exaggeration, is almost sustained throughout the course of all nine innings in Japan. You have a culture where people work so hard, they're so reserved, they're disciplined, and they hold their emotions in, and then they get to the ballpark, and they just let it all out. They have this moment of freedom to let everything go from the day and just embrace their team. I've wondered countless times, *Who goes home more tired—the players or the fans?* Away from the ballpark, Japanese fans are pretty respectful. If you're out in town, they will come up to you and talk to you. They will not hesitate to do that, but they're not over the top. If they see you out in town with your kids, they're just like,

"Hey Matt, just saying hi." They are pretty chill. They recognize that you have a family.

The world of baseball has realized, probably for a long time, that the quality of the Japanese game is very good. But some things were certainly different and kind of stood out. I was there for six years. The first year I came over, there were four different official balls! They had done that for a long time. One of them was a little bit more juiced or had a little more life to it than others. In my second year, they decided as a league that they wanted to go to a uniform ball. So, they had to determine how they were going to regulate that baseball. Anytime you start making changes, there are periods of learning and adjustment. So that year was very difficult for not only me but for a lot of guys because of the new ball. The other thing that you noticed on Japanese balls was that they were a little tackier out of the box. The type of leather they used was tackier, so pitchers had a better grip.

The American game is built off the ability to get multiple bases with one swing to score runs. The idea behind this is that it takes fewer hits to score a run as compared to having to string together multiple hits. The Japanese game is predicated on the principle of creating run-scoring situations with a single hit, or even no hits, by moving up base runners. The second-hole hitter in Japan usually can handle the bat well and can lay down bunts with a high rate of success. It is very common in NPB to witness the leadoff hitter get on and then try to advance to second base by either a steal, or more often a bunt, right out of the gate in the first inning. It is more of a run-at-a-time approach, but it reduces the likelihood of a big inning, and studies show that the team with the biggest inning over the course of a game tends to win more often than not. This one-run approach is so prevalent in Japan that on defense, even in the early innings of games, corner outfielders are asked to play in and in the hole to cut down runs at the plate on singles, a position that leaves you exposed to getting beat on balls over your head.

When I came into the big leagues in 2005, pitchers were taught to get guys out in three pitches or fewer. That was their mindset because they tried to get deep into games. I remember Greg Maddux telling me, "My goal is to pitch into the seventh inning of every game to give myself a chance to win." To do that, you're attacking with the fastball early and then maybe expanding the plate as you go. In Japan, when I came over, they didn't think that way. All bets were off. They may throw a breaking ball on

Matt Murton. Courtesy of Matt Murton.

the first pitch, then expand the zone to make your eyes bigger, and then throw a two seamer or a ball that's off the plate with enough movement on it to come back over for a called strike. They weren't as worried about pitch counts and would run pitch counts up. They also weren't afraid to walk you as much as they were in the United States. It really forced me to rethink the way I looked at counts because I was wired a certain way, and I had to reprogram my mind. What was funny is when I came back to U.S. baseball, I never fully recovered from that mentality. I kept thinking that a breaking ball was coming, and they kept throwing fastballs.

Lately, we've seen a little bit of a shift in Major League Baseball. I don't know if it's the influence of the Japanese pitchers who have come over and done well, but guys are more willing now in the United States to pitch what we would call backward, like throwing off-speed earlier in counts and then when the pitcher is in the driver seat, like on a two-strike count, throwing fastballs.

For the most part, the rules in NPB and MLB were the same, but there were unwritten rules, like gentlemen's rules, that I didn't fully understand at first. They didn't really take anybody out at second base. In the United States, if you didn't take the guy out at second to break up the double play then you weren't giving a good effort. I remember Tsuyoshi Nishioka, a middle infielder who had played for the Chiba Lotte Marines, who came to the United States. When he played for the Minnesota Twins, he broke his leg while trying to turn a double play because he wasn't accustomed to getting out of the way.

Japanese pitchers have tremendous control. They're known for that. They didn't hit very many batters, and typically if they did, they would tip their caps, like, *I'm sorry, I didn't mean to do that*. It was just a way of paying respect. Pitchers in the United States would never do that. Sometimes when I was hit, I felt that the pitcher meant to do it, but he's still tipping his hat. *If you meant to do it, don't tip your hat!*

Japanese and Major League managers are, in certain ways, very similar. There's a certain line that you still feel, whether you're in Japan or you're in the United States, that's inevitable because he's the manager and you're the player. That's just the way it is. But that line is a little fuzzier in the United States than in Japan. After I spent some time in Japan, I started thinking, *You know what this feels like? Amateur baseball at a professional level, in terms of how these players sit under the authority of these managers.* The players submit themselves to the manager. There is a more submissive posture to authority in Japan, even at a professional level, than there is in the United States. I think that's just the nature of the culture. The managers who I had didn't speak to you a lot. They were great guys. They would take us out to dinner, but on the field, there was not a ton of interaction. You would also see coaches unafraid to challenge a player, whereas in the United States you don't see confrontational challenges as much because they might start a scuffle.

The relationship between players and umpires was also very different. In the United States, umpires will allow you to ask questions a little bit more freely about called strikes or what they saw. There's a little bit more back and forth. In Japan, it's expected that there will be no back and forth. They're the authority. They're going to tell you what's going to happen. Japanese tend to be very good at internalizing their emotions. It's seen as a lack of control or discipline if you allow that emotion to come out. In U.S. culture, we allow emotion to come out a lot more freely. So interactions with umpires are distinctly different both culturally and even in how it plays out on the field on a day-to-day basis.

On a typical home-game day, I would head over to the ballpark in the late morning. I started out in the indoor facility working on my swing. Then, we would have batting practice. Afterward, there would be a lunch that was prepared for us. It was phenomenal. Most days it was *katsudon* (pork cutlet on rice), *tamago* (omelet), *katame* (firm noodles) for me. Then we would have a scouting meeting—every day. We'd sit in that meeting for probably twenty to thirty minutes going over the day's starter, and at the beginning of each series we would go over every bullpen arm. Then we'd go back out, and we'd have our second warm up. There was a lot of warming up where everything was done together as a team, so there's not a whole lot of free time in Japan; most of it is programmed for you. And there's not a lot of time in the clubhouse. We were in and out in a couple of minutes, so there's not a ton of interaction with your teammates. You talk some, but just not much. It's very work oriented. We were not there to hang out. We were there to get stuff done. In the second warm up, we took ground balls or fly balls and threw them to the bases as outfielders. Then I would go in, and the trainers stretched me out and made sure I was ready to play.

The trainers in Japan did a great job. Massage therapy was really a part of the Japanese game. That was new to me because in the United States, only veterans were doing that. It was kind of like a no-no. In Japan, if you're not doing it, you're not taking care of your body, and you're not really preparing yourself for the game. It was an expectation that you would get on the table.

After the game, I took notes to prep me for future meetings with these pitchers. What were the strengths of this guy? What things did he expose me on? Where did he have success, or where did I have success? From there I would usually have some dinner, and then I would lift in the weight room. One thing I didn't do initially, but I started getting into over time, was taking a warm bath. It was totally relaxing. Then I went home. There would be some days where I didn't feel like my swing was dialed in. On those particular days, I would stop by that indoor facility after the game and work on the swing and/or check out some video. If there was something on my mind, or bothering me, I wanted to put it to bed that night so that when I came in the next day it was back to work as usual.

Away games in Japan were a unique experience. We stayed in a hotel like we did in the United States, but we would change into our uniforms, and we would have our scouting meetings at the hotel. They would also provide the team breakfast and lunch at the hotel. In the United States, you figure out how to get your own breakfast and lunch, and we never got changed at the hotel. We would go to the field in our street clothes, change at the ballpark, and the clubhouse attendant would wash our stuff, and then we'd change back into our street clothes and head home. Well, in Japan, no. We'd get dressed at the hotel, go downstairs, and have our meeting. Then the foreigners would jump in a taxi and go to the ballpark while the team took a bus. I think that was because they could smoke on the bus and we weren't used to sitting in the smoke. After the game, we would go back to the hotel in full uniform. If I was diving around the field, I'd be a mess walking back into this nice hotel in my uniform, like I'm a kid in the United States. At the hotel, we would take our showers and throw our clothes into laundry baskets out in the hallways. They would clean them and fold them neatly into plastic coverings and set them in front of our doors the next morning for us to get dressed to go back to the ballpark. We had visiting locker rooms, but they were very sterile. You would find a spot in the locker, you sit down, you get yourself ready for the day, you pack up your stuff, you go back to the hotel. We also had to carry all of our equipment to and from the ballpark every night.

Baseball in the United States is very big, obviously, but in Japan, there are not as many things to compete for everybody's attention. For generations, baseball was one of the main focal points of Japanese culture, so every day, baseball is front and center in the papers. A lot of people are following what's going on with their local team, so the press is very prevalent. In the United States, the press stays out of the clubhouse for thirty minutes after the final pitch, so guys can get their thoughts together before the press would engage them at their lockers. In Japan as soon as we finished, we went to the locker room, where the guys would gather their stuff before they went out. The press is not allowed in there. But we only stayed there for a handful of minutes. As soon as you walk out of that room, you're walking in the hallways either to the bus at the end of a visiting game or back to the clubhouse at Koshien Stadium. Reporters line the hallways, and they're grabbing you. You go from a final out to the press asking you questions within a handful of minutes. When somebody grabs you, a whole cluster of media will surround that interview. You have one individual, or maybe a couple, asking questions, but tons of people taking notes. Everybody who wants to be involved is involved. So, as you can imagine, if you're not disciplined and controlled, it can lend itself to sound bites or quotes that aren't necessarily favorable. You have to learn to become much more guarded and use fewer words so that you don't get yourself in trouble.

What's crazy is that you can almost outfit your entire home at the team shop. It has whatever you want, whether it's pillows or your blanket or the curtains on your window—you name it, they've got it. Of course, they sell jerseys. Jersey sales are really big. But they will also market a whole line of things for you as an athlete. There will be key chains with your depiction, or a cartoon depiction of you as an athlete, and your name and your number; and towels with your name and number; stickers; everything. They made T-shirts my first year with a picture of Florida because that was where I was born. One of the things that was kind of cool is we each had a meal at the ballpark named after us. They asked us, "What do you like?" And then, they produced it and sold it at the ballpark. The Murton was katsudon, tamago, and katame. So, they marketed even their food that way. They don't leave any stone unturned when it comes to the marketing of memorabilia. If it's produced and people use it, it will have a Tigers emblem on it.

I worked out in the off-season with Ben Zobrist, Chase Headley, and Logan Forsythe. Well, Ben played in one of the tours that went over to Japan. He played at Koshien, and he goes in the team shop. He sees all my gear. He buys all my gear. After he came back to the United States, the guys walked into the training facility wearing a whole slew of Matt Murton memorabilia and started giving me a hard time, like, "What is all this stuff?" So, even these American ballplayers were taken aback by how much stuff was out there for Matt Murton.

After my last game in Japan, I wrote a letter. I knew there was going to be another American the next season and the Americans usually took the same locker. I had no idea who the guy would be, but I wrote a letter and just poured my heart out to a guy whom I didn't even know. I said that this is going to be one of the best places you will ever put on a uniform, and it's going to be one of the most difficult, so just embrace the journey. Do not be afraid to swallow your pride. Do not be afraid to do something different. Remember, you signed up for it. You put your name on the dotted line, so embrace the culture and do whatever they ask you to do. And just enjoy the culture, enjoy the people, and experience the things off the field.

I think if guys go over there knowing it's going to be difficult but with an open mindset, and they embrace the journey, they are going to have some wonderful moments, memories that they'll never forget.

3 / Shungo Fukunaga, Minor League Player

After playing three years in the Japanese independent leagues, Shungo Fukunaga was drafted by the Hanshin Tigers in 2016. He spent four years with Hanshin, playing mostly on the farm team, before playing in Mexico and Taiwan.

◆

Players usually enter NPB by being scouted in high school, often at Koshien, or college and then being selected in the NPB amateur draft that takes place each October. But I followed a more unusual path.

At first, I attended a very well-known high school that often made it to the Koshien tournament. When I started playing baseball in high school, I was aiming to become a professional, but I experienced a couple of injuries, and it reached the point that I didn't want to keep playing baseball. I was ready to give it up and just move on with my life. So, I moved to Clark High School, which didn't have a baseball club. I finished my high school years without playing baseball. I did not even pick up a ball.

Right after I graduated, I turned on the TV and I saw guys who were my age playing in the Koshien tournament. And I thought, *It sure would be nice if I could play baseball again.* I didn't have any serious aspirations at that time, just a wish to play again. I wasn't even sure if I was good enough to play, but I wanted to give it a try.

I started out by getting myself in shape. I wanted to play catch, but I didn't really have a partner, so I just threw the ball against a wall to practice my throwing. About six months later, I heard that tryouts were taking place for the Kansai Independent Baseball League. I went to the tryouts and received an offer from the 06 Bulls. I joined that team and played with them for two seasons.

After the 2014 season, I heard that there were tryouts for the Shikoku Independent League. The level of play in Shikoku was much higher than it was in Kansai. I was still hoping that I could be drafted and turn pro, and I knew that my chances would be better if I went to Shikoku. So, I tried out and joined the Tokushima Indigo Socks for two years. The Shikoku League put together a team of representatives that went to North America to play in the Can-Am League (Canadian American Association), which was principally in New Jersey and in the Ottawa and Quebec areas of Canada. I was on that team for two seasons.

I feel like my experience playing in the Can-Am League is connected to where I am right now, in the sense that when I went to play there, it really helped me see baseball in a different light. It was my first time seeing baseball being played in a different country, and it left an impression on me. Baseball wasn't just what I thought it was while I was playing in Japan. One example of that was the stadium atmosphere. This is just my personal interpretation, but it seems like baseball in Japan is about going to the games to cheer. That's the purpose of going to baseball games. Whereas in America, it felt more like families went there to have family time together, to enjoy a meal together, and to be entertained by the baseball that was happening on the field. The league just presented a completely different version of the game. It started with practices before the game, which were different than they are in Japan. Of course, we practiced hard. We took it seriously, but it just had a different feel than it did in Japan, as did the game itself, the crowd, and the stadiums. It really opened my eyes to a different version of baseball that I hadn't seen up until that point. Because of this experience, after my NPB career I felt comfortable playing in Mexico and Taiwan.

I also saw a different style of play. Japanese baseball is a team game. Teams are always looking for a way to score one run at all costs. They'll do whatever they can to get that one run across home plate. In Japan you see a lot of guys swinging for contact or fouling off pitches on purpose to stay alive at the plate. That really didn't happen in America. In America, guys would stay true to their hitting style. No matter what, they were going to swing all out, hard every time. They didn't swing for contact, or just to stay alive at the plate. They want to make sure that if they went down, they went down their way. What that meant for me as a pitcher was that I had to make sure that every pitch was my best, because they were going for it. At first, this was a little bit scary because every one of their swings was going to be hard.

In my second season with the Indigo Socks, I was putting up some good numbers. Right before the draft, scouts from multiple teams came out to watch. If a team is interested in possibly drafting you, they will give you a form that you need to submit back. It's like a resume of your baseball past. I received forms from multiple teams indicating that they might draft me.

In Japan the players do not attend the draft. Instead, the team that you are currently playing for sets aside a room for you at their particular institution. So, if it's a school, there will be some room in the school where the student can watch the draft live. If you're working for a company and you're playing industrial baseball, the company will have a room for you just to watch the draft as it goes along until you're chosen.

I was playing in Tokushima, and I was in a back room at the Youme Town shopping center with my teammates, the team manager, the coaches, and the team representative. We were all watching the draft live in that room, and the players who were possibly going to be drafted sat in the front row. Once we were selected, we went into the mall itself where we had our press conference to make remarks about being drafted. I was selected in the sixth round by the Hanshin Tigers.

The team representative from Tokushima and the Hanshin scout who had scouted me then arranged a date for the scout to come to our team facility, where I signed an agreement—not the official contract, more like a precontract. Then in early December, Hanshin had a press conference welcoming the new players to the team. All the players who were drafted attended, and we received our uniform numbers and signed our official contracts.

At that point, I moved into the team dormitory. As a basic rule, all players were required to live in the dorm when they joined the team. But some players were already married when they were drafted, so they were given the choice whether or not they wanted to live in the dorm.

The farm team plays in Nishinomiya, a bit south of Koshien, and the team dorm was right next to the farm facility. Each player had his own room, a one bedroom, about eight tatami mats in size (about 133 square feet). There was a bed, a desk, and a closet, and then there was a space to have a TV or some sort of entertainment system, but that's about it. The bed was a Western-style bed, not a futon, but we were not provided with a mattress, so it was just the bed frame. We had to bring in our own mattresses. There were bathrooms on each floor. On the first floor there was a large Japanese-style bathing room with showers and a large tub, a gym, and the trainers' facilities, where we could receive massages or any kind of physical therapy that we needed. There were also lockers that we used on game and practice days. There was a parking lot for players who had cars, but during your first year on the team you were not allowed to have a car, and if you were drafted straight out of high school, you had to wait three years before you could have a car.

The cafeteria was in the farm facility. We were allowed to eat whatever we wanted to, but we had information sessions on what different types of foods would do for our bodies. So, we learned about nutrition. Also, on the cafeteria walls there were a lot of posters that explained the nutritional value of various foods.

There was a kind of dorm supervisor, but there were no specific rules regarding wake-up and lights-out times. However, breakfast was at a designated time, and we were told that we needed to be at breakfast every day. We did have a curfew. On nights before a practice or game, the curfew was 10:30 p.m. If we had the next day off, our curfew was midnight.

The Tigers were quite strict, so there weren't incidences of young players going out and doing anything wild or falling into temptation because of their new freedom. We actually were required to attend sessions to inform us about what was acceptable and not acceptable.

At one of these information sessions, they had told us about a first-year player several years prior who took the money from his signing bonus and bought a very expensive car. But he had spent so much on this new car, that he wasn't able to pay his income taxes the next year. So, the team changed the system. Now, when a player receives a signing bonus, the team withholds the amount that will be taxed the following year to make sure that it doesn't get spent. Legally, Japanese professional baseball players are independent contractors. So, we are responsible for doing all of that tax work and declarations on our own. We are also responsible for finding and purchasing our own insurance.

Decades ago, rookie players had to do a lot of extra work, like clean the veteran players' clothes and shoes and take care of all the equipment. It was a form of hazing. But that doesn't happen anymore. There was no hazing at all, and the only extra work that first-year players had to do were small things, like bringing out the netting for batting practice, or things like that.

Typically on the farm, games started at 12:30 in the afternoon. I would wake up around 6:30 a.m. Either before or after breakfast, most players would spend time soaking in the bath. Then around 8:00 a.m., we would go to the ballpark and do our personal warmups, training, stretching, etcetera. By 9:00 a.m. the team would be doing warmups together. The whole team would work out together and practice until around 10:30. Position players would take batting and fielding practice. Pitchers would do various prep work, including playing catch and warming up our arms to be ready for the 12:30 game. Starting pitchers who were not scheduled to pitch that day would throw their bullpens. Usually on the day after a start, pitchers would just play a little bit of light catch. Then, the day after that was a complete day off. Three and four days after a start is when we would do the bulk of our bullpen workouts. We would throw 60 to 70 pitches at about 70 percent strength. The day before the next start, we would do our final preparations for the upcoming game, making sure that all the pitches were working and the mechanics were okay. We would throw about 70 percent of our full strength, although a few of the final pitches might be at full strength.

In our bullpens, we used Trackman technology and analytics. When pitching, it's hard to know for sure how much movement I've got on my pitches. Using Trackman allowed me to see the height of my point of release, how far off the plate my pitches were, how much movement I had on them. I could check on each individual pitch and better analyze them and fix issues.

After the game, we would often hit the gym and lift weights. I did a lot of weightlifting. To work my lower half, I did squats, lunges, and hip thrusts. For upper body, I did just basic things like bench presses and lat pulldowns, things like that.

On May 3 of my first season, I was told that I was being called up to the first team and would start against the Hiroshima Carp in three days. A couple of days before the start, I went to Koshien Stadium just to get a feel for the noise and the atmosphere of the game. I also looked at the data on the other team's hitters.

On that day, I didn't really feel anything different until I got to the ballpark. As time went on, I began to get more and more nervous. Before the game, I went out and played catch, and that's when the nerves really started to hit because I looked around and saw just how many fans were there. It was a sellout and so there were over forty thousand people in the

Shungo Fukunaga. Courtesy of Shungo Fukunaga.

stands. After playing catch, I had to go back to the locker room, and I was so nervous that I lost my way.

When the game started, I was so nervous that I couldn't even feel my legs. I just went blank. The veteran players gave me words of encouragement. They talked to me from when I arrived in the morning, all the way through to when I was on the mound during the game. But I was so nervous I can't remember a thing they told me. Even when they were speaking to me, nothing really sank in.

In large part because of my pitching, the team was in a huge deficit right from the start. We were way behind. But after I left the mound, the team actually pulled off a miraculous comeback and ended up winning the game. It was a very important game, as we were fighting for first place against the opponents, so I'm glad that we won, but I was disappointed with my own performance. After the game, I was told by the pitching coach to go to the manager's office, and he told me that I was being sent back down to the farm.

After the season, we had fall camps. As far as I know, the American system does not have required autumn camps for the players. In October there was a special development league for the farm team, and then November was the fall camp for the first team. Those training camps were excruciatingly hard, and I was so sore after practices that I wasn't able to move. For the next three seasons, I was mostly on the farm team, but each year I was called up and pitched a few games for the Tigers.

Many Japanese athletes have their own superstitions. For example, the day before a game, pitchers might eat the same meal as last time, and on the day of the game, they might eat or drink the same things. Some players even have detailed routines, like the order in which they put on their socks. Some wear the same underwear or outfit and follow the same route to the stadium, stopping at the same convenience store to buy the same items. On the field, some athletes have specific rituals, like which foot they step onto the field with first. I had similar habits when I was a starting pitcher, but after becoming a relief pitcher, I became less concerned about them. In my case, I would eat soba noodles for lunch, wear the same undershirt, and change shirts during the game in the third, fifth, and seventh innings. I also made sure to wear the shirts in the same order that I had changed them previously.

After my NPB career was finished in 2020, I signed a contract with the Rakuten Monkeys in Taiwan, but because of the COVID-19 pandemic the contract was cancelled. I still wanted to play baseball, and because of the pandemic it was difficult to play in Asia, so I decided to go to Mexico. There, I was met with a series of surprises. For example, unlike in Japanese stadiums, there isn't a big fence between the bullpen and the stands in a Mexican ballpark. In my first game, I was warming up in the bullpen and a fan handed me a scorpion lollipop. It had a scorpion stuck on a stick and was coated in transparent candy so that I could see everything. I didn't resist it and decided to accept it as normal, so I put it in my mouth without fear. An old man watching the game near the bullpen smiled when he saw that.

Another difference was in the managers. Japanese managers, generally, in both practice and games, stand at the front of the dugout giving orders, telling the coaches what to tell the players. Whereas in the Mexican league it seemed like it was more about the players coming to the manager with their ideas of what might work for them. They would tell the manager what they would like to do, and then the manager would make the schedule based on what the players have asked for.

The locker room behavior was completely different. Before the games in Japan—and this is mostly true in Taiwan as well—players would quietly do their own thing. They would eat meals, or they would put on their headphones. They might look at their iPads, either watching YouTube or checking video footage of different players. Some of them will put on an eye mask and take a nap. That's kind of the standard in Japan.

I really experienced culture shock when I went to Mexico and the locker room there was a completely different story. First of all, there was loud music—really loud music. A player might put on some kind of virtual-reality headset and would play a game. People would be screwing around and just messing with each other. Some guys would have Segways, and they would be zooming around the locker room on them. It was just really loud and noisy atmosphere in the Mexican locker rooms. I would say it's pretty close to zero horsing around like that in a Japanese locker room.

After playing in Mexico, I played in Taiwan's industrial league and the CPBL (Chinese Professional Baseball League), Taiwan's professional league, before becoming a coach in the CPBL. I definitely feel that baseball does a great job of uniting different cultures. Just looking at this from my own personal experiences, if baseball didn't exist across various cultures, I would not have been able to play the game in these different countries. I would never even have gone to these countries, let alone played in those places. By playing in these different countries, I was able to make friends with my teammates as well as other people. Even to this day, I'm still in touch with some of the players from when I was in the Mexican league. These experiences also made me realize how much I took for granted when I lived in Japan. By going to other countries and playing baseball in these different cultures, I've been able to experience new cultures, and that has enriched my life.

4 / Natsuo Yamazaki, Umpire

An NPB umpire from 1988 until 2010, Yamazaki officiated 1,451 league games. His seventeen ejections are the most by any NPB umpire in history.

◆

I love baseball. I think Japan is a country that values partnerships and relationships. Baseball, being a team sport, brings that to the forefront. It's a bunch of individuals who are playing the game, and they've got to do things on their own, but the ultimate goal is team victory. Even the players who don't get into the game, who remain on the bench, are cheering on their teammates. Even if they're not participating, they still want to contribute to the team's victory by encouraging their teammates. And this goes beyond just the players on the field—there are people behind the scenes who are contributing. Everybody is contributing to the good of the team, and I think that matches well with the national character of the Japanese people.

As I grew up loving the game of baseball, I wanted to become a professional baseball player. In high school I played in every game and every inning for three years. I continued to play at Hokkaido University, but during my third year I fractured my right ankle, so I had to abandon my dream of becoming a professional baseball player. I still loved baseball, but I also loved writing. So, I decided to become a journalist and cover baseball as a sports journalist. I joined *Nikkan Sports* but, unfortunately, they put me in the sales department. I had to endure that for three long years of agony. I didn't enjoy it at all, but I realized one day as I was watching baseball that there might be jobs for umpires.

At that time, there were three ways that you could become an umpire. The most common of those—and this was the case for over two-thirds of the umpires when I became an ump—was that you were a former professional baseball player, and after you retired from the game, you would be recommended by the team to become an umpire. The second way was if you were an amateur umpire and worked some of the big tournaments and were recognized as skilled at the job. Then you could be recommended to move up into the pros. The third way was through a public audition. A lot of people would go to these auditions, but it was hard to find good umpires in this way. On a side note, currently, of the fifty-six umpires who are in NPB, only eight of them are former pro players. These days there is really only one way to become a professional umpire, and that is to go to the NPB umpire school, which was started in 2013. They get about 150 applicants every year, and only about three or four make it all the way to become NPB umps.

Well, the year that I decided to become an umpire, there were no open auditions. So, I went directly to the president of the Pacific League and asked him if I could be a professional baseball umpire. Of course, he rejected my request because of my lack of experience. At first, I was depressed, but I realized that I really wanted to become an umpire. The next day, I submitted my resignation and left *Nikkan Sports*. I memorized the 250-page rulebook, and I approached an active umpire, who taught me the skills and techniques. Then, I went back to the president. Maybe it was my passion, maybe it was just the way that I looked, but I convinced him to make me kind of an intern. I was allowed to go to the umpiring camp and try it out. I had a hard time with it for a month, but after the camp, the president handed me a one-year contract. So, my way of becoming an umpire was unique. There's nobody else that has done it that way, before or after me.

It took me eight years in the minors to become a regular member of NPB's major league umpire crew. At first, my annual salary was only ¥1.6 million, the lowest among the one thousand people in NPB, including the players, so I had to work part-time to support my family. But that has changed. Now, when you become a new umpire, the pay is basically the same as a new recruit for any company straight out of university—about ¥4 million per year. In the beginning, there are no raises, and it takes about seven to eight years to make your way to the top level of professional baseball. At about ten years, if you are in the majors, your salary might be ¥10 million per season. But even the best umpires will never reach ¥20 million for the season. The age of retirement is fifty-five. Unlike baseball players, there's no signing bonus when we first become umpires, nor is there any retirement fund. So even though the annual pay might be a little bit higher than the average person's salary, considering these other factors, it really isn't that high.

In 1993 I went to the Jim Evans Umpire School. It started in the first week of January and ran for five weeks. The Pacific League Commissioners Office sent me because they wanted me to learn umpiring techniques from the best in America. This practice continues to this day. They still send two umpires over every year. Currently, they're sending them to the Harry Wendelstedt Umpire School. When I went to the Jim Evans Umpire School, I was really impressed by the first thing that Jim Evans said in the very first class: "The most important thing about being an umpire is being respected." That is something that I have always focused on. The time that I spent at the school was a wonderful experience, and it's still a treasure of my life. It helped me form my umpiring policies for the twenty-nine years that I was a professional umpire.

Until 2010 umpires were separated by league. There were Central League and Pacific League umpires. To decrease the amount of travel between cities and to have a more consistent product, the two umpire groups were merged in 2011. So, they're all lumped together as one now. Fifty-six umpires are active in 2024, plus five supervisors and one head umpire. The five supervisors watch all the games, including farm games, and evaluate the umpires. At season's end, the seven umpires who rank the highest are chosen to be the umpiring crew for the Japan Series.

We work in five-man crews, with four umps on the field and a backup umpire. The head umpire puts together the crews. Of course, some umpires work well together, and some don't work so well together, so the head umpire asks the crew chiefs who they would like to work with, and he can grant the requests. Usually, three of the umpires will stay together for most of the season and the other two may change every three to four series. Sometimes, there are young umpires on the farm who are doing a really good job, so they will get a chance to come up to the major leagues for a little while. In 2020 and 2021 during the pandemic, the five-man crews stayed together the whole season to decrease the risk of transmission of COVID-19.

The umpires in NPB travel a lot less than MLB umps. Teams play two three-game series each week, so generally speaking, the longest road trip for an umpire crew might be six games or six nights. There are five stadiums in the Tokyo area: Meiji Jingu, Tokyo Dome, Yokohama Stadium, Seibu's Belluna Dome, and Chiba's ZOZO Marine Stadium. So, the umps who are based in Tokyo don't have to travel that much. Whereas for the umpires based in Osaka, all they have is Koshien and Orix's dome nearby, so they naturally have more road trips. The longest stretch that we have on the road is actually during spring training, when we would be away from home for the entire month of February. If you add up all of the road trips plus spring training, we're looking at about between 100 and 120 nights a year on the road. NPB takes care of the hotels. They have a contract with the hotels for the entire year, so they are set up well in advance. But transportation is up to the individual. Some umpires prefer to get to the ballparks nice and early, others would rather take their time and get there as late as possible.

On a typical day with a night game, I would get up around 7:00 in the morning and have breakfast with my kids. After they went to school, I'd go back to sleep until around 10:00. From then until noon, I would do some training. To have the stamina to get through an entire baseball game, you need to be in good shape. Umpires are very thorough about that. We work out daily, just like the players, so most of the umpires are in very good physical condition. I am 183 centimeters, or 6 feet, and 90 kilos (just under 200 pounds). That's probably about the average size for an umpire. Umpires are also pretty fast runners and have good stamina. You won't find any umpire in Japan who's trying to tuck in his stomach because it's protruding. There's no such thing in Japan.

After training, I would eat some lunch, take another nap, and, between three and four o'clock, head off to the ballpark. Generally speaking, we don't meet before games and talk about the pitchers or anything like that. We stay in the umpires' room and just relax and chat with each other. We might stretch. Some umpires like to practice a little bit, but that kind of stuff usually gets taken care of at home. The umpires are responsible for preparing the balls by rubbing them with dirt to get rid of the finish on them. We'll typically start the game with seven dozen balls that need to be prepared before the game. Depending on how many balls we need, there could be up to three dozen extra balls that must be prepared. The backup umpire prepares the extra balls, should they be needed. If it's a rainy day, we could go through as many as fifteen dozen balls.

Natsuo Yamazaki. Courtesy of Natsuo Yamazaki.

Of course, in Japan it rains a lot. The umpires are the ones who make the decision as to whether to call for a rain delay or to call the game off. The most important consideration is actually the fans. If possible, we try to keep the delays to thirty minutes or under. If after thirty minutes it still doesn't look like the rain is going to let up, we'll call the game off. The teams themselves usually want to finish the games. If we call that game off before the fifth inning, then the game doesn't count. It has to be played all over again, and that means the club has to return money to the fans. So, the clubs want to, as much as possible, play at least until the fifth inning. That makes the decision hard if a game gets delayed in the fourth inning when it's getting close to becoming official.

If it's not raining in the summer, it's usually hot. The biggest thing is to stay hydrated, so drinking a lot of fluids, especially between every inning, is important. Some umpires, because of all the sweating that we're doing, change their uniforms during the fifth-inning break. The black umpire uniform, obviously, retains heat, so in the summer months we have a sky-blue uniform. The color makes it a little bit easier to deal with the heat. By the way, the home plate umpire wears five to six kilograms worth of equipment, so working there is a more physically demanding position than on the bases, especially in the heat.

The games start at 6:00 p.m. and usually end between 9:00 and 10:00. After I take a shower, we have our postgame umpires meeting. The lengthier ones might take up to thirty minutes, but if nothing major happened during the game it might just be a ten-minute session, where we would ask each other, "What did you think about this call or about this play?" The younger umpires sometimes will get to the ballpark early the next day to go over video and review some of the closer calls. I would get home sometime between 11:00 p.m. and midnight, perhaps have a beer, watch some TV, eat a little bit, and be in bed by 1:00 a.m. We have to launder our own uniforms. When we are on the road, the hotels have coin-operated laundry machines. Even though I would bring three uniforms with me, I always wash my uniforms daily. So, I would usually wake up early the next morning and get it done before the next day's game.

For an umpire there's an expectation that you get things 100 percent right. If you call a perfect game all the way to the bottom of the ninth inning but you make a mistake at the very end, that one mistake is going to stick with the fans, and they'll remember that. So, it doesn't matter that you've called a game perfectly up to that point.

Of course, humans aren't gods; no matter what, we can't be perfect, so in the game of baseball there are going to be disagreements and arguments. No matter how good of an umpire you are, there are going to be mistakes. The best you can probably achieve is 99 percent accuracy. To maintain control as an umpire when you make mistakes, you need the respect of the players, managers, and fans. That comes from building up a strong character. You need to build up the trust from others and build up your likeability, and that comes from treasuring the people you meet, as well as trying to become an excellent person by reading books and learning and gleaning things from movies. Besides that, umps must make sure that they are physically fit and ready for every game. I make sure that every day I do something to make myself better in those respects.

In addition, I was always aware that when I was on the field I was being watched. Fans would have their eyes on me, and so that meant wearing my jacket right, wearing my uniform properly, having pleated slacks, making sure my spikes were spotless and shining, making sure I was wearing my equipment right, and not partaking in small talk with the players that might look unprofessional—just always conducting myself as a professional.

When I did make a wrong call, I would never apologize to a player. If I were to do something like that, it would be time for me to resign. About 80 percent of the time when I made the wrong call, I realized it right away, and I felt bad, but I would never voice it. I would even feel depressed about it that night, but I would always try to shake it off. I could shake things off pretty quickly and come back the next day with a fresh mind. I feel that to be a pro umpire you must be able to do that. You can't let things drag out, and you can't hold on to stuff like that. I would never make up for a wrong call later in the game by giving a player a favorable call. I would never give him a ball when it was a strike just because I had made the wrong call earlier. That just doesn't fit with being a professional umpire, so I would just shake off the bad call and continue to call the game the best that I could from that point forward.

Umpires go to the stadium by car, and the parking lots have a special exit from the stadium, so we don't encounter fans after the games. As a result, I never got into an altercation or was threatened by fans. However, there were times that I would get phone calls, anonymous phone calls, at my home when I would pick up the phone and somebody would say, "You suck! You need to quit your job" and then hang up. And sometimes there's anger that gets deflected onto the family. I live in Chiba, not too far from the where the Chiba Lotte Marines play. At the school that my kids attended, all their classmates were Marines fans. Sometimes when I made a call against the Marines, my kids would get picked on by other classmates. They would say, "Because of your dad, the team lost" or things like that. It's not really publicized very much, but because of incidents with fans or because of the pressure was just too much, there have been some umps who have resigned or had to quit. Some have checked themselves into hospitals. Many of them have sleepless nights.

I think umpires in the United States are required to control things much more so than they do in Japan. From my point of view, it seems that the teams and the umpires in the United States are in opposition, whereas in Japan it's almost like a partnership between the teams and the umpires. Consequently, there is less conflict over some of the calls. Also, in the United States a rule states that a manager or a player can't argue with an umpire about balls and strikes. If they do, it can result in automatic ejection. There is no such rule in Japan, so umpires generally will listen to what the managers or players have to say. But there's an agreement that any protest that lasts more than five minutes will result in an ejection. The ump will first listen and may issue a warning, and if the person still doesn't calm down or doesn't accept the decision, then that might be grounds for ejection. Most ejections now happen when a manager exceeds the five-minute limit. In recent years, video review has had a real calming effect on everybody. It's created a better relationship between the teams and the umpires. For example, in 2023 there was not a single ejection in an NPB game.

But back in the day, when I started, things were a little bit rougher than they are at present. It was more common for managers and players to yell things at the umpire from the benches. And it wasn't just that people were harsh and rough with their words. Sometimes they were violent. It would turn into fisticuffs at times on the field. There's a saying in Japanese that if there is a fight, then both parties are at least partially to blame. I think umpires understand that, and they take it to heart. So, if something has happened that has caused a manager or a player to get angry, then the umpire is partially responsible, and he doesn't want to eject that manager or player automatically.

I expect that rules are going to be followed, and if players are not following the rules and if they cross the line—for example, if they call me an idiot or they say that I suck or something like that—that's grounds for ejection. During my career, I ejected seventeen people from games. I think that is a record. But I also feel like the average umpire in MLB probably ejects seventeen people per year. So, by comparison, seventeen is really not that many.[1]

One time, during a game between the Lotte Orions and the Nippon Ham Fighters in May 1991, I called a close pitch a ball on a Fighters' batter. It was a very intense game, and Lotte's manager Masaichi Kaneda was clearly frustrated with my call. He came out of the dugout and called me an idiot. I said right back at him, "I'm not nearly as much of an idiot as you are!" And I ejected him. Well, the next day before the game when the managers were exchanging lineups, he came to me and said, "I realized, sir, that you graduated from university, and so you're not an idiot, and I'm sorry that I called you one. What I should have said is, 'You suck!'"

But nowadays, players and managers have much better manners. I would say that the complaints are very few and far between. I think there is a better relationship now than there was then between the teams and the umpires. Part of the reason for that might be that umpires these days are taking their jobs really seriously. They study, they try to improve their techniques, they try to learn from their mistakes, and they review things a lot more frequently. I really think the level of umpiring in NPB in recent years has really taken huge strides.

I retired as an active professional umpire in 2010. I then became an instructor for NPB umpires until 2018. I love baseball, so I still watch a lot of baseball. In fact, last season I went to around one hundred games. I've also started umpiring again, at the amateur level. I umped about forty games last year. Besides that, I'm a writer and a public speaker. I probably had fifty speaking engagements last year, and I have four monthly columns that I write. I've published two books. The first book, *Behind the Scenes of a Professional Umpire*, is a collection of stories from my career. It explains how I became an umpire, and it talks about the players whom I witnessed. In the second book, *All Around Passion! The Truth about Professional Baseball Umpires*, I write about what it takes to be a good umpire. I also talk about the current condition of the game and what professional baseball should do in the near future. I have plans to write a third book, concerning my current work.

I have appointed myself the Umpire Cheering Squad Leader, kind of the oendan leader for umpires, because I feel that umpires are so necessary and yet they're so underappreciated. We need to support them. I've taken upon myself to give lectures, write articles, and make videos to improve the appreciation and authority of umpires and promote the healthy development of baseball. I hope to be able to continue doing this at least for the next five years. It's something that I feel is very important. In order to have a good game, whether in baseball or any other sport, it can't only be done with two good teams. There's a third team involved in every game, and that would be the umpire team. Umpires are very important in creating games for everybody to enjoy, and so that's another reason that I've spent the last eight years of my life developing and training young umpires to become more competent at their jobs. I really feel that the world of umpires and developing good umpires is my life's work.

5 / Trey Hillman, Manager

A long-time MLB coach, Hillman managed the Kansas City Royals, the Nippon Ham Fighters, and the SK Wyverns, winning championships in both Japan and South Korea.

◆

As a lover of baseball my whole life, I always dreamed of being in the big leagues. Growing up, I wanted to be the starting shortstop for the Texas Rangers. After three years of playing in the Minor Leagues, I realized that being a Major League player was probably not in the cards. And then God kind of took over from there. The Cleveland Indians offered me an opportunity to come back as an AA utility man or take a scouting position and be one of the youngest scouts in the country. I thought about it for twenty-four hours and decided to take the spikes off and become a scout. So fast forward to opening day at the Seibu Dome in 2003. It hit me during the Japanese national anthem. It hit me right in the face: *This is my first day in the big leagues! Here I am on the other side of the globe listening to the Japanese national anthem.* And I felt just appreciation and gratitude.

I was the director of player development and the field coordinator for the Texas Rangers when Toshi Shimada, the director for the Nippon Ham Fighters, called me in June 2002 to ask me to manage the Fighters in 2003. I asked him exactly what he wanted me to do, and he said, "We want you to build a sustainable championship-caliber system." And he offered me a one-year contract. Even though it was a big pay raise from my Texas Rangers salary, I said that I don't believe that I could do that in one year. I don't believe that I'm that good, nor do I believe anybody is good enough to build sustainable team in one year. I also knew that they were moving to Hokkaido in 2004. I wanted to be a part of moving to an island that had never had its own franchise. So, I told him that I wasn't going to come to Japan with only one year of guaranteed money; to make this commitment, he was going to have to guarantee me at least two years. A couple of weeks later, he called back and said that he couldn't believe they did this, but the board agreed to the two-year deal.

So, then we started talking specifics. I was very detailed about what I could and could not do, what I would have control over, what I would not have control over. I would have control over the roster and what we implemented on the major league field. I also needed autonomy over what was being taught, especially for team play-by-plays, defensive positionings, lineups, hitting philosophy, and pitching philosophy. And I needed some sort of control over the minor league team so that the guys there had an understanding of the philosophy and the procedures operating at the major league club. I told Toshi up front, "There's just going to have to be a level of trust that I will continue to communicate and try to combine East with West and come up with the best solution for moving the organization forward."

Before I went over, I read *You Gotta Have Wa* by Robert Whiting, and then I read Warren Cromartie's book, *Slugging It Out in Japan*, and I watched *Mr. Baseball* multiple times. I watched *The Last Samurai*, which had a couple of really good nuggets in it about the history of Japan and how the cultural mind thinks over there. (When I tell people that, they're surprised.) Once I got over to Japan, I read *Bushido: The Way of the Samurai*. That was very helpful. And I read a ton of Japanese history, all the way back to the Edo period. I told my wife, "I feel like I'm back in college." I reached out to Bobby Valentine, who was incredibly gracious with his time. He helped me with fine-tuning my thoughts and points in my contract. I also had a lot of conversations with many people to make sure that my presentation was appropriate, professional, and proper in that culture. I probably could have done more, but I just didn't have enough hours in the day.

When spring camp began, I was a little bit awestruck. As I said, I prepared, but you can't really appreciate Japanese baseball until you see it in action—the commitment of the players, the work ethic of the coaching staff, the amount of preparation. I joke about this all the time, but it's not a joke. It's actually true. We would have meetings to decide when the next meeting was. I had to get used to that part of the culture, try to let go as much as I could of my American mind, and stop rolling my eyes and going, "Are you serious?" One of the things that I had to remind myself and my American coaches, Mike Brown and Gary Denbo, was, "We're in their country."

I was amazed at how long the hitters could continue to do reps in batting practice while maintaining balance and maintaining good swings. That blew me away. On the pitching side, I was amazed at the same thing—how many pitches they threw in their bullpen sessions. I tried to shorten the practices and make them a little bit more westernized that first year, but my shortstop, Makoto Kaneko, met with me and did something that is very unusual for a Japanese player. He asked for permission to talk freely. We sat down and he said, "Hey, look, we really appreciate what you're trying to do. We really do. But the part that you're not understanding as a Westerner is that if we don't have a certain number of swings, or a certain number of base drills, or a certain number of ground balls, or a certain amount of time on the clock, then our spirit doesn't rest well at night. Then we're not getting good rest." I had shortened the practices, but after that meeting I expanded them back to their comfort level.

Managers manage, coaches coach, players win championships. I've known that since I was a young manager. I didn't create that, and I don't know who originally said it, but it's very true. I really didn't want to be the focal point and the center of attention; I wanted the players to be that center of attention. My belief system, and I would say that it's aligned with all managers if they're doing their job, is to put the individual players in the best possible situations where they can have the highest ratio of success. There's a lot of ego in any managerial job; it's just a matter of how well we manage our egos. If you keep that at the forefront, you can focus on the players and putting the guys in the best situations to be successful the highest percentage of the time. And then, through communication, you can help the players understand you want success for them.

I've been accused, even when I was a coach with the Yankees, of getting too close to my players. But I think every manager would tell you that, to some degree, it goes back to building the relationships and the trust. Maybe mine went a little bit deeper than the norm. It's all about connecting with people and making sure they understand, if your intentions are well-meaning and pure, that this guy actually cares. Then you can get to know them better, and as you get to know them better you can better help them succeed.

The biggest difference between me and a Japanese manager was I needed direct contact. I needed that eye contact. I needed to be able to read the

Trey Hillman. Courtesy of Trey Hillman.

player's body language, his mannerisms, to get what I hoped was an accurate read, whether or not he was talking to me from his heart, because that was the bottom line. Japanese managers would send messages to their players primarily through a coach, usually the bench coach, but I wouldn't hesitate to go out on the field and talk to somebody if I saw something that I thought needed addressing, whether it was positive or negative.

I hate to lose. But mentally and physically, there's a balance that we all have to continue to go through, and it's a fight to maintain the right balance where the performance will consistently graduate to championship caliber. This starts in the mind. It starts with your preparation. And then you fight your butt off to stay as consistent as you possibly can, day in and day out. When it has been a positive day and you've had positive results individually and collectively as a team, there's got to be some reflection. How did I do that? How did we do that? Now, simply put that together again and do it again tomorrow and the next day and the next day.

I tried to spread joy, tried to spread energy to the coaching staff, to the front office, to the players through my actions and my extroverted personality. Looking back on it, I probably came across as abrasive, because that's not the norm—the hugs, the slapping players on the butt, the high fives, the knuckles. Japanese managers at that time typically didn't do that. I raised a lot of eyebrows, probably made a lot of traditional Japanese people cheer against me.

The other thing that probably bothered some of the cultural traditionalists was my emphasis on getting the ballplayers' families to the ballpark. The primary goal of my first year in 2003 was to make my players love coming to the field. We had to try to break that inherent cultural feeling that when they went to the stadium that they had come to work. I told the players, "We're professionals, we get paid to do what we do, and we've got a great company, and you have a responsibility to properly represent this uniform; however, I want you to try as best you can to really look forward to the atmosphere in which we get to do those things." So, we encouraged them from day one to bring their families to the stadium. I tried to get to know the players, and I told them, "I would love to meet your families. I'd love to meet your moms or dads, your wives, your kids, aunts, uncles, whomever. If they're important to you, then I would really like to meet them." Then I would ask, if they still had their parents, "How's mom and dad doing? How's their health?" It's just about caring, caring about people. And that was a shock, for the wives especially. They didn't come to the workplace even as fans, even as a support, but some of the players actually got comfortable with that, and their wives enjoyed it. I can honestly say that by the end of the first year, the joy factor was much higher than what it was when I arrived.

For a typical game, I would prep the night before, get an idea of what I wanted our lineup to look like. I would think about who might need a day off; the ebb and flow of momentum, or lack of momentum, during the past week; the attitude and energy level of the team. All those things would be part of prepping for the next day.

In NPB you could keep up to twenty-nine men on your roster. These extra roster spots allowed managers to move players up from the farm team for an important series. It especially helped with bullpen matchups, so you could get more mixing and matching. For example, at the back end of their bullpen, Bobby Valentine and his Chiba Lotte Marines had some incredible seventh-, eighth-, and ninth-inning right-handed guys. The statistics told me that their right-on-right stats outweighed their right-on-left stats. So, I would try to bring up an extra left-handed, or even a couple of extra left-handed, hitters to try to combat that. Or if you were facing a starting pitcher who did not have good release times and you wanted to utilize a little bit more speed, you could bring up somebody who was a little bit faster, to give you an advantage.[1] In the morning, I was usually at the ballpark by 11:00 to 11:15 a.m. I would make a few notes on the lineup and study some statistics, and then I'd go work out. The team's pregame practices were run by the coaches under the supervision of my head coach, Kazuyuki Shirai. My philosophy in both the Major Leagues and in Japan was quite simply to hire good coaches and let them do their jobs. As a manager, you need to be aware of what's going on, so the individual area coaches will let you know if there's anything of major substance that's going to change or that you're going to see in competition as far as mechanical adjustments. They need to let the boss know those things, but the minutia—let the coaches worry about the minutia. If there is something that's going to rear its ugly head, then they'll let the manager know. There was just a trust factor that these were good baseball men.

The afternoons were usually pretty calm, and then we had the pregame interviews. I actually had a lot of fun with the Japanese media. They were engaging. Sometimes I didn't understand why they would ask specific questions, and I didn't understand why the photographers with $2,000 lenses with incredibly huge circumferences had to get so close to my face to take a picture. Occasionally things might bother me a little bit, but honestly, I had a lot of fun with the media over there. I thought before going to Japan that things would take twice as much time because of interpretation. It actually takes two-and-a-half to three times as long to get things done because you have to discuss things with the interpreter. And then with my Texas redneck vernacular, sometimes I'd have to explain exactly what I meant. So that was a challenge for my interpreter Ken Iwamoto, and he handled it with tremendous grace.

The games were longer in NPB; that was something that took getting used to, but otherwise they were similar to MLB games. The big exception was that NPB managers played the most sacrificial baseball I have ever witnessed. Many times, I watched the opposing team bunt early in game with a runner on first, or first and second, with no outs—even at times with their number three hitter. There's a cultural emphasis to sacrifice for the good of the team if you can get the lead and possibly gain the momentum toward a team win.

I was probably a little more aggressive with movement than the Japanese managers. Everyone tried to steal bases, but I had a little bit more confidence with putting the game in motion with the guys who I knew could get the bat on the ball with the hit and run. Japan's the only place where I've ever put on a two-strike hit and run. The reason I did that is because I knew that Kensuke Tanaka could put the ball in play, and he did, and the play actually worked.

After the game, you didn't really have a cool down. The time from the last out to the postgame interviews was less than two minutes, and then you're standing in front of the whole group of media. You had to do some mental gymnastics, especially after a frustrating loss, in the hope that your presentation would be calm and professional. After the interviews, we had postgame meetings, and I would sit in on the first part of those. Then, there would be more discussion after my exit, to provide an opportunity for the coaching staff to raise any issues. Later, I would have a one-on-one conversation with my bench coach, Shirai-san, to get a feel for the staff and what their concerns were. Shirai-san had really good discernment on what he brought to me and what he didn't bring to me and how to present it to me and when to present it to me.

After my first year, we moved to Hokkaido. The promotions department and the marketing department were exceptional, and they weren't afraid to be different. We were up on our own island. We were a new franchise. We decided to do things that none of the other eleven teams in Japan had even thought about doing. On opening day, we had plans to be in uniform and spread out throughout the stadium to greet the fans as they came in after they opened the gates. Our players were nervous about it. They were afraid that nobody was going to show up, so they'd be standing there and it would be an embarrassing situation. I told them that with the media following I could guarantee that there would be people; there may not be a lot, but we would see. This was our initiative to reach out to the community, greet the fans, and let them know that we wanted a personal relationship with them. We were the first team to do that in Japan, and we did it every year after that. Then we got out into the community. The mascot, Brisky Bear, visited schools, and we would have players or staff members go with him, whether it was a reading session or a Fighters pep rally, to meet and greet and sign autographs. The fans were thrilled, and it was a good connection for us.

Japanese baseball is obviously undergoing a lot of changes, but I think it's just going to continue to grow. It is still the national pastime in Japan. I think the United States has gone through some ego management and realizing through the WBC that, "Wow, these guys are better than we thought they were." So I think internationally the respect level has continued to increase. And it's made our world grow closer. There are countries playing baseball that have never played baseball before. For example, back when I was with the Fighters, we played against the Chinese national team. I think Japanese baseball is at the forefront of spreading baseball worldwide, and partnering with MLB will really help grow the game. Korea is right behind in third place. But I think their goal is to strive to be neck and neck with Japan. MLB is looking at the East and thinking, "There's Korea and Japan; we'll use both those guys, and we'll collaborate and figure out how this trifecta can make something great for the game of baseball and the business of baseball." At the end of the day, it's still all about the money, but it's all about the money for the right reasons and promoting what I think is the greatest game in the world.

Part 3 / **In the Ballpark**

6 / Jim Allen, Sportswriter

A journalist with nearly thirty years of experience covering Japanese baseball, Jim Allen has been a columnist for the *Yomiuri Shimbun* and *Kyodo News*. He cohosts the podcast *Japan Baseball Weekly* with John E. Gibson.

◆

I had always wanted to be a writer, since I was a kid. I saw myself being a writer in a foreign country, like a novelist in Ireland. Studying Japanese history at university changed the trajectory. I came to Japan as an English teacher for a private language school. They hired me straight out of college. I had no real desire to be an English teacher, but it did get me overseas.

When I came to Japan, I saw the graphic box scores in newspapers. They're essentially scoresheets. They blew me away because where I came from the box scores in the papers only had at bats, hits, RBIs and home runs. I was a fan of Bill James, and I thought, *Wow, I can do something with this.* So, I started snipping the box scores from the papers every day, and I kept them in scrapbooks. I just was building up this pile of data.

My students were mad about baseball. One asked me, "Who do you think is the best second baseman in the Pacific League?" At that time there were a number of really good ones: Hatsuhiko Tsuiji, Daijiro Oishi, Junichi Fukura, and Kazuyuki Shirai. I thought that's a question I could actually answer. I could do what Bill James did and write statistical analysis about Japanese baseball. My student said, "Well, why don't you?"

And I thought, *Wow, you know, why don't I? I've got time. I've got this wealth of information.* So, I sat down one day in 1993 and started writing. My first analytical guide to Japanese baseball came out in 1994, and I did that in different forms for five years.

I advertised my book in *Stars and Stripes* and in the *Asahi Shimbun* and the *Asahi Evening News*. So, a few people knew about it—not many, but a few. I thought the powers that be within Japanese baseball were going to hate what I did, but I found out that a lot of people who work in Japanese baseball are incredibly dedicated and sincere about what they do. Hiroshi Yoshimura, who was the assistant secretary general of the Pacific League, bought a copy and introduced me to his former editors at *Nikkan Sports*, who asked me to write a few stories here and there, and I got work with the *Japan Times* and *Slugger* magazine. And I started a blog.

Eventually, I landed a job with the English-language newspaper the *Daily Yomiuri*. At first, I was kept away from baseball because Ken Marantz was the guy who wrote baseball. He would write about the players he cozied up to—mostly foreign players, and the big games, like Opening Day, the All-Star Games, and the Japan Series. And that was his baseball coverage. I wanted to go to games every day, but my boss didn't want to annoy Marantz, so he kept me as far away from baseball as he could.

My colleague was saying, "All you ever do is spout off about Japanese baseball. You've got to write a baseball column." So, one time when my editor was away, I wrote a baseball story. My buddy, who had his own soccer column, said it should be a column, but my boss said no because he didn't want to annoy Ken. Finally, he said, "It's going to be Ken's decision." Ken thought it was a great idea, and then it took off from there. I started covering baseball games regularly and writing. I had a column basically every week from the summer of 2000 to 2009.

I studied Japanese in university, but I was not a particularly gifted language learner. At first, some of my interviews were difficult. I'd ask a player a question, and he'd give me an answer. But if he didn't understand the question, he might answer what he thought I wanted. I wouldn't notice because my Japanese listening ability was not good enough. So, I had some interviews where we were talking at 90-degree angles from one another. Sometimes, I was asking players things they'd already answered. It was awkward. But my Japanese got better and better every year. I feel more comfortable talking to Japanese players. I went from never asking questions in the press conferences in Japanese to understanding enough to ask and do follow-ups.

Around 2012 *Yomiuri* cancelled its contract with Kyodo News. It had been a Kyodo News subscriber and used Kyodo's stories for domestic news and especially domestic Japanese sports. At the time, I wasn't getting along with a new editor, and she cancelled my column. When *Yomiuri* cut the contract, Kyodo said, "Well, Jim, you no longer work for our customer. Why don't you come work for us?" So, since 2012 I've been working with Kyodo.

In 2014 I started going to MLB's Winter Meetings in the United States to cover the Japanese players going to the Major Leagues. When I was there, I met people like John Thorn and Rob Neyer, who encouraged me restart my blog, which I had abandoned because it was just too difficult. So, I started my website Jballallen.com. I'd already been doing a podcast with John E. Gibson called *Japan Baseball Weekly*.

The Japanese baseball print media is divided into the mainstream national and local newspapers, the evening papers, the sports dailies, and the weekly magazines. I don't really see the English media as part of the equation. The English-language media is small, so people will say things to the English media that they would never say to the Japanese media because they know nobody cares what we write. For example, I once asked a league executive how big the under-the-table signing bonuses for top draft prospects were in excess of what they're allowed to be and he told me, "Two to four and a half million." He's not supposed to say that. But he had no hesitation because he knew whatever I wrote would never get any carry in the Japanese media. So, I wrote it, and nobody cared. Nobody cared.

The regional and national newspapers are pretty conservative, and they don't write about anything people do that's deplorable, unless it's illegal. If you're a restaurant critic and you find that a restaurant chain is adding ridiculous service fees and overcharging, you're not allowed to write about it because it's technically not illegal. The baseball media is more or less the same. They don't write anything bad about someone, unless they break the law. These guys are real journalists, but they're constrained by the limitations on what mainstream media is allowed to do in Japan.

Then there are the evening papers, which are a whole different breed because they can't write about game results, so they write about people. And that is not always something that's very comfortable for the teams, which would prefer everything be kept on the field unless it's controlled by their media people.

The sports dailies, of course, focus on sports and other entertainment. But they tend to go for big splashy headlines, so it's often "click-bait" stuff when there isn't much going on. To do that, they crow about records that are really dodgy. In 2020 Tomoyuki Sugano set a "record" of 13-straight winning decisions "from Opening Day," and the sports papers and even some of the mainstream media ran with it. But it was made up, because

Masahiro Tanaka went 24-0 in 2013. The papers used the fact that Tanaka hadn't pitched on Opening Day that year—after the World Baseball Classic—to create a record to write headlines about. What they are really good at, though, is presenting tons of information and data about players and games, and various backstories.

The real baseball journalism in Japan and the breaking news generally takes place in the weekly magazines, like *Shukan Bunshun*, which are essentially scandal sheets because they're not constrained like the mainstream media. When they get stories, they write them. Of course, everybody threatens to sue the weekly magazines for essentially printing the truth. I don't say they're always true; sometimes they tend to cut it a little close to the edge of believability. But I would say that the weekly magazines break 99 percent of the news in Japan. Once they print a story, teams react, and then the mainstream journalists can jump on the bandwagon. But the mainstream journalists are not allowed to tackle something until it becomes public. Once it is, then it's fair game.

Pre-COVID-19, reporters would show up at the park in time for practice, which technically starts at 3:00, but some teams start early. Now everything's on the internet, so they no longer have to input yesterday's box scores into their computer spreadsheets or clip score sheets as they did back in the day, so they just go to the ballpark and check the news. Some teams' managers meet the media before the game. Some don't. But most managers will meet the media after games. In Japan, reporters are not permitted in the clubhouse like they are in MLB, so they stand on the sidelines and wait for the players to come out.

Of course, that changed during COVID. Reporters were kept off the field for three years. Then on May 8, 2023, when coronavirus was no longer a national health emergency in Japan, most of the teams switched from coronavirus protocols to safety protocols. It was now considered unsafe for reporters to cover the players from the sidelines, where they had been for seventy years. At Tokyo Dome, they crowd the reporters into the photographers' box next to the dugout. There are two direct entrances from the dugout to the clubhouse, so the Giants players who don't want to talk to the media use the exit farthest from the camera box and pretend they don't hear the questions. Pitchers have to do a lot more work to avoid you because they do their pregame practice in center field and have to walk

Jim Allen.
Courtesy of
Jim Allen.

past you to get to the dugout. The upshot is that most of the teams want to restrict media access to players to where they can keep an eye on who's talking to whom. To me, that means they want to shut out the weekly magazines and the evening newspapers.

While the reporters are waiting for the players, they've got ideas percolating in their minds about possible stories. If they're beat writers, they follow the team every day, so they've got questions based on things that are going on and other news events that might be related to a specific player. So, they figure out whom they want to talk to—batting coaches or pitching coaches or individual players.

They'll also have a list of questions that their editors require them to ask. These might include asking players to comment if their high school has done something significant in one of the national tournaments; asking what a player intends to do when he qualifies for free agency; or, if a player or manager has achieved a record or is on the cusp of it, asking for a comment. They probably don't want to ask these questions because they know they're going to get pat answers, but the outlets want to print the meaningless answers because that's what people do. Everybody prints them.

Sometimes the players give you an honest answer, but mostly answers are the rote lines that they are required to say, or feel they are required to say, so that it gets them off the hook. A lot of baseball players don't really want to answer questions to begin with. Baseball quotes, in America and Japan, depend on a willingness to tell white lies. The reporters need a story, and the players need to say something. Everybody's happy. Nobody's satisfied, but nobody's supposed to be satisfied. It's just, you know, your job. Cliches work the world over.

My beat-reporter friends tell me that every player will have some reporters he can vent to. This year one player told me that he values being able to talk to reporters because they are not teammates and not coaches and not former players, and he can just spout off and sort of work things out in a neutral environment. It's sort of like free form poetry. He said, "When I'm doing badly, I find talking to reporters helps me clear things away." He really missed not having reporters on the field before the game because he was having a terrible season and really needed to vent and express himself to get out of his funk.

So basically, the reporters mill around in front of the home team's dugout from 2:00 p.m. until about 4:00 p.m., when the home-team players disappear into the clubhouse to eat and change out of their practice duds and into their game uniforms. Then they'll go over to the other side of the field, and they'll do the same thing with the visiting players. I find the visiting players more interesting because I don't get a chance to see them that often. I usually have something in mind about some phenomenon, statistical or cultural, that I want to ask about to make a story. I really enjoy asking the foreign players, "What have you learned about Japan? What have you learned about yourself? How do you deal with adversity?" These questions, to me, are the most fun. Sometimes I get silly answers but, by and large, people want to tell their stories.

Then the game starts. The reporters go to the press box, watch the game, keep score, and start a story—just the bare bones of what's happening in this game: who was pitching, what happened, who was the star, who drove in the winning run. You'll write a bare-bones game story, and then you'll write a hero story. You'll prepare those as the game goes along.

The Japanese media and American English media are so radically different because the demands are different. Japanese newspaper stories tend to be short. They have lots of small stories. English papers tend to have one game story and one sidebar—bingo, bango, you're done. So it's a different thing.

You file a short story at the end of the game—this is what happened, this is the score, and this is what I have to say about it. Then, we go and get players' comments as soon as players are available. The winning team will have an on-the-field hero interview, so you get those quotes. Other players may or may not be available to the media, depending on the teams. We then go to a pressroom and crowd around and wait for manager and maybe some players. In general, you want quotes that fit your storyline, although sometimes you'll learn stuff that changes your story. A reporter will ask a question and you might think, *You know, wow, I never thought about that.*

After the interviews, you finish the story. There are things you want to add, things you want to cut, and things your editor tells you to write about. We're writing until basically last train time, which is midnight throughout most of Japan. You leave the park about 11:30 and get home around midnight or later.

Social media has changed how we do our coverage because now if you work for a media outlet as I do, you'll be on a social media chat group. At a big event like the Japan Series, reporters will upload audio and transcriptions from the people they're talking to in the chat group. I used to spend half my time running around looking for colleagues to find out what they had about a certain player. Now I just open my iPhone. That's amazing. It's become extremely efficient. So, if a game ended at 10:00, I used to be done at 12:30. Now I'm out of there by 11:00. It's wonderful. That's the postgame stuff, something I don't do much anymore because there's not a big demand for English-language game stories except for the Japan Series and the WBC.

The Yomiuri Giants beat writers would tell me horror stories about getting calls at 3:00 and 4:00 in the morning from a *Yomiuri* executive complaining about the story they just filed because it was too objective. So they would have to rewrite it to be more team friendly.

The teams in Japan all have tremendous control over some aspects of the media. Part of it is the same as it works in MLB through broadcast contracts. People who work for MLB affiliates do not have free reign to say whatever is true. They can be fired. That is the same in Japan. But in Japan the teams are part of economic groups, where a bank works with a trading company, which works with a media company, which works with an advertising company, which works with a movie chain. And these companies hold stock in each other's companies. For example, the *Yomiuri Shimbun* owns the Yomiuri Giants. They also own Nippon Television and the *Sports Hochi* newspaper and are connected with movie theaters. So, they are connected to a variety of media outlets. I think that nearly every Japanese baseball team has a part owner that is a media company. The DeNA BayStars are partly owned by Tokyo Broadcasting System (TBS) which is affiliated with the *Mainichi Shimbun*, and the Swallows are partly owned by Fuji Television and they have a newspaper, *Sankei Shimbun*. So, they're all intertwined. This involves their rights, but it also involves obligations to the team, such as sitting on bad news. If a reporter writes something that the team dislikes, there are consequences.

Oddly enough, when I worked for *Yomiuri*, my column was often critical of the system that the Yomiuri corporation ruled over, with barely a peep about my being too harsh. That changed when the newspaper business hit a wall in 2019; salaries were cut, and I was told specifically that any stories about the Giants or the NPB system would have to be cleared with Yomiuri's PR department.

I never got into any trouble for any story I broke until 2019, when I was with Kyodo and broke a story about the Giants posting a player for the first time in team history. *Slugger* magazine, a Japanese-language magazine that writes about MLB, sometimes asks me, what do these scouts say about this player? So, I call up my little network of scouts, they tell me, and I write a story. Scouts and reporters are part of an ecosystem. We depend on each other, not because the reporters find players but because reporters are there day in, day out, reading the local sources, talking to local people. We know stuff that the scouts can't possibly know. So, we exchange information on a very informal basis. Scouts are not allowed to talk to the media officially, but they do. The information just can never be attributable. They don't say where they got their information. We don't say where we got ours. That's the way it works, and it's mutually beneficial.

In November 2019 a scout told me that Shun Yamaguchi was going to be posted to MLB. Now that's news, not because of who Yamaguchi was, or because MLB teams were interested. It was big news because he played for the Yomiuri Giants. The Giants at that time were one of the two teams that had never posted a player and had taken a public stance against the posting system.

So, I tweeted that an MLB source told me that Shun Yamaguchi will be posted by the Yomiuri Giants. That was huge. The Giants were furious. They went ape shit. They said it's absolutely not true, even though it was absolutely true. The reason they went ape shit was that the Japanese media was sitting on the story until it would be released upon the conditions of Yamaguchi and his agent. I didn't know that.

There's the difference between Japanese and American media law. In Japan, if I write a tweet and I work for Kyodo News, that tweet is considered legally a Kyodo News story. In America, it's a tweet by a guy who happens to work for Kyodo News. Because of this media law, my company descended on me like a ton of bricks, not because the story was wrong—we knew it was right—but because the Giants complained. That mistake cost me hundreds and hundreds of dollars in lost pay and pay increases over the next four years.

At the end of the season, I get to vote for the player awards and for the Hall of Fame. As far as I know, I'm the only non-Asian who votes for the Japanese Baseball Hall of Fame. You need to be a writer for fifteen years as a member of the sports *kisha* club, and you have to be nominated by a media company. The eligibility requirements for the players' ballot are essentially the same as they are in MLB, except players are allowed to stay on the ballot until twenty years after they've retired instead of ten, as long as they get the minimum required number of votes. I think in MLB it's 5 percent. If you don't get 5 percent, you're off the ballot. In Japan if you don't get 2½ percent, you're off the ballot.

The Japanese system created a huge backlog of stars from the 1990s, because you had to have been out of uniform for five years to be on the ballot. So, players who retired and then became a coach and then became a manager weren't eligible. Guys like Sadaharu Oh, Katsuya Nomura, and Shigeo Nagashima didn't get into the Hall of Fame until they hadn't been playing baseball for fifteen years. But now they've changed the system to eliminate that "in uniform" bottleneck.

Now they have two ballots for players, one, the Players Division—where I vote—for when they become eligible five years after they retire regardless of whether they're still in uniform as a coach or manager. The second ballot, called the Experts Division, can look at players, coaches, and managers who haven't played for twenty years and who are no longer in uniform.

Now what happens with the vote? The vote is largely a matter of a how good your numbers are, how well liked you are by the media, how free of scandal you are, and finally how popular you are with the Tigers and Giants beat writers, who make up probably half of the pool of all baseball writers in Japan. I think that's the reason why Tuffy Rhodes hasn't been elected. He spent two years with the Giants. During the last year he was hurt and got into to a fracas with one of the coaches, which harmed him with the Giants' beat writers. He's probably the most qualified player who isn't in the Hall of Fame right now. Nobuhiko Matsunaka is another qualified player who is getting very little support because he was not well liked by the media. He was a wonderful player, but he had an edge to him. He could be irascible.

The big question is why Japanese baseball doesn't want to get bigger. Why is a country with the infrastructure and education and economic development and know-how and passion for baseball satisfied with not being the best? It's remarkable. The resources that could make Japanese baseball the best in the world are at hand. The money's there. The desire is there from the fans. The knowledge base is there. The interest level is there. So, what's lacking?

The short answer is that the teams are an advertising arm for promoting the larger companies that own them. You cannot overestimate how much value the owners get from this advertising. Nippon Ham famously was Japan's third-largest meatpacking business before they bought the Fighters in late 1973. Within a decade, they were the number one meatpacker in Japan. They considered the Nippon Ham Fighters a very good value for the money, even though you could count the fans at the Tokyo Dome on a bad day. So, the reason things are the way they are is not because Japanese baseball can't be better, but because the owners have already gotten what they paid for. They're not interested in investing millions of dollars to become one of the best baseball franchises in the world, as they are already getting a huge advertising impact for the parent company and then writing off the losses for the baseball team as a business deduction. They're losing money, and they are happy about it. They're not winning, and they're not happy about that, but they can live with it.

The problem with that formula is that the SoftBank Hawks exist. The Hawks desire to be the best baseball team in the world. Unfortunately, you can't do that by being the best baseball team in a second-tier major league because the lack of competition will preclude that. But there are teams that do not want to finish runner up to the SoftBank Hawks every year. The Seibu Lions are spending to keep up with the Hawks, not necessarily to be best in the world, but at least not to be last. Now, with their new stadium, the Nippon Ham Fighters have put themselves in a position where they could be hypercompetitive if they choose to. The Pacific League teams are beginning to suck up most of the free agents, and the Hawks and Fighters are beginning to delve into international amateur markets.

The Pacific League teams can now make money selling baseball. Four Pacific League teams own their ballparks, and two have long-term operating leases that allow them all the concessions, ad revenue, and ticket revenue. The more people who come into the ballpark, the more money they make.

So, there's the possibility Japan could have the best baseball league in the world. The sky is the limit if Japan would throw open its restrictions on import players. There would be no stopping them from building the best stadiums in the world and having the highest quality baseball on the planet. They could be so good that the Japanese players who want to move to MLB will do so because they want to see America and not because they want to make more money. MLB players, on the other hand, will be saying, "We want to go where the best baseball in the world is, so we're going to Japan. And the food's better as well!"

7 / Jennie Roloff Rothman, Superfan

Jennie Roloff Rothman is senior coordinator of teacher professional development in the English Language Institute at Kanda University of International Studies. She has been teaching in Japan since 2004.

◆

Was I a baseball fan growing up? No, absolutely not. I'm originally from Seattle, and I grew up a long-suffering Seahawks fan. In 1995 the Mariners had its first playoff run ever. It swept Seattle absolutely by storm. As you might imagine, I also got kind of swept up in it. As you'll probably discover, I don't do anything halfway. It's either 0 or 150. So when I got into baseball, I *got into baseball*. I followed the Mariners when I was in college, but I lost track of baseball when I first came to Japan, but rediscovered it, obviously.

Toward the end of college, I heard about the Japan Exchange and Teaching (JET) program. My boyfriend, now husband, had graduated a year ahead of me, and he was getting his master's degree in London. I told him, "I'm thinking about this JET program. You got a year in London. I want a year in Japan."

So, I came here in 2004. About two months in, I was like, "I might have found my place." I found my authentic self here in Japan. The longer I'm here, the more it's true. It's the classic JET story. It was only going to be one year. But then I was like, okay, just two years. I was planning on returning to the United States when my boyfriend said, "Maybe I should just go over there and teach English?" He did, and that's all she wrote. I have been here for nineteen years. I got a job at Kanda University of International Studies as a lecturer, then taught at International Christian University for four years, and in 2017 moved back to Kanda. I'm now in charge of teacher professional development and proselytizing baseball—the more important job.

We got hooked on Japanese baseball in 2016, but we actually went once in 2009. I had just moved to Chiba. My husband, who has loved baseball his entire life and grew up a dedicated Mets fan, was like, "You know, there's a baseball team here. Why don't we go?" So just on a whim, we bought cheap tickets. Little did we know, we ended up in the Marines cheering section. Everyone was getting up and sitting down and jumping. We were like, "Wait, what is going on?" People weren't really talking a lot to us, but they were like, "Oh, you need to stand up now. You need to do this"—sort of helping us and guiding us. We didn't understand, but we just rolled with it. It was so not what we were expecting, but it was really fun. But we never went back after that first game, which is strange because we both liked baseball.

Then in 2016 a friend asked, "Does anybody want free baseball tickets to a BayStars game?"

My husband was like, "We've always talked about going to baseball again. Why haven't we gone? Let's just do it!"

And, you know, I loved the experience! I loved the atmosphere, the hamster mascot, and the cheer for Yoshitomo Tsutsugo because I'm a language person. I love puns. I love word play. Everyone was cheering, "Go, go, two, two, go," as they held up their hands to show five fingers, then two, then two, and then five. You see, his number was 25 and his name sounds like "two, two, go (the Japanese word for five)." And I'm like, "That's amazing!"

Afterward we were like, "Why don't we go to another game." We ended up at a Swallows game, and we decided to become baseball fans. As I mentioned before, we don't do anything halfway, so we decided before we settled on teams to go to every stadium once and be a home fan of every team. We got through eight stadiums, and by that point our loyalties were solidified. My husband said, "I'm a Marines fan because of Bobby Valentine." I was trying to decide between the BayStars and Swallows. It was going to be one of those teams, but I couldn't really tell which one it would be. And in the end, it was the hamster ears that did it.

I really love the hamster mascot in Yokohama. It's so ridiculous. It's baseball and a hamster? Are you kidding me? That's not the normal animal that you're imagining for a sports team. Oh, the vicious hamster! You know? But I really love the character. We were at a game, and my husband went for a walk. When he came back, he said, "I got you something," and he handed me the ears. I put them on and—I know this sounds absolutely ridiculous—the minute I put the ears on, I was like, "Yeah, this is it!" It was like the Harry Potter wand moment. You know, the wand chooses the wizard. It was the ears that helped me decide that I was going to be a BayStars fan.

After the first few, I don't think I've ever gone to a game with no gear. The few times I've gone with just a BayStars towel to wave, it felt weird. For most of my first season, I only had one jersey. That has since changed. I joke about it, but we have three carry-on-sized suitcases full of uniforms. One is just BayStars uniforms, another is Lotte Marines, the third is Samurai Japan and other teams. Off the top of my head, I think I've got ten to twelve BayStars jerseys. I probably have about five or six that are in the rotation that I'm wearing in the stadium.

When you're living as an expat, you try to connect with the culture to show that you belong or that you're a part of a community. We overtly show our connections to things. I always have my baseball key chains and things on my backpack. I don't take them off year-round. When I go to games—it's a ninety-minute train ride—I will wear my BayStars uniform all the way through Tokyo just to show I am a part of this community. There have been times when coming back from Yokohama—again, it's a ninety-minute ride—I forget that I'm wearing my ears. We get off at our home station, and I realize that I've been on public transportation for like almost an hour and a half wearing hamster ears! I'm okay with it, but at the same time I know this is a new level of ridiculous.

In 2016 and 2017 we really went full bore. We went to seventy-one games during the 2017 season. Those first couple of years, if we were not in a stadium, we were watching the game on TV. I was working in western Tokyo and had a ninety-minute commute, so I would hop on the train and watch the game until my battery died. In 2017 the BayStars went to the Japan Series. So, I really got into it because, as a Mariners fan, I've never experienced a team getting into a World Series. I was just beside myself. I was like, not only do I love baseball, but wow, this is incredible.

At first, my husband and I went to most of the games together. Then we met another foreign fan named Steve. He's now one of our very close friends. I don't go to Marines games by myself because a lot of my coworkers and friends are in the area, so it's easy to find someone to go with. But I sometimes end up going to BayStars games by myself. I'll even go watch a game by myself in the rain. I've got a towel on my head and a poncho, and I'm just drenched, but I'm like, "I'm here for the team." Sometimes as people realize you understand the cheers and you know about the players,

Jennie Roloff Rothman and Gerome Rothman. Courtesy of Robert K. Fitts.

they will start talking to you, which is less likely if I'm with other people. So going by yourself can actually be a little bit more fun.

My favorite place to sit in Yokohama and Chiba is in *gaiya*. Simply put, gaiya means "outfield." *Naiya* is "infield." But we often refer to the right-field stands, where the home team's cheering section sits, as gaiya. Formally, the oendan is the cheer group recognized by NPB, so the core of the right-field stands is the oendan, with the trumpets and drums and everything like that, but the rest of people in the right-field stands also participate in the cheers. So gaiya is the cheering section, led by the oendan.

If you are sitting in the infield (the first base line is typically for the home-team fans and the third base line is typically for the visitors), you don't have to cheer, you don't have to clap along. You can just sit back and watch the game, but if you are in gaiya, it's expected that you're working. When the players are at bat, you're standing and participating in all the cheers. If you are not planning to do those things, you should not be sitting in gaiya. It's an immersive fan experience.

It's kind of fun as foreign fans to go right into the middle of the cheering section. No one will say anything. But the Japanese fans are like, "There are foreign people here. Do they know what's going on?" You can hear them quietly talking about you. But I'm wearing a uniform, and then I'm doing the cheers and they're like, "She knows what she's doing." I can see the facial expressions change from, *Are we going to have to help these people who don't know what's going on?* or *Are we going to ignore them?* to *Oh, she's cool.* As the beers flow in gaiya, people will start talking to you. Now, I'm actually more likely to engage the people next to me because I'm more comfortable with my Japanese. So, when someone makes a comment, I'm like, "Oh yeah, totally right. I know he does this all the time." And soon they start high-fiving and things.

The word for foreigner in Japan is *gaikokujin*, literally "outside country person." And there are places within the culture where you get locked out. Often, language is the barrier, and it's used strategically. Job ads will not be in English. They will only be in Japanese to block out certain people. A lot of it's quite subtle. But in other places, it doesn't matter as much. That is one of the things that both my husband and I love about baseball. Nobody cares where we're from.

I've contemplated joining Seiha, which is the oendan, the official cheering group, for the BayStars. But it's hard for me to commit the amount of time needed, being an academic and also living in Chiba. As I mentioned before, I don't do anything halfway. Japan is a country of that. There's no such thing as a casual hobby in Japan. There would be no halfway in this. You'd have to prioritize the club, be at the practices, be at the meetings, be at the regular rehearsals; otherwise, you would not be welcome. It could be really fun, except that I cannot guarantee that I will be at every home game. I'd have to be there by 3:00 or 4:00, and if I'm teaching until 6:00, I can't. You know, I'm a diehard fan, but I am actually an academic first.

You cannot have Japanese baseball as we know it without the cheering sections. In many ways, they are what makes Japanese baseball Japanese baseball, as much as the concept of small ball makes Japanese baseball *yakyu*. I think they're indispensable. The pandemic really showed that. My husband is a diehard fan, but during the pandemic he lost interest in baseball because we were not allowed to cheer. In 2020 and 2021, no cheering. So suddenly ZOZO Marine Stadium was silent. It was so weird. My husband was like, "I love the team; I love baseball. But I just can't get into the season because there's no cheering." It's a fundamental part of Japanese baseball and as a fan; it's what helps you feel connected. It's one thing to watch the game, but when cheering I feel like I'm contributing. I feel like I'm participating in the atmosphere. Being a Japanese baseball fan is not passive. Even the casual Japanese baseball fan will still be clapping along with walk-up music or just clapping because other people around them are clapping. I think it's much easier to be a passive MLB fan.

We've had experiences both in Yokohama and in Jingu where visiting American baseball fans will boo or they will be drunk and rowdy. They do things that, as we like to say, disturb the *wa*. When that happens, we resolve to act more Japanese to prove that we are not like them. There's a Japanese phrase, *ba no kuuki wo yomu*, or "reading the air." It's a very important concept in Japanese culture that I think Americans and many Westerners either don't possess or are greatly underdeveloped in it. There's an element of emotional intelligence, but a lot of it is reading the room. Most Japanese are highly attuned to the people around them, just the way somebody breathes in means "no." You have to be attuned to these things. So when we're around people who are not doing that, we feel like we have to be model citizens.

It's not that there's no booing. One year, I sat in a gaiya where fans yelled at the team on the last day of the season as they came out to bow and thank the fans. Fans in gaiya were yelling, "Give us our money back!" You can be critical of your team, but other people can't be critical of your team. At the end of the day, as much as we love this, it is just a game. There's a lot of emotional intensity, but it's just a game. So, if you're ruining it for other people, if you're ruining the atmosphere, if you're making other people uncomfortable, you shouldn't do it. And again I go back to ba no kuuki wo yomu, or reading the air. Yelling something about another team is going to make the fans of that team annoyed or angry. And if that happens, you don't know what's going to happen. What if they start a fight? It just ruins the experience for everybody. So as intense as we're into it, it's still just a game at the end of the day, and we're all hopping on a train and going home. But people in gaiya are more likely to jeer because, among like-minded hardcore people, it's not going to cause a problem.

My husband tested this theory. It was our first year of fandom. And we heard you're not supposed to boo. But like, really? So he's like, "I'm going to test it." So we're in Yokohama Stadium, and we're on the first base line, in between home and first. Brad Eldridge, who played for Hiroshima, had just struck out. My husband, who has nothing against Eldridge, stood up and yelled, "Sit down Brad!" And, icy chill, immediately, in the atmosphere around us. No one said anything. No one said a word. But you could feel the chill. We were both like, "Okay, so now we know. We don't do that." The thing is it's supposed to be fun. And if it's not fun, what are we here for? We slag off our teams. That's what fans do. But it's how you do it and when you do it.

It's been interesting for me to experience baseball as not just a foreign fan but also a foreign female fan, because sometimes people don't know what to do with me. Many people say, "If you look at the number of women in certain positions, there's this huge gap in the gender equality balance. Japan's terrible for women." On certain metrics I'm not going to dispute that, but statements like that suggest a shallow look at the culture. If you take a deeper look, you'll see that a lot of things are more egalitarian. I think often people look at Japanese culture through a Western lens, and they see what they are used to seeing. If you don't fully understand what you're looking at, you're going to be interpreting based on your perspective, perceptions, and experience. I don't think I saw it when I first came here. The longer I'm here, I see the dynamics; I see how it works. There's a lot of things within Japanese culture where the gendering is subtle.

Women are actually fairly active in Japanese baseball. I teach a class on international baseball. We did a deep dive into women's baseball, professional and amateur in Japan. My students were like, "We don't have much." And I'm like, "Oh, contraire. Look at all these websites and teams." They had no idea there was so much women's baseball in Japan.

There are also women who are just as dedicated and as active in the pro fan base as any man. They travel everywhere, and they've got fifteen different versions of the same player's uniform and all the other stuff. They sit right in the front, and they're always taking pictures of their favorite players. There's this pair of BayStars fans, two women. They go on all the road games, they go to fan events, they go everywhere. They even go to *ni-gun*, or farm team, games. They're ever present and just as dedicated as anybody.

Where I start to see the clear gendering is in the leadership positions. There's only one woman who is a club owner, Tomoko Namba of the DeNA BayStars. She achieved this after studying at Harvard and starting a company that became a powerhouse. She recently became a vice chair of the Japan Business Federation too, but she only got into baseball *after* cracking the glass ceiling in business. Other than her BayStars, a few teams have hired female strength and conditioning coaches or trainers, but I think the number of women across NPB can be counted on one hand.

If you look at the crowd at Yokohama Stadium, it's about 50:50 men to women. But in the BayStars' gaiya, I would say it might be 70:30. And there's maybe one woman as an actual oendan leader. Lotte's gaiya has women cheering, but none in oendan leadership, to my knowledge. I believe Nippon Ham has a woman in the leadership of their oendan. On broadcasts and in ZOZO Marine Stadium, I've seen her leading cheers.

I was recently interviewed by the Chiba City tourism board, and they asked, "As someone who's been living in Japan for a long time, what's your advice for newcomers?" My advice is to give everything a try. It's making connections; it's making links that makes life interesting. I've got my complaints and issues with Japan and the culture as well, but I love it here. We realized after about a decade or so that Japan is home for us. Why is Japan home? Well, we have made efforts to connect with the local culture and the local people and make links.

For me, baseball is one of these links. Again, we met this guy Steve in the Marines' gaiya, and we're like, *Cool, we have another foreign person to sit with*. We had no idea when we first met him that he would become one of our closest friends. We now have a small group. These people are some of my closest friends in Japan because we love baseball so much, but beyond baseball we built connections, and we do other things. But of course, these are foreign fan connections.

Because of baseball, I can start conversations with pretty much anyone now that my Japanese has improved. When I meet someone, I'll ask, "What team are you a fan of? Who's your favorite player?" One time, we met some random Japanese people at a table next to us. We noticed they were watching the same game on their phones that we were watching. I asked, "Are you BayStars fans?" So we now we meet up for dinner, or we say hi at the games. These are not deep relationships, but they don't have to be deep to make me feel like I belong. And that's important.

There's a Japanese guy who comes and sits with us at Marines games. He comes just to talk with us. Every time we're there, he comes and sits for at least an inning, and we just chat in English. He's like, "Do you know the background of this song?" He started explaining the background of the music and the cheers for us. He started sending us the links, like for the pachinko music that is the basis for Shogo Nakamura's cheer. One time he said, "Let's go to karaoke." We had a karaoke day where he put in all of the original songs for the cheers. So we're in karaoke singing the actual cheers, but with the music coming from the speakers. Not only did the experience give me a deeper understanding and appreciation for the nuances of Japanese baseball, but also the friendship makes my life richer.

It's these friendships, these connections, that are important. Of course, friendship doesn't have to be through baseball. But sports are universal. And I think baseball is—and I know soccer fans will argue with me—the world's greatest sport. And baseball has made my life richer.

8 / Yasuro Karibe, Oendan Leader

Yasuro Karibe has been a Hiroshima Carp oendan member for over thirty years and heads the National Hiroshima Toyo Carp Private Cheering Federation.

◆

In the oendan our role is to take the lead and conduct the cheering that goes on at the stadium. We're like the conductor of an orchestra, if you will, at the ballpark. We are at the stadium not so much to cheer on the team ourselves, but rather to enable others to do so. It's almost like we are stadium staff or team staff in that respect; we're doing this as a service for others so that we can have better joint cheering as a stadium. But we pay for the tickets with our own money, and we pay the same price as anybody else.

The cheer groups probably started roughly a month after the formation of the team back in 1950; however, the form that the oendan takes now started somewhere around 1970. Back at its beginnings, it grew organically as people who supported the team would gather at the games. They weren't in the outfield organizing the cheering, but they cheered together and little by little started to form these simple songs; they started to blow whistles, and before they knew it, they were an organized cheering group. Carp fans are passionate. There's real community pride in Hiroshima, and on game days the whole town is painted red.

The National Hiroshima Toyo Carp Private Cheering Federation was formed in 1997. There were various unaffiliated oendan clubs at that time, so to help with organization and to ensure that things were being done properly, a single organization was created. We currently have eighteen groups within the federation with a total of about 190 people. Because these groups are spread out across the whole country, we've never had all eighteen at a stadium at the same time. But several groups might attend a game, especially at Mazda Zoom-Zoom Stadium in Hiroshima.

I'm the head of the federation, but I'm also part of the Higoikai (National Red Carp Union). The Higoikai has five of those eighteen oendan groups. One of them is an all-Japan club, then there's a Tokyo group, a Nagoya group, a Kansai group, and a Hiroshima group. Each of those groups has a particular territory that it is responsible for. Games that take place in Tokyo would be attended and led by the Tokyo group, and so on. So those five groups very easily cover the Central League games. If we're playing interleague up in Hokkaido or in Sendai, then the Tokyo group would send a team up there. If we're playing in Fukuoka against the Hawks, then the Hiroshima group would send a team.

When we go on the road, there is a limit on the number of us that can be at a game. For example, a stadium might say you can have no more than thirty oendan members. Because we have a specific section in those road stadiums, different oendan clubs will end up sitting together, and other people are not allowed entry. We actually have tags hanging around our necks on lanyards showing that we have permission to be in those seats. We tell the host team how many seats we need, and they set them aside for us, but we still pay face value for them. Even at Koshien Stadium, where every game is sold out this year, they still set aside a certain number of seats to ensure that we're able to have people attend the game, and those tickets won't get sold to the public.

I was born and raised in Tokyo, and I had zero connection whatsoever with the city of Hiroshima or with the Carp. But when I was a little boy, my grandma bought me a red baseball cap. Most of the teams had black ball caps, but a black cap attracts a lot of heat, and she thought that wouldn't be good. So, the choices were either a blue Chunichi Dragons cap or a Hiroshima Carp hat. She just happened to choose the red one. At that time, it was rare to see a little kid wearing a Hiroshima Carp hat in Tokyo. There were no other Carp fans around. Because it was such a novelty, I got noticed by some of the elderly folks in the neighborhood, and they would ask me, "Oh, do you like the Hiroshima Carp?" And since they thought it was cute or unique, they would give me snacks and candies. So, I immediately associated being a Carp fan with getting good things, like it's good to be a Carp fan. I had never even seen a Carp game on TV before, and I didn't even really know who the Carp were. I just knew that wearing this cap was getting me good things. That's how my journey with the Carp started.

That time was the golden age of the Yomiuri Giants. They were in the middle of their dynasty, and only Giants games were broadcast on TV every night. The only games that I was interested in watching on TV were the Giants versus the Carp. Of course, I wanted to attend a Carp game, but there were no fellow Carp fans around to go with me. When I was about seventeen years old, getting close to graduating from high school, I still hadn't found anyone to go to a game with, so I realized that my best bet to go to a game and feel comfortable would be to join an oendan. That way, I would have people to cheer alongside. My cousin was in the oendan for the Lotte Orions, which is now the Chiba Lotte Marines, so I had a positive image of oendan. I felt that being part of an oendan must be a wonderful thing. Of course, that image got shattered when I joined one because it was a pretty rough world.

At that time, the hierarchy in an oendan was very strict (which is no longer the case), and seniors were to be obeyed. What seniors said was absolute. That old worldview was very stern and rigid. The outfield bleacher seats were general admission with no assigned seats, so as a junior member I often spent the entire night in line waiting to buy tickets for the next day's game. The oendan's way of life was all about spirit and guts. Looking back now, I feel that Japan back then had rather inappropriate rules compared to today. I think I lasted because I had been toughened up in the baseball club during my school days.

When I became an oendan member, you would get invited into the oendan if you were seen at the stadium often enough as a regular fan. They would approach you and ask, "Do you want to join us?" That has changed, obviously. Now it's much different. A lot is done through the internet, through websites and social media. We put out an announcement that we're looking for new members. We get a lot of people who are interested, a lot of applicants, and then we interview them to make sure they are suitable. We really are strict about who we let in because if they are a person who cannot be trusted or who can't follow the rules, not only might they get kicked out of the stadium, but also the entire oendan might lose their privileges. Many apply, but few are actually accepted. There are quite a few rejections at the interview stage.

The rules are fairly strict right now as far as cheering goes. When I first joined the oendan thirty-two years ago, there weren't a lot of restrictions.

Yasuro Karibe. Courtesy of Yasuro Karibe.

But now it's quite hard to make sure that we adhere to all of the rules. For example, we're not allowed to drink alcohol at all. We're not allowed to use bad words. There are limits on what we're allowed to say and certain rules about what we can't say. But more than specific rules, it's the feeling that we're constantly being observed and that people are constantly looking for something we might be doing that is out of line. If we break the rules, we would receive a notice from the team, and in some cases people would get kicked out of the oendan. These people might be allowed to come to the stadium as regular spectators, but in the worst-case scenarios, they would be banned from the stadium outright. So, it is very strict, and we really want to make sure that we follow the rules.

It's our job to pump up the players, to give them that extra push or that extra jolt of energy, but we only cheer when our team is at bat. There is no oendan cheering for pitchers. This was born out of respect for the other team's cheering squad to give them a chance to cheer for their team. Now, it's actually become a rule that we're not allowed to cheer while the other team is at bat. The exception is, we can give a vocal cheer for our pitcher if he needs that extra push, but we're not allowed—it's forbidden by rule—to play the trumpet or anything like that while the other team is at bat.

Being part of an oendan means you're working with a group and as a group. There's a strong sense of camaraderie. We are busy with the games every day, but we all cooperate and cheer each other on. Outside of the games, members socialize with each other, and often we'll go out for meals or drinks together. We have people from different walks of life; we have some students, and we have some that work regular jobs. So, there's no rule about how many games one needs to attend as a member of the oendan. You go when you can. We just make sure that we have enough people at the games. If it's an unpopular day or opponent or whatever and we don't have enough members, we make requests to ensure that we get enough people.

In our group, there are no practices. I think there might be a few oendan that gather together and practice on occasion, but we don't. There might be a meeting before the season starts if there are new player songs that we want to practice, but other than that you practice on your own and just come to the stadium and get the job done. There are times when people, especially actual musicians, say to us, "Your musicianship is terrible." Whether or not they're right is a different point altogether. From their perspective, the trumpet is a refined and sensitive instrument, and so it makes sense for them to say those things. But when we're playing the trumpet in a large stadium without microphones, there's a certain way that we have to play that might differ from how a true musician would play the instrument. So, the trumpeters have to practice on their own to make sure that they're ready to do things that work well in the stadium. But that's not something that we do as a group.

There are no tests or requirements to become an instrument player, flag bearer, or cheer leader. In fact, when people join the oendan, the ideal person would be able to do all of them, and a lot of people actually do all of these things. However, it's not easy to do this. It requires a lot of energy and, of course, if you are the cheer leader it requires a very strong voice. You have to be able to yell out directions to the crowd. In the performance seats at Mazda Stadium—that's where the oendan sits—there are up to two thousand people in that section with us. And you have to be able to be heard by all those fans, without using a microphone. So, you're only going to be able to last about an inning. We have a rotation, and everyone has to be able to do that job. You do it for roughly one inning, and then you move on to do something else. There have been games that I've gone to where I'll take the lead for one inning and then for the other eight innings, I'm playing the trumpet or whatever is needed. So at any given game, we see who's in attendance and who can do which jobs, and from there we decide our roles throughout the game.

The oendan create the cheer songs for the players. Of course, we're not professional musicians, so that limits who is able to make songs and the quality of the songs. We generally ask people who have some musical ability—maybe they play the piano or whatever—as they might be able to make a better song than someone who doesn't. But recently there's a video game called Powerful Professional Baseball, or Power Pros for short. Within this game, there is crowd noise, and the crowd noise includes songs. They're not the official oendan player songs. Because of copyright issues, they're not allowed to use the actual songs, but they are similar to the official songs. You can actually enter data into the game, and it'll create a song for you. In recent years, that's been kind of a shortcut to make new songs for the actual players at the actual stadiums.

These days, we put the new songs on the federation website and use social media, and we also create YouTube videos. So, it's pretty easy to get people familiar with the songs because almost everybody's using social media and can hear how the songs go. Back in the day before the internet, though, we would decide on a date when we would present the song in front of everybody at the stadium during an exhibition game. That would be like the unveiling of a new song, so those in attendance would be able to hear it and somewhat remember it. Then as the games continued during the exhibition season, more and more fans would hear the songs, and it went from there organically. By the start of the regular season, the fans knew the new songs.

I've been watching baseball since I was a little kid, so I've been seeing the oendan in action right from the very start. Sometimes when I watched baseball games, I was watching the oendan as well. I was taking that in as part of the baseball experience. I don't think that Japanese baseball is complete without the cheering. If you go to an MLB game at a Major League stadium, people cheer at the right moments in their own way, in an individual style. That fits American culture, but that wouldn't really go over so well in Japan.

Japanese people like rules and like following rules. When we go to a baseball game and somebody is leading the cheers and telling you this is how to cheer, this is the song we sing, it's easy for Japanese people to ride that wave, to jump on board and say, "Okay, I can do this confidently." I feel that if nobody were leading the cheering, then nobody would cheer at all. Our cheering is so rule driven, it really suits the Japanese people and our style. It allows us to let loose because there are certain rules around how we can let loose.

Foreign fans who come to our stadiums see the Japanese cheering style and say, "Wow, this is so much fun. This is so unique and so refreshing." But if they were to come to all 143 games, would they still enjoy it because it is so rule driven? A couple of World Baseball Classics ago, we went to San Francisco. I believe it was the first time in that stadium that a game was played with trumpets blaring and an actual oendan preforming. A lot of people were really happy to see that, and they said, "Wow, it would be really cool if we could do this in America too." But I got the feeling that if that we were to do it over the course of 162 games, it would actually become the source of anger and frustration for the fans because it would get on people's nerves. It just doesn't fit with the American style.

Here in Japan, sometimes we get criticized by people who say, "You're not even watching the game. You're not paying attention, you're just cheering. You don't even know what's going on in the field." There is some truth to that because sometimes we've got our backs to the game itself, and we are cheering without actually seeing what's going on. When our team gets a big hit, or when we score some key runs, we can't actually get excited and rejoice together with the rest of the fans because we're too busy doing what we do. It's like we're at work. Some people actually quit being oendan members because they realized that it's really hard to be at a game and see those key moments and not be able to cheer in the way that regular fans do. I sometimes wish that we were able to enjoy the game the way that U.S. fans do, actually watch the game and take in the moments and cheer spontaneously at the right times. Maybe this is a case of the grass being greener on the other side. I look at American baseball and the fan experience and kind of envy it, but Americans look at the Japanese style and envy it as well.

But I think just sitting and watching baseball would be really hard for me to do without the oendan cheering. I might be able to do it for thirty minutes or an hour, but I think it would be really hard to do it for nine full innings. I'm very Japanese by nature. I'm pure Japanese. My heart is Japanese. So I think that watching and cheering baseball in the Japanese way comes naturally to me and feels good to me. For me, it brings about a sense of responsibility, a sense of obligation, that I've got to do this for the sake of the other fans. I've got to do my job so that others can rejoice during the good times. When I hear other Carp fans say, "It's so much fun to be a Carp fan. It's so much fun to cheer for the Carp." That's when I know that I've done my job well, and that makes it worth it.

9 / Taylor Foote, Mascot Team

Taylor Foote has performed as a mascot for about ten years. From 2019 to 2023, he was part of the Hiroshima Carp's mascot team.

◆

I work as a consultant for the Hiroshima Toyo Carp doing translating, interpreting documents, and checking the English grammar and spelling on products and advertisements, and I'm part of the mascot team. I assist the mascot Slyly at his appearances. Slyly does not speak the same language that everyone else does, so we need a specialist like me to help him communicate.

My sophomore year, I played rugby for the University of Oklahoma but suffered some injuries and quit. My friend Nick said, "Hey, if you're not doing any extracurricular activities, I think you'd be a great mascot, so you should come to tryouts." I had no experience at all, just a charismatic and outgoing attitude, I guess. There were two mascots, Boomer and Sooner, so we had a pretty big team. I think there were ten of us. We were full-time college students, so we split the responsibility for all the sporting events: wrestling, volleyball tournaments, basketball, baseball, and of course football—both home and away games. We also did commercial shoots. I went to New York to be on *Good Morning America* a few times.

By the time I graduated, I knew that I wanted to be a professional mascot and work in professional sports. Before my senior year, I did an internship with the Chicago Blackhawks and spent the summer working with their mascot, Tommy Hawk. So, I gained some more experience. After I graduated, I worked for the Tulsa Drillers for one season as their mascot, Hornsby. We won the Texas League championship after a twenty-year drought. Not sure if that was because I joined the team or not!

Nick, the friend who suggested I try out as a mascot in college, was working for the Hiroshima Carp. The Carp's president, Mr. Hajime Matsuda, had studied abroad when he was in college. When he was in America, everyone was very hospitable and helpful. As a way to pay it forward, when he took control of the Carp, he started recruiting Americans to work as interpreters and translators for the organization. So Nick reached out and said, "Do you want to come to Japan and work for the Carp?"

And I said, "Yeah, tell me what I gotta do." I went over in April of 2019.

The first week or two, I just got my bearings. I went to the stadium and met with all the people in the office. And I met with Slyly and saw how he worked. Even before I came to Japan, I had watched every video I could find and memorized his movements, his antics, and things like that. The first few games I just sat and watched as a fan to get a feel for Japanese baseball and the atmosphere. Nick introduced me to a couple of his English-speaking Japanese friends, and they would explain what was going on. I knew about baseball. I played baseball. So, I knew the rules. But they explained the traditions and the cheers and dances and things like that.

After a few weeks, I started assisting Slyly during the games. We'd do a pregame greeting with fans. Then, I would be on the field, taking video of Slyly for the big scoreboard screen or pictures when needed. Soon I became part of the performance team.

In the mascot world, in the United States and Japan, many organizations want to keep the integrity of the character intact. That means not making any sort of admission that it's a person in there. There are some U.S. colleges where they are so secretive that a person can only tell their family that they are the mascot. They insist that they not tell anybody else until they graduate. If they do and they are found out, they get kicked off the team. I agree with this because it keeps the fantasy of the character special.

Slyly is an alien from Shirohima, a planet in a nearby galaxy. He looks similar to the Phillie Phanatic, except Slyly's fur is blue instead of green. According to the stats on his baseball trading cards, Slyly weighs 100 kilograms and is 210 centimeters tall. He premiered on July 29, 1995, after he arrived in Hiroshima due to a GPS error. He had meant to type in Shirohima into his spaceship navigation system but accidently typed in Hiroshima. If you look at the stadium, you will see that the top closely resembles a spaceship. Mazda Zoom-Zoom Stadium is Slyly's spaceship. He just happened to land there and then figured, "Well since the Japanese people love baseball, why don't I turn my spaceship into a baseball stadium and make

Hiroshima my new home." The Carp then asked him to be the ambassador of the Hiroshima Toyo Carp.

Slyly is a bit rounder than many of the other mascots. As much as he loves doing sports-oriented performances, he has a hard time keeping up with the other mascots who do backward handsprings during the games. The Saitama Seibu Lion, Leo, just broke a Guinness World Record for the most handsprings by a mascot in thirty seconds. Instead, Slyly loves gyrating his big old blue belly, and his act is a tasteful mixture of mischievous and kawaii (super cute or adorable). He likes ribbon-twirling gymnastics, dancing, and pulling pranks. He does a balance-beam act. It never works. Every time he tries it, the wood beam always breaks. And he always hurts himself. But one of these days, maybe, maybe he'll land it. Who knows?

I've seen videos of mascots from the 1990s and early 2000s, and it was kind of a free for all to do whatever you wanted. Baseball wasn't taken as seriously, I guess. But I think baseball culture has changed quite a bit since the early 2000s. It has become much more serious, and it's not as open to mascots doing those sorts of things. If you look online, there's a video of Slyly stepping up to bat in the batter's box during a game, and he actually hits a ball! If that happened at a game this season, it would not go over well. I'd probably get fired or scolded really bad for letting it happen.

From our perspective as performers, most home games follow the same routine—except for the COVID season, which was a bit different. Weekend home games usually start at 2:00 p.m. on a Saturday, and 1:30 p.m. on a Sunday. Weekday games start at 6:00 p.m. On weekdays I usually get to the office in the late morning. We go over the schedule for the game. We'll have different sponsors, and they'll want a photo on the field with Slyly, or they'll play a video on the board before the game, and we will dance. They have a lot of accolade ceremonies in Japan, so if a player just got his 2000th base hit, or 100th stolen base, or something, they might have a little ceremony for that player. So, we talk about positioning on the field, where Slyly should be standing, where they're going to take the pictures. They're very, very detailed. Everything has its place and its spot.

They don't really have giveaway days like they do in American baseball. You know, if you're one of the first five thousand fans, you get a Mickey Mantle replica or something like that. In Japan, they don't really do that, which is a bit disappointing, but I can understand there are a lot of logistics that go into doing giveaways. But we do have headband dances. Each year we'll give away a red headband with a different animal associated with it; in recent years we've had a bee, we've had a koala, we've had a fox. Before the game, there will be an announcement that says, "Okay, everybody got your headband? We're going to practice the dance, and we're going to dance again in the fifth inning." So Slyly will be on the field, right behind home plate, and I will be there with a Handycam on him. We'll have a choreographed video that they'll put up on the board, and we'll kind of talk the fans through a very simple dance while Slyly is doing it on the board. Then in the fifth inning, everyone will have their headbands on, and we'll do the dance. So that might be a part of the game schedule.

After we go through the schedule, we go through Slyly's performance. We are told how much time we should have for each performance. But sometimes that changes once we are on the field. They may say you've got four to five minutes, so we plan for four to five minutes. And then we get down there and they're like, "No, you've only got a minute or two," and we have to shorten it to two minutes. Or sometimes, a ceremony goes by so fast that we planned on two minutes and we have five, so you got to milk it. We just make it work. We then take the music for Slyly's performance—say he's doing a dance to *Thriller* by Michael Jackson—up to the music guys. We tell them, "Play it starting from here." After that, we'll eat lunch and just chill. Sometimes I'll go out and field BP when the Carp are hitting, just to get a little workout.

If it's a six o'clock game, gates open at 3:00. An hour before first pitch, we have our first greeting, signature, and photo session with fans on the concourse. In right field at Zoom-Zoom Stadium, there's a huge gym called Renaissance Gym. Inside, they have this big viewing area where they have a whole bunch of treadmills, ellipticals, and bikes lined up. You can watch the baseball game while you're working out at the gym. I've never done it because I've been working every game, but at some point I'd like to go up and see what that's like. Underneath that gym is our concourse goods shop. Our first greeting is there. We take pictures with fans. We do signatures. Recently we haven't been doing signatures as much, but Slyly is the boss. If he wants to sign something, we'll get him a marker, and he'll sign it.

After that, we take a break. Slyly comes back on the field for the pregame ceremonies. Besides the sponsor and player ceremonies that I already men-

Taylor Foote and Slyly. Courtesy of Taylor Foote.

tioned, we have a flower ceremony, where they give flowers to two players from each team and take a picture. Before the first game of every three-game home series, they play the national anthem. If we have a lot of time after the ceremonies, Slyly dances to "Take Me Out to the Ball Game." That adds just a little bit of an American flair to the Japanese baseball games. On a side note, the Carp, out of all the NPB teams, have the most Americanesque environment. The team aesthetic, the stadium, the ballpark food, the atmosphere were all modeled after American baseball.

If there's nothing special scheduled, we perform on the field before the game, right after the ceremonial first pitch. Slyly works with two *kuroko*, two guys who dress up in all black. The idea was borrowed from Japanese Kabuki theater. In Kabuki, kuroko dress in black so that they sort of blend in, and they move scenery, hold props, and things like that. Here, they assist Slyly, or they'll compete against him. Usually, they are the butts of Slyly's jokes and pranks. I think they add a lot to the performances and Slyly's character, especially because no other team in NPB has kuroko except us. Sometimes, they'll do the limbo. Slyly will do a limbo blindfolded first. When it's a kuroko's turn and he is blindfolded and doing a limbo, Slyly will just take the limbo pole and just go back to the dugout with the other kuroko. The first kuroko is still in the outfield trying to figure out where he is. Then he takes his blindfold off and realizes they are all gone.

There's a Japanese game called *kamizumo*, which is paper sumo. It's a game that kids play on New Year's. You make little sumo guys out of paper and put them in a ring, and you just bang your hands on the ground. The one that falls over loses. So Slyly does this. He goes in the outfield, where he has his big sumo ring. He's throwing his salt and slapping himself, and one of the kuroko is his opponent. Then they'll go in the ring, and Slyly will just stand there. He'll look at the crowd. He'll kind of teach the crowd what to do. They don't really get it at first, but then they start clapping, and Slyly and the kuroko will start moving around, and they do a life-size version of the paper sumo.

After the pregame performance, Slyly takes a rest, then comes out in the third inning for another greeting with the fans. Sometimes we visit the suites, and Slyly hangs out with kids or whoever is in the suite. The fans go crazy when they meet Slyly—like fangirl crazy! They lose their minds—absolute insanity. We can't even go into the crowd unless it's a controlled greeting on the concourse. Slyly is loved by all of his fans (except for maybe the ones who are still too small to know that he's not a bad alien). He gets a surprising amount of fan mail from all over the world too!

Slyly comes out again in the fifth inning for the CC Dance, which is a dance we do every game with all the fans. All the beer girls line up at the front of the sections, and they're all dancing along as well. Then right after the CC Dance, we go into bazooka time. Slyly has a T-shirt bazooka that shoots T-shirts or towels to fans. After that, he goes back in for a break.

In the summer when it's so hot, Slyly loves streaking naked. He will be out on the field and just take his jersey off, throw it on the ground, and start streaking across the field. The kuroko chase after him with the jersey. Other times, he'll just take a nap on the field if he's tired. He kind of just does whatever he wants.

Then he comes back out in the seventh inning for Lucky 7. Slyly used to ride out on a Segway, which was difficult to get used to, but after a while you can ride it without your hands. Slyly rode the Segway across the warning track, from left field to right and then back to left, while waiving a large koi flag as the Carp's song played in the background. Slyly stopped using the Segway about two years ago and started riding on a custom hot rod. A kuroko drives while Slyly rides on the back, which is a lot safer and way cooler than the Segway. He's very excited about that.

During this time, all the fans are blowing up these special red balloons. Then when the song is over, they let all the balloons go. They're elongated balloons designed to fly straight up and then come back down. I think it's one of the coolest things in Japanese baseball. Seeing all those balloons, thirty thousand balloons, especially when you're on the field, is amazing. The balloons are specially made because the Shinkansen (the bullet train) and the local train tracks are right behind the stadium. They were designed so that they would not fly far and reach the tracks. The odds of any reaching the Shinkansen are impossible. But in Japan, safety is especially important.

Slyly comes back out in the eighth inning for another greeting with fans, and then comes the postgame performance. If we win, he goes out to celebrate. We have a hero interview, and somebody from the PR department takes a picture of the hero with Slyly. That's not done in American baseball. It's a postgame interview on the field with whoever is hero of the game. Then Slyly will make his rounds on the hot rod and say goodbye to the fans. That's it for a win. If it's a loss, Slyly is very sad, and you can tell because his eyes show his sadness. If you look closely, he has different eyes for when he's sad.

That's one thing I really love about Japanese mascot culture compared to that of America. When I was learning to be a mascot in America, even if your team is losing, you had to be energic and positive. You know, "They're gonna come back! They're gonna win!" I didn't like that. But in Japan, Slyly gets sad. When the Carp lose, he doesn't even put his head up to take pictures with people just because he's so sad. And the fans love it. They eat it up. They're like, "Slyly, feel better." "Slyly. It's okay; we're going to win tomorrow. It's okay, Slyly." And he's just like, "No, I'm done!" and he'll lay down on the field and throw a temper tantrum.

If we have a walk-off win, Happy Slyly comes out of the dugout. He gets so ecstatic and excited that his color changes to pink. And then he goes crazy. He runs out like a madman, running in circles. He'll run the bases with this giant koi flag, even bigger than the one he has in the car.

Road games are different. Slyly's schedule depends on the hosting team's schedule; however, there are a couple things that are included in both home and away games. The CC Dance and Lucky 7 are performed at away games when Slyly is in attendance. Usually, we also have a greeting with the hosting team's mascot(s) and cheer team. Sometimes we also perform a stage show before the game outside the stadium for the fans. Other teams also have designated dances during their games, and Slyly will go out and dance along with their mascots.

Fans in Japan just love mascots. They're just obsessed with them. Every company has a mascot. Every city has a mascot. Everything has a mascot. The NPB mascots are at the top of the hierarchy of mascots, aside from others who have made a name for themselves and built a huge following, such as Hello Kitty, Pikachu, Kumamon, and Chiitan.

From what I've seen and experienced, Japanese mascots are appreciated far more for their character and personality than in the United States. Characters in the States place more emphasis on entertainment value and how big of a stunt or how many backflips through a flaming hoop they can do, especially in the NBA, where they are doing backflips off thirty-foot ladders and doing big trampoline dunks and doing insane choreographed dances. American fans love their mascots, but they want to see something, they don't want the mascot to just stand there and look cute. Whereas in Japan, there are numerous characters that can't even touch their own faces but have thousands of fans and followers on social media, simply because they are cute and the character and personality they have developed is unique and engaging. It's kawaii culture—unbearable cuteness. I'm obsessed with some of them. One of them is DB Starman, the hamster from the Yokohama BayStars, and he can't even touch his face; his hands stick out the side of his body. It's just the cuteness of the character. The companies that make the suits do such a good job.

The most famous mascot in Japanese baseball is on the Yakult Swallows. His name is Tsubakuro, and he has been around for nearly thirty years. He is a giant swallow in a batting helmet. And he does nothing. He just stands there. He's a witty, funny kind of guy. He writes jokes, things like that. Other than that, he doesn't really do anything. He dances, if you could call it dancing, as it's just him barely moving. Tsubakuro barely moves a muscle, but the fans are obsessed with him. Whenever he comes to visit our stadium, we have to set up stanchions and cordon off this huge area because fans would just rush and try to get pictures with him. We have a huge line of people waiting to get pictures as they bring him gifts. He's more popular than the players on the team for the most part.

I am a firm believer that Japanese baseball is way more entertaining than American baseball. In America, you have the people who are really into it, who watch the game, and then you have people who are just there for the dollar beer night. Not that I don't like American baseball, I just think NPB is far more entertaining. It's the atmosphere. There's something going on the entire game. The players have their own chants when they're up to bat, every stadium has a "performance section" for both home and the visiting team fans. These sections consist of trumpets, drums, and such to play songs and chants during the game. There are the mascots. You've got dances. You've got cheerleaders—well, except for us. We're the only team without cheerleaders. Again, they want to make it as American as possible, and in American baseball there are no cheerleaders. Regular-season Japanese baseball has the same energy as postseason American baseball. Everyone is watching the game. Everyone is way more into it.

And I think Hiroshima is special. It's a great place. I've been to all the stadiums, so people always ask me, "What's your favorite stadium?" I might be biased, but it's Hiroshima. Not only because of the American feeling of it, but when you're up in the nosebleed seats, it's the perfect picturesque Japanese image. You have the shinkansen going by in the background, and you have the local trains right underneath that. You've got the mountains in the distance, and then you've got baseball. And that's Japan. It's the bullet train, mountains, and baseball! It's just so beautiful. I love it!

10 / Saori Ogure, Cheerleader

A member of the Hokkaido Nippon Ham Fighters cheerleading squad from 2008 to 2013, Saori Ogure has been the director of the Fighter Girls since 2014. In 2022 she created the routine for the Fox Dance, which became a national sensation.

◆

My father is a huge baseball fan, so I've always had baseball in my life from the time that I was a very young child. I took dance lessons from age seven onward, so when my father heard that the Nippon Ham Fighters were holding auditions for cheerleaders, he reached out to me and asked if I was interested in auditioning. I was twenty years old when I auditioned to be a Fighters Girl in December 2007. I passed the test, and then training began in January so that we could prepare ourselves for the season.

We stayed in Hokkaido for the preseason training. There was a training room within the stadium, which is where we spent our days, just training the whole day. We did a lot of dance practice, but we were also preparing our bodies in terms of body strength and stamina for actual game-time cheerleading. We practiced basic body movements, and then also we practiced the choreography for roughly ten songs. The squad was composed of about twenty cheerleaders, and when I joined the Fighters Girls, I didn't know any of them. So, the biggest challenge was not the dancing or the workouts but the mental approach, getting motivated and just figuring out how to fit in and achieve unity in this group of twenty girls whom I had never met before.

There was no dormitory for the cheerleaders, and there still isn't today, so we were left to find our own places to live. Most of the girls were from Hokkaido, so some found apartments, while others were still living with their folks. When I first joined the Fighters Girls, there actually was no pay. It was volunteer work, which meant that a lot of the girls had to find other work. I worked a part-time job on the days when we didn't have games.

Now cheerleaders are able to make a living, or at least survive, on the pay that they get from doing the job. It's taken fifteen to sixteen years for that to happen, and that's because the status of cheerleaders has grown and the recognition they receive has enabled them to achieve this salary.

Now, the Fighters Girls can supplement their salaries by teaching at the Nippon Ham Fighters Dance Academy. The academy conducts classes for all ages. We start with preschoolers and also have elementary school, junior high, high school, and university students, as well as adults and even professionals joining our classes. At present we have roughly one thousand students enrolled at our various locations. We have several within Sapporo; one in Kitahiroshima, where the team currently has its home stadium; and others in the cities and towns in the surrounding area. The girls themselves are the instructors. We look at the squad to see who has good technique and skills and also the ability to teach. We will then recommend her to one of the schools and dispatch her to that school as an instructor.

When I was a cheerleader, we would gather at the stadium about four hours before the game began. For a night game, that would be around 2:00 p.m., and we would spend about two hours training, preparing, warming up. We had a dressing room, but it was very small and simple, with just a long table and folding chairs. As Sapporo Dome was rented by the team, we had to set up equipment and our belongings before each homestand and clear everything out after each series, which was a very labor-intensive task. Now, at Es Con Field, the Fighters built a dedicated dressing room for cheerleaders. Each cheerleader also has her own locker, so it is an excellent setup. Furthermore, we have been provided with a dance studio, allowing us to train at any time, which makes us very happy. Each girl does her own hair and makeup. We only have a professional stylist come in when a girl first joins the squad, to show her what hairstyle and makeup suits her best. After that, it is up to each cheerleader to do it herself.

Back then, fans were allowed into the stadium two hours before game time. We then lined up at the gates to greet the fans as they entered. This was an opportunity for fans to have interactions with the cheerleaders and even take pictures with them. Right before the game was to begin, we would do the opening dance. Then, we came on the field three times during the game. In the first half of the game, from the first to fifth inning, we would do some type of performance and then another right after the fifth inning, then there was one more during the second half of the game. And finally at the end of the game we would come out and make our final appearance.

Things have changed a lot since then. There's a lot more for the cheerleaders to do now. The gates now open for the fans four hours before game time, which means that the cheerleaders have to get there roughly seven hours before the first pitch. We still do our two hours of workouts and warmups, and we still greet the fans when the gates open. So, we're basically spending three hours greeting the fans and taking photos with them. Before the game we still have the opening dance, but then in the first half and the second half of the games we're coming out onto the field twice each time instead of once each time, and we still come out at the fifth inning and after the games.

Although dancing is the cheerleaders' primary job, Fighters Girls are also involved in fan service to increase support for the team. The Nippon Ham Fighters have become a real part of the community here in Hokkaido, as we're a very local team. The players do their part by making appearances, but during the season it's hard for them to get out into the community because they're busy playing. So, the Fighters Girls fulfill that role, especially on the off days during the season, by getting out into the community to encourage community spirit. We visit nursery schools, preschools, kindergartens, elementary schools, junior high schools, and so on. We conduct dance classes and attend festivals. So the number of tasks that a cheerleader needs to do has increased significantly, and it's not enough just to be able to dance anymore. Now cheerleaders are more seen as staff, and like staff they interact with the fans and deal with the media at times.

I think the Fighters Girls do a lot more work than the cheerleaders on other teams because we're in Hokkaido, which is a vast land. There are hundreds of cities and towns across Hokkaido, and a lot of them make requests for us to come and do PR appearances. So, on days that we don't have games, we are often at these towns doing events. We also get a lot of requests from the local media, and we try to respond to as many of those as we can.

Because the popularity of cheerleaders has been on the rise and the number of our appearances has increased, so has our exposure on social media. Now there are people who are just cheerleader fans, and they end up treating or seeing the cheerleaders like Japanese pop idols. With that has come different types of troubles from guy fans being interested in the girls as idols. It's something that we are working on right now. When it comes to the girls' social media accounts, even though these are their private accounts, the team is overseeing them and is being very careful about what is allowed to be posted. That might help to prevent some of the troubles from happening. As far as in-person incidents, which have been on the rise, we make sure that there's always somebody there who is able to intervene if things get out of hand.

Interaction, dating, and communication with players are strictly prohibited. Cheerleaders are only allowed to greet players if they meet them in the areas within the stadium, and no other contact is permitted. If any interaction with players is discovered, the cheerleader's contract is immediately terminated.

There are twenty-four cheerleaders on the squad this year [2024]. The number of cheerleaders changes from year to year depending on the auditions. If we find a number of girls who seem qualified, we'll have more cheerleaders on the squad that year. If there aren't as many qualified applicants, there might be fewer cheerleaders. The auditions are held every December, and that's when we change the personnel in the cheerleading squad. Even the current members of the squad have to audition each year if they want to continue. Some of them pass the audition, and some of them do not. We do this because the auditions are a unique and emotionally difficult process. We don't want the current cheerleaders to forget that feeling. We want them to keep trying to improve themselves and build themselves up to have the emotional strength to get through the audition. Last year, we had about three hundred applicants. That was about the same as the year before, but the number of applicants really saw a huge spike a few years back when the Fox Dance became a big hit. We probably doubled the number of applicants after that.

There are three stages in the audition. The first one is just a regular application. They submit paperwork with their resumes. We're looking at what their experience is, where they live, to see if they will be a good match or not. In this process, roughly half the number of applicants are cut out. The second stage is face-to-face audition where we give them a song that they need to prepare a dance for and then perform it in front of us. And again, in that process the number gets cut in half. Then, the third stage is a Q & A—type interview.

Saori Ogure. Courtesy of Saori Ogure.

    I believe that the Fighters Girls cheer team is unique, quite different from other teams. I believe that the other teams that have cheerleaders are looking at technique and dancing skills first and foremost. We, of course, do look at the technique, but we're also looking at other attributes. What are their speaking skills like? What are their facial expressions, their body types, and their personalities? Do they have something interesting or unique to offer or things that they can do? In fact, we've hired some girls who can't even dance. They can pass the audition without that ability. They've got quite a rigorous work and training schedule to get on the same page as everyone else in front of them, but we have hired such girls before.

    Every team has a different concept of what their cheerleaders should look like. There are the sexy ones, the ones that try to look like idols, or the young lady look. And some teams will go for the traditional or orthodox cheerleading team. The Fighters Girls have been designed keeping our fan demographic in mind, which has a lot of elderly fans. We want to create an image where the cheerleaders are like the daughters or the granddaughters of these fans. So, we have kind of a country-girl type of image, where the girls are down-to-earth and very approachable.

For the uniforms, we ask an external costume-production company to handle the design and creation. I provide specific requirements such as color scheme, sleeve length, shape of the top, skirt length, number of pleats, flare width, and so forth. The production company then submits around ten designs based on these specifications. I choose the one that matches our image, and we finalize the design. We change the uniform design every three years.

The training for cheerleading, the dancing, the practices, and all that are definitely not enough to help them to maintain their physical condition, so we expect—and we tell them quite often—that they need to keep themselves in good shape. The cheerleaders aren't allowed to use the training facilities at the ballpark, so each cheerleader is responsible for either finding a gym on her own or just doing workouts in her own home.

During the years that I worked as a Fighters Girl, I was the cheerleader captain. When I was ready to retire from the cheer squad, a team rep approached me and asked me if I was interested in working for the team. So now I'm officially employed by the Nippon Ham Fighters as part of the Guest Relations Department. I'm responsible for the cheerleaders in a more official manner. I coordinate their events, interviews, and schedules and run the auditions, create the dance routines, and direct the squad.

As the director, I try not to tell them what to do or just bark orders at them. Instead, I'd rather to have them think about things themselves. I just direct them or guide them. I feel that a good leader is able to be a good facilitator and a coordinator—someone who watches over what's happening, as opposed to directing everyone in a very strict or specific way. The girls often say that I am like a mother figure to them, and in fact I see them as daughters in a sense as well. I strive to be someone who they can very easily approach and they can talk to about anything. It feels a bit strange to say this myself, but I do feel like I'm really good at seeing details. I notice the small things about each of the girls from day to day. And I think that I'm a pretty good communicator; I'm very proactive when it comes to communicating. So from being close to them every day, being able to see the smaller details of their lives, and actually trying to take care of them maybe is what causes them to see me as a mother figure. I think it's an honor.

When we create a new routine for the cheerleaders, we want to produce something that [not only] the fans can participate in but also gives us a chance to show our own dancing skills. The song needs to be catchy, so that from the first time the fans hear it, it will stick with them, and they will want to join in with the dance. After I've got the song and the concept, I create the choreography. And again, I want to make sure it's something that fans can easily join and have fun doing. This process takes about a week, and then I'll teach it to the cheerleaders, and we'll spend a whole day perfecting it. After that, we're ready to go.

In 2020 and 2021, baseball was, of course, interrupted and changed because of the COVID-19 pandemic. There were times when no fans were allowed in the stands, and then even once they were allowed back in, all the fan cheering that was once in place could no longer be done. There were no trumpets. There were no cheer songs being sung. It was a really quiet environment. So, I wanted to create something that fans would be able to participate in and enjoy without having to use their voices, since that was forbidden.

The idea that I had at that point was somewhat vague. The inspiration came from the team mascot Frep, who is a fox. I thought, *Can we create some sort of dance with the content connected to the fox?* My next step was to choose a song. I did a search with the word *kitsune*, the Japanese word for "fox," and of course the word *fox*, on YouTube. And I stumbled upon a song by the Norwegian duo Ylvis called "The Fox (What Does the Fox Say?)." The first time I heard it, I was enraptured. It was so catchy. I decided right away that this was the song we wanted to use. When I watched the video, I noticed that they had a catchy dance as well, and if we rearranged it a little bit, it would be usable. So that's what we did.

It's a rather unique song and a unique dance, so when we first performed it, the fans were quite confused. Rather than there being a positive response, there was just a murmuring among the fans. I felt like it had failed. But rather than packing it in, I thought we should just keep on doing it. As we did it more and more, the players wanted to try the dance as well. They thought it was catchy. So, the team created a video for their official YouTube site with some of the players also doing the fox dance. From there, it really took off. It became the most viewed video on the team's official website and YouTube account. It eventually had over four million views and became a national sensation. The shock that I felt when I thought that it had failed was still lingering inside of me, so I really wasn't prepared for it to become a big hit. Then I saw the number of plays it was getting on YouTube, and the media started to pick up the story and started calling for interviews. I was just so surprised as it was completely unexpected.

With its success, my personal life changed a lot. I had a lot of media offers and all of a sudden a lot of friends, acquaintances, and people from my past contacted me. Even strangers recognized me outside of the ballpark and said, "Hey, are you Miss Ogure? Are you her?" The success of the Fox Dance also led to a boom in Fighters merchandise sales. The team recognized that, and it cast a positive light on me, so I was very happy to have been recognized for that as well.

I've been thinking a lot about the role of cheerleaders in Japanese baseball. Last offseason I was able to go to the United States, and I was able to take in some NFL and NBA games. Everything was impressive: the music, the lighting, the scoreboards, the sounds, the cheerleaders. I feel like Japan still has a lot of catching up to do. But I think if we try to just replicate what NFL or NBA cheerleaders do, it won't work because it's not Japanese. Cheerleaders here need to match the Japanese spirit. Two things come mind when I think about that. One is hospitality, which really matches the Japanese spirit, and the other one is to put the fans first and think about their wants and their needs and respond to them. I'm not sure exactly what the role of NFL cheerleaders is and how much they interact with their fans, but in Japan cheerleading teams place high importance on fan interaction and getting to know the fans and letting the fans get to know us. So, I would like to invite you to come to Japan, come to a ballpark, and interact with the cheerleaders. In recent years at Es Con Field, we've had a lot of foreigners coming to the ballpark, and we definitely make sure that we interact with the foreign fans as well. So please come out to Es Con Field and meet us!

11 / Keiko Suzuki, Uriko (Beer Girl)

From Osaka, Keiko Suzuki worked for two years as a uriko at Koshien Stadium.

◆

As uriko, our job is to help the fans to enjoy the game of baseball at a higher level. Within our group, we do not call ourselves workers or beer girls or servers; we refer to ourselves as the cast. We see ourselves as part of an important cast that puts on a performance of sorts for the fans to enjoy the game even more. I think that uriko represent Japanese hospitality at the ballpark. We bring that aspect of Japanese culture to the game.

I'm from Nishinomiya, which is the home of Koshien Stadium, so I grew up around baseball and have always been interested in the game. When I was in high school, I was one of the helpers for the baseball club. So when I heard that uriko (beer girls) get paid fairly well and that it was a part-time job, I was interested in applying. I did an internet search and applied online for the very first one that came up. It was really simple. I then went in for an interview and was hired. Uriko are hired by the beer companies, not the stadiums or the teams. I was hired by Asahi; it sells beer and other products, and it has a contract with Koshien Stadium.

I only worked at Koshien. I did the job for two years. In my first year, I didn't work at every single game. But last year in my second year, I worked at every home game, so roughly twelve to fifteen times per month and sixty-eight games in total. When I started, there was no real training session. I was just told to do what the more experienced girls were doing and just to do my best. The first five times on the job were a kind of a probation period.

The products sold by the vendors are varied. There's beer, chuhai, and whiskey. And then there are soft drinks and ice cream. Within the soft drink and ice cream categories, guys make up about 10 percent of the sellers. As far as the beer and chuhai goes, it's 100 percent females. The age range is from high school students to university graduates, but there are a few that are in their late twenties or early thirties. The drinking age in Japan is twenty, but you can start the job at sixteen years old.

Night games start around 6:00 p.m. I would arrive at the stadium before 4:00 p.m. to go to the changing room to put on my uniform. We didn't have our own uniforms. Every day they would just give us one and then at the end of the day when we changed out of it, we'd give it back to them. They would clean it and prepare the uniform for the next workday. There were only two sizes that were set out for us. We would just pick the one that was going to fit. As you can imagine, the girls take time to get ready physically, meaning that they're making sure their hair is tied neatly and their makeup looks good. In my case that would take about thirty minutes, but it would depend from girl to girl.

A lot of the girls put something in their hair or on their hat to identify themselves and separate themselves from the other girls. They might have a flower or a ribbon or something like that. I put a big ribbon in my hair, and on my cap I had a plushy of the game character called Kirby, so I was easily identifiable.

At 4:00 we would have a brief meeting. We would talk about the sales from the day before, and we would talk about the expected weather conditions for that day and the expected attendance. There were some basic rules that we had to follow. We were told to make sure that we didn't block people's view of the game, especially as we were pouring beer. They were quite strict about that. Also, each uriko had her own section or her own set of stairs that they would walk up and down. We were told not to step into other girls' rows and to make sure that you stayed where you were supposed to be.

The stadium is divided into seven areas. For the infield seating, there are three sections: first base, middle, and third base. In the outfield there are the first base and third base Alps (the bench seating down the lines in the outfield) plus the left-field stands and the right-field stands. There were about 10 uriko who worked in each of these areas. I worked in the outfield stands.

Obviously, there's a huge difference in fan behavior and atmosphere between the outfield and the infield. In Koshien Stadium, the right field is where the Hanshin Tigers oendan is, and so it is a very boisterous atmosphere. And left field is where the other team's oendan is, but it's got a different flavor to it. It's maybe a little bit milder than the Hanshin oendan. And then in the infield—I personally don't have much experience with sales there, so I can't say this for sure—it seems like people are more intent on watching the game. It's a little bit more of a quiet, subdued atmosphere. So as salesgirls, we wouldn't have to necessarily yell out and make calls for sales because people there are more attentive to their surroundings.

The outfield stands are probably the best places to sell, but it really depends on the day of the week and the conditions. In rainy weather, sales in the outfield suffer, so that's not the best place on those days. On the other hand, on the weekends when there are more people in the stands, it's the best place to sell. You can get assigned to an area in different ways, but it's often out of our control, and a company employee will make the final decision. They may assign you based on your personality, deciding that a particular area really suits you. Or someone that you get along with might suggest that you come to her area and join her. And then some people actually put in a request that they want to work in certain parts of the stadium.

After the meeting, the first group of uriko would start selling at 4:30, about ninety minutes before first pitch. A second group would start at 5:00, a third at 5:30, and the last at 6:00. We signed up to be in the group that best fit our schedule. I would sell until the bottom of the eighth inning, which means I was usually working until about 9:00. I was responsible for selling chuhai, which is short for "shochu highball." It's a canned cocktail made with shochu, seltzer, and lemon. So, I didn't have to carry a keg on my back. I had a tray hanging from my shoulders that rested around my waist. It contained thirty-six cans of chuhai plus the ice, the cups, and the money. I don't have an exact weight, but it was very, very heavy. I would say the same thing about the beer kegs. They're very heavy. When full, they weigh about fifteen kilograms (thirty-three pounds). The Asahi kegs hold ten liters of beer, enough for twenty-seven cups.

Being a uriko is an extremely fatiguing job. On your first day of work, they allow you to carry less than a full tray because you're still learning the ropes. So, I was duped into feeling like, *Oh, I can do this; it's not so hard*. But as I started to understand how the ranking system worked and that the more you sell the higher your ranking, I wanted to carry the max. That's when the fatigue really started to set in at the end of the day. I probably lost five to eight kilograms (eleven to seventeen pounds) since starting the job.

We're allowed to take breaks whenever we want to, but doing so means no sales, so very few of the girls actually take breaks during the game. So every now and then, we will stop in the entryways between the concourse and the stands and just take a sip of water, or tea, or a sports drink that we bring from home.

Like all the uriko, I would start my sales at the bottom of the aisle. I would turn to face the fans, then bow before climbing the stairs. I would also raise my hand and wave the drink sign until I made eye contact with a customer who wanted a drink. Once I found a good row where I thought I could sell a lot, I made sure I went up that row at least once every two times I climbed the stairs.

I didn't really make any changes in my sales routine based on what was happening in the game. I would go up and down the stairs no matter what was happening on the field, unless I could see that it was not the best time to sell and I needed to get more chuhai. For example, if I only had a few drinks left and the Tigers were at bat and doing really well and the crowd was into the game, then I would use that time to go and get refilled.

It usually took me about twenty to thirty minutes to sell out my tray, and then I had to go back to our base to get resupplied. We had two refilling stations on the second concourse of the stadium. There's one on the third base side of the stadium, and there's another one in right field. I would walk past all of the stands and all of the shops on the second floor right to the very end to receive more chuhai. If I was working in left field, I would have to go almost halfway around into the third base section to get replenished and then go back to the left-field stands. That round trip and being resupplied took over five minutes.

Asahi has its beer stations in the same place as I got my chuhai, but Kirin has its station in a different place, right in the center-field area down on the first floor, so their girls can get replenished quickly. Changing the kegs for the beer girls is a bit like changing the tires on a Formula One race car. There's a team of people, guys and girls, who work hard to make sure that it's as quick of a transition as possible because we want to get back out and sell so that we do not lose out to the competition. They don't refill the beer keg while it's on the girl's back. Instead, they take the empty one off and put a fresh one on. It's a very fast process. I think the record for the quickest change is only thirteen seconds.

When I went to the refill station, somebody was there to keep track of the sales. They would count the number of cups that I used and the number of empty cans, which should always be the same, and enter that number into a computer. But I also kept track; I usually knew exactly how many I sold each day.

At the peak of summer when sales are high, like in July, I sold around 200 cups per game. But earlier in the season, in April and May when it's colder, I sold closer to 170 cups. Based on the pace of the game, the number of sales can change. For example, when Shoki Murakami was pitching, the game tended to be faster paced, which means that our sales went down. The Tigers winning or leading didn't necessarily lead to more sales. In fact, if the Tigers are losing, that sometimes means the other team's time at bat is a little bit longer, which leads to longer periods of sales because fans are focused on cheering when the Tigers are at bat. On my best day, I sold 276 cups. It was a really hot day in July 2023, and the game went into extra innings. It was a very long game, and maybe that's what enabled me to sell so many. As far as I can remember, the Tigers lost that day.

We received an hourly wage of ¥1,000 (about $6.47 in 2024). So, if we worked five hours, that would be ¥5,000. But as the sales go, for every cup that I sold I received a ¥30 (about $0.19) commission. Basically, that means if I sold 150 cups, the commission plus my salary would work out to about ¥10,000 (roughly $64.50), and if I sold 200, then I'd get around ¥12,000 (about $77.50) for that one day.

In each part of the stadium, the girls who ranked in the top three in sales for chuhai or the top five sales for beer got an armband that displays their ranking. This was measured over the course of one month. That means if you missed a game, you missed out on one day's worth of sales, which was going to hurt your rankings. For the company that I worked for, if you continually ranked in the top over the course of a half season or a full year, then you would receive gift certificates, or you could choose gifts from a catalog. So there were incentives to be a top seller. I heard rumors that other companies gave prizes out for the monthly rankings, but that was not the case for my company.

There's a strong sense of rivalry between the uriko. During the games, we track our sales compared to our rivals to make sure that we are not on the losing end. I haven't experienced this myself, but sometimes the girls will actually glare at each other. Kind of saying, *Stay out of my territory!* just from the look in their eyes when they stare each other down.

Many of our sales come from regular customers. Season-ticket holders are going to be at every game, and so they are a good target to try to gain as repeat customers. Over time, I got to know them. I tried to remember their names and remember their drink preference. Some of the regular customers would wait for me to come around. This is why we added distinctive accessories to our uniforms, like my ribbon and my Kirby, so that they could distinguish us from far away. But others might not wait. So, as I was doing my job, I was always checking for the right time to go back to them. But I also had to make sure that I had enough cups for when it's time for me to go back. I had to get my timing right.

When I poured a drink, I always smiled. Customers are coming to watch baseball and have a good time. Our purpose is to help them enjoy their experience, which includes drinking. So, I tried to make it as pleasant as possible for them. I would often talk to the customers, especially if they are regulars. I sometimes talked to them about the weather, or I would talk about the other team a little bit. We might talk about yesterday's game. At night, after the games, my face usually hurt from smiling—from keeping my muscles in that same position all game.

Men tend to drink more on the whole than women, so there might be more interaction with male customers, but if I was selling to a couple, I made sure that I talked to the woman. Guys tend to buy beer from the same girl based on how the girl looks and because they like the way the girl looks. So, if I was approaching a couple, the girlfriend might make that assumption about her boyfriend. Well, jealousy might kick in, and she may not like it if he keeps calling me back to buy from me. Making a good connection with the girl allowed me to be able to go back and sell to those customers over and over again.

Sometimes single guys asked for a way of contacting me, like they would ask if we could exchange social-media information. In those cases, I would either tell them that it was forbidden by the stadium or that I forgot my email address or social-media account information. Luckily, I've never been really harassed, but I have heard of some other uriko who have had guys almost stalking them. There was one instance of a guy who kept taking unwanted pictures of the uriko. He was reported to the stadium staff, and then he was told to leave the ballpark. I don't know what happened after that, but he was not allowed to stay at the park that day.

Many tourists who come to the ballpark ask to take pictures together with us. As a rule, that is not allowed by the company, but I personally didn't mind. I feel like it's a chance for them to make a good memory and for them to enjoy themselves. So, I was okay with taking pictures with them, even though technically it was not allowed. As for people taking pictures freely without asking first, I got a little bit uncomfortable because I was not really sure what their motives might be. We wore kind of short skirts and so I was a little bit leery about them just taking pictures without asking first. But overseas fans should remember that the uriko girls really want the fans to come to the game and have a good time. I feel that a Japanese baseball game is a unique experience. If they're coming to Japan to experience Japanese culture, baseball is a very important way to do so. We're there to help them if they don't know what's going on. We are on their side.

Being a uriko really presents a great opportunity for the girls. Anybody can do this job if she's interested in it. Of course, it's a hard job. You need to have strength. You need to have that competitive fire in you. A lot of girls quit. There's high turnover, but the pay is quite good, especially for university students. And it's a very rewarding job. If you do this job at Koshien Stadium or one of the other big ballparks, you can experience baseball in a different way than you would as just a fan.

12 / Kenjiro Kajita, Ballpark Security and Intern

A history major and varsity pitcher at Grinnell College, Kenjiro Kajita has worked as a security guard at Meiji Jingu Stadium and has been an intern with the Yomiuri Giants.

◆

I started playing baseball with T-ball when I was really young in the States. I think from that moment on I was committed to playing baseball for the rest of my life. I was born in Japan, moved to Connecticut when I was four because of my dad's job, and moved back to Japan at eleven years old. Then, I moved to Malaysia for all of middle school and then back to Japan for high school. Now, I'm in college in the United States. It's been really fun having all these weird baseball experiences that probably no one else has had.

I saw my first professional game at old Yankee Stadium. [Hideki] Matsui was still there. I was a diehard Yankees fan. I'd go home from school, turn on the TV, and start watching the YES Network. It was kind of a golden era for the Yankees with Mariano [Rivera], [Derek] Jeter, [Andy] Pettitte and [Jorge] Posada. I watched them win the 2009 World Series. Then, in the summer of 2012, I got to see Meiji Jingu Stadium and Japanese baseball for the first time. I really liked it, and we kept going back there.

I've played baseball all my life, but playing middle school baseball in Malaysia was really different. The only team for middle schoolers in the entire country belonged to the Japanese school. Although I didn't attend the school, I played on the team and became the captain for two years. It wasn't very serious. Our parents were the coaches and we only practiced on Sundays—even then many of the kids didn't show up because they had to go to cram school!

My high school in Japan was in a rural part of western Tokyo. It's an international-friendly school where you get a lot of kids like me who were foreign-exchange or expat students. I started high school in Japan in the second term. I was late, so I kind of walked on to the baseball team—well, everyone walks on to the team because there are no tryouts in Japan. Anyone can play. But for tournaments, the rosters shrink down to eighteen or twenty players. The baseball team was serious. The kids had played baseball all their lives and were committed. Our coach had been a backup catcher for the Yakult Swallows.

So I came in as a small Japanese kid who doesn't really speak Japanese too well and is kind of like out of his sphere—I think people find me an oddball anywhere I go. But here I am, and all the kids on my team have shaved their heads. They believed that it was a new era for the team and we were going to Koshien. And I come on with a full head of hair and I'm just like, "I don't know why you want to shave your heads. It doesn't really change anything." And, "Let's be realistic, we're not going to Koshien. It's not going to happen for one hundred years." So there I was judging everyone's dreams. I don't think my seniors liked me too much at first. But yeah, that was me. I did eventually shave my head because my coach told me to. But then when I became a senior, I suggested we stop shaving our heads and everyone grew a full head of hair. And I was like, "I told you, it doesn't matter."

Our practices were pretty tough. We'd finish school around 3:00 p.m. every day, and then we'd be practicing until 7:00 or 8:00 p.m. on weekdays, and on weekends we'd be playing from 7:00 in the morning till like 7:00 at night. We did a lot of running, like traditional Japanese teams. We'd have 8K runs every day. In the summer we'd have games, so that was fun, but in the winter all we did was running and physical stuff. I didn't really enjoy that part of it.

Our team followed most of the traditions of Japanese high school baseball. We would bow to the field before taking it. It's a sign of respect that we are able to be out there playing the game. We'd fix the diamond all by ourselves. There was no one to do that for us. We had a dirt field, so we'd rake it after practice. We had a kind of forest in our outfield. So everyone would spend what seemed like an hour picking up the balls that went in there. If we had an indoor practice, we would clean the gymnasium. The younger players would clean the toilets. The old standard existed within my team where the younger players did all the cleaning while the older players did their own thing. At the end of a game, we would bow toward the field and say, "*Arigato gozaimashita*" (thank you). And we said thank you to the opposing team, the umpires, and the parents who came to watch. There's a lot of gratitude within baseball in Japan. You're taught to be respectful and have gratitude when you're growing up.

Before my last game of my senior year, I got recruited by a company that did ballpark security for high school and professional baseball games. They employed a bunch of high schoolers to work part-time at multiple stadiums. I thought it was interesting and I was like, "Yeah, sure, I'm down." I started after my season ended. I worked about twenty games at Jingu Stadium that summer. My title was part-time ballpark security staff. There were probably about a hundred of us, mostly high school and college students. We didn't have an official uniform, just a polo shirt that said "STAFF" on it.

I really like Jingu Stadium. I think one of the best things about Jingu Stadium is that it's cheap. It's really affordable for any fan. I think the outfield seats, when I was a kid, used to be ¥500, which at that time was like $5. Now it's up to ¥1600, but even that's still really affordable. The Swallows fans have this thing where they use an umbrella—it's a see-through green, plastic mini umbrella. Whenever they get a run, they start this chant, and they sway their umbrellas. I think one of the best parts of being in Jingu is getting to see everyone pop out their mini umbrellas and do this. And then there's the mascot Tsubakuro. He gets a lot of showtime on the screen and a lot of time entertaining fans. They portray him as kind of a comedian. He likes to write posters and show them to the opposing team. He's probably the Phillie Phanatic of Japanese baseball in the sense that he'll do anything to get laughs. It's also an open stadium, so in summers you'll get fireworks, and then you'll have cheerleaders dancing everywhere too.

On game days, I'd arrive before batting practice. All of us would clean up the stadium first. Then we'd stand in the outfield bleachers during batting practice to get the balls that came in and throw them back onto the field. When the fans started to come in, about an hour into batting practice, we'd have to blow a whistle for their safety so that they wouldn't get hit by any balls. The thing with Japanese baseball is that it costs a lot of money to get baseballs, so you can't keep batting practice balls. If fans grab one, we have to go and ask them for the ball back. That's the most awkward interaction because they're so excited to get a ball, especially if it's a young kid. But then here comes these high schoolers who are just working part-time, and they say, "We need the ball back." So that was one of the weirdest interactions.

People were really understanding, but it wasn't fun to take balls away from people who came early to just see batting practice.

After batting practice, once more people started to come into the stadium, we would guide them to their seats because Jingu Stadium is small, and you can't see your seat number until you get there. During the games, we would stand by the staircases or somewhere where people don't really see us.

I usually worked in left field. The left-field stand is basically reserved for the visiting team's fans. That's common in any NPB stadium. The fans are divided into right field and left field, and that's where they have their own cheer group with their trumpets and flags. When it's time for their team to hit, everyone stands up and cheers them on. The Yakult Swallows fans are kind of relaxed and are just there to enjoy the game. But the Hanshin Tigers fans, or any sort of fans from western Japan, are really rowdy, and they'll start yelling a lot. That's when it's no longer fun to be standing there watching baseball. Sometimes you get fans from the home team who accidentally sit in left field. That day they probably have the worst baseball experience they've had in their entire life.

Part of our job was, if something happened among the fans, like a scuffle or anything, we had to go and intervene. But the thing is, we were high school and college students, and they're full-grown adults. They've had a couple drinks, and the game is going badly, or they're not seeing what they want to see, so they're not in the mood to listen to us. We usually had to get our supervisors, who wore police-like uniforms so that they have more authority, to tell them off. That was one of the most nerve-racking experiences, when you were close to those scuffles and you're told to stop them. I was like, "I don't want to do that." That actually happened quite often.

Some days in the summer they'd do fireworks in the seventh or eighth innings. They would ask me to go down to the visiting bullpen. I'd stand right behind the gate of the bullpen so I'd be able to watch these pitchers, whom I've idolized growing up, throw bullpens, and I'm just feeling that this is the sickest experience ever. When the fireworks ended, we'd run on the field to pick up any remaining burnt scraps or anything else that was on the field and then run off as quickly as we could. That probably took ten minutes, and then we went back to our stations until the end of the game, watching what people are doing and keeping an eye on everything.

Kenji Kajita. Courtesy of Kenji Kajita.

From the time we got to the stadium, we usually were unable to eat until after the game. We did get a break time, when they told us we could eat, but we had to get the food from the local convenience store or something like that. They didn't provide us with stadium food.

After the game ended, we had to pick up all the trash that the fans left. If you watched the 2022 soccer World Cup, you saw that Japanese fans are really good about keeping the area clean. They often bring their own plastic bags for trash and gather everything and bring it to the stadium trash cans and throw it out there. So, we didn't find a lot of stuff in the seats. But we did have to sweep the bleachers. Then we went to the trash disposal place, and we had to divide all the trash that people left—put the plastic bottles together, the aluminum cans together, and so on. That was definitely the worst part of the job because it stank of alcohol and everything. After we finished with that, they might tell us to pull down some displays, and then they would tell us to go home. On a quick day that would be around 10:30 p.m., but some days we'd be there until midnight.

I got to work with a lot of other kids who played high school baseball. My final season was the COVID year, and everyone was talking about their COVID experience playing baseball. I learned a lot. My school went to the Round of 16 in West Tokyo, but some kids were from schools that were Koshien-bound. So it was really interesting to hear their stories and the types of practices they did and all that. That was one of the most interesting experiences, just talking with these kids who I thought were beyond my reach within baseball.

I knew when I went into high school that I wasn't going to stay in Japan for college and that I wanted to go to the United States. I went to Grinnell on a scholarship from the Japanese Foundation. While I was there, I played on the baseball team. College ball in the United States is very different from high school baseball in Japan. The practice hours are so much shorter, and it's not too intense either. I find practice kind of easy because I've been through much harder in Japan. But I did find it surprising that my coach is teaching a more Japanese style of baseball where we're bunting and everything, instead of playing a more dynamic, American-style baseball that focuses on slugging percentage and hitting home runs.

Within the Japanese Foundation is a person that works for the SoftBank Hawks as an assistant general manager, named Shun Kakazu. I met him in 2022, and I told him that I wanted to work in baseball. I tried to get an internship with the Hawks, but that didn't work out, so Kakazu-san talked to his colleagues, and I got a summer internship with the Yomiuri Giants data-analysis group. I was with the farm team for most of my time, and that was super interesting.

The farm team is located in Inagi City, about twenty-five kilometers from downtown Tokyo. The farm team has two teams, the second team and then the third team. The second team plays with other NPB second teams, but the third team plays with college and independent teams. When the third team played, all the amateur scouts came, and they'd be talking over who's good and who's not, which was super interesting. After college, I want to work in baseball operations for an MLB front office, but the main thing is I want to be a baseball scout. So, I really liked the days when the scouts were there because I could ask them a bunch of questions. I got to learn a lot about scouting from them.

If it was a game day, then the players would practice the morning. If it wasn't a game day, then practice would usually be in the afternoon. After the players warmed up, the pitchers and hitters were divided. The hitters would go straight into hitting or fielding practice, and the pitchers would throw. There were always a lot of drills. With Japanese baseball in general, it's always about fundamentals. There was also a lot of running. Some days, they'd be running poles [running from foul pole to foul pole]; other days, they'd be doing shorter sprints. In Japan everyone does a lot more running than in the States. After the group workouts, the players had individual practice time. A lot of players would lift weights. Some pitchers would go to hit in the cages. Then they would go to the training room to do some rehab or core exercises or whatever. Then they'd be done for the day.

The Giants data-analysis group was a small team. I think there were six full-time people. There's one person who's always with the top team, but then the rest moved between the teams, depending on schedules and availability. There were usually four people with the farm team. The team does everything from taking video, being responsible for the technology, clipping videos, doing the coding, and everything to get the numbers. There's also a biomechanics person.

On nongame days, I'd be at the ballpark from about 8:30 a.m. to midafternoon. I'd first come in and set up our Trackmans in the bullpens, and then I'd set up our video cameras. Trackman is a digital device that sits on a tripod. It uses Doppler radar to track the ball. We connect it with an iPad, and it gives us a monitor screen where it tells us everything from velocity to spin rate and axis, along with release angle, horizontal movement, location—anything that can be numericized from one pitch. All the data is downloaded into CSV files. When the pitchers came in, I'd select the Trackman for each pitcher and start the videos. It was the same for the hitters, except we used a device called Rapsodo, which is a camera-based tracking system that does a really great job at measuring spin tilt and efficiency. So, I'd place that for the hitters for when they hit batting practice, and I set up cameras for that too.

When they were done, I'd get all the videos from both the hitters and the pitchers and go back to our room and start clipping the videos on the Charlyze system. Charlyze is a video-editing tagging software that moves frame rates within a split second or two, so you can get an accurate timing of each video, and then lets you view them in a slow mode. Then once I finished the videos, I uploaded them onto our server so that the players could see them.

On game days, we would start the game at 6:00 p.m., and I'd go down to the basement of the stadium to set up our game Trackman and video cameras. I was responsible for filming all the game videos, which I could do with a click of a button from our PC. I'd watch the game, and my supervisor sat next to me operating the Trackman software and teaching me how to use it. That was interesting. After the game, around 10:00 or 10:30 p.m., I'd go back our room and clip all the videos from the game for each hitter and each pitcher and upload them to the server. And that would be the end of the day for me, around 11:30.

I'd also get to talk with players to go over their videos. That was really a fun part for me. You can pair the data from Trackman with the videos so that they can see all of the metrics. For example, you can take videos of your pitchers from the side or your hitters from the side and analyze the swing while looking at the numbers. That's now a really big thing within the baseball industry. Every MLB team has it. Every Minor League team has it. Every Japanese team has it. It's something that people in the baseball industry can't live without. Most of the hitters were interested in exit velocity and launch angle, just like in the United States. But in Japanese baseball there's always a sense of trying to fit into a player's style of hitting. So, some players wanted to look more at their swing path and swing speed rather than being too focused on launch angle and hitting home runs. I think our team did really well to try and engage with each player's specific requests.

To generalize, many of the older coaches don't understand the analytics. The only thing they understand is velocity. That's pretty much the only thing they care about. Once you start to explain to them what pitch movement is, what spin rate is, and what spin axis is, they get lost because they've never cared about those things numerically. For them, if it looks good, then it's good. They don't care if it's numerically good or numerically bad—they just want to see how it works with their own eyes. I think a lot of the younger players in Japan don't really know too much about the numbers within baseball either. When they look at their own pitching data, they can't explain it for themselves. The data-analysis group has the knowledge to explain to the players what's going on. We can approach their pitching or their hitting from a numeric standpoint, not just from the human eye. We can improve things based on that data and video clips to make their numbers better and make them better players in general.

I also got to translate for some of the foreign players. A really interesting part of it was seeing how differently they think compared to Japanese players. We had a foreign pitcher who had a totally different approach to pitching than what the coaches wanted him to do. There was a bit of an argument between the coaches and him. He had played in MLB, and his stuff had worked in the past, but he had not been doing that well in NPB. He wanted to go back to MLB, so he wanted to keep his approach. On the other side was a sixty-year-old coach who had played baseball only in Japan and only knows Japanese baseball. There was frustration on both sides. That kind of disagreement doesn't happen between a Japanese player and Japanese coach.

On a personal note, even as an intern, they let me use their training facility, and they taught me stuff too. I learned about baseball and pitching from players and the coaches who are teaching the pros. That alone was just a dream come true for me.

The Hanshin Tigers cheering section at Tokyo Dome. Courtesy of Robert K. Fitts

The Hiroshima Toyo Carp oendan at Mazda Zoom-Zoom Stadium. Courtesy of Robert K. Fitts.

Carp fans during the Lucky 7 festivities at Mazda Zoom-Zoom Stadium. Courtesy of Robert K. Fitts.

Takero Okajima of the Tohoku Rakuten Golden Eagles slides into home. Courtesy of Robert K. Fitts.

A close play at third base at Seibu's Belluna Dome. Courtesy of Robert K. Fitts.

The Hiroshima Carp cheering section at Tokyo Dome. Courtesy of Robert K. Fitts.

Concession stand at Mazda Zoom-Zoom Stadium. Courtesy of Robert K. Fitts.

Stadium food at Es Con Field in Hokkaido. Courtesy of Robert K. Fitts.

Wataru Karashima of the Tohoku Rakuten Golden Eagles lays down a sacrifice bunt. Courtesy of Robert K. Fitts.

Celebrating a "sayonara home run" at Rakuten Mobile Park. Courtesy of Robert K. Fitts.

Munetaka Murakami of the Tokyo Yakult Swallows at Meiji Jingu Stadium. Courtesy of Robert K. Fitts.

Part 4 / **In the Clubhouse**

13 / Toshihiro Nagata, Data Analyst

Toshihiro Nagata has worked in NPB for almost twenty years as an interpreter, international scout, and data analyst for the Yokohama BayStars, Hanshin Tigers, and Yakult Swallows.

◆

When I graduated from high school, I wanted to become an English teacher. So, I moved to the state of Washington, and I went to Pierce College for a few years, before transferring to Sophia University in Tokyo to get a teaching certificate. In the end, I decided to first get a job in the corporate world and then become a teacher. When I started job hunting, I wanted to be involved with sports because ever since I was in high school, all I did was play baseball and study English. I came across this interpreting job for the Yokohama BayStars, and I had to take it. The team was owned by the TBS TV broadcasting company back then.

On my first day of work in February 2007, I met Junji Kako, who was in advanced scouting. He said, "Hey, I heard you understand English. Can you translate this for me?" And he handed me a sheet of sabermetrics about DIPS, Defense Independent Pitching Statistics. I was like, what? What the heck is this? That was my first contact with sabermetrics. Over the next two years, he taught me a lot of different things. He taught me about [the book] *Moneyball*, and I started helping him with the analytics. I was also fortunate to be able to help the people in baseball operations. So, I was like a baseball operations assistant and scouting assistant and minor league interpreter. That's how I got started. When I wasn't interpreting, I was learning about sabermetrics. I did analysis on the foreign players who we were thinking of signing, and I also helped out the player evaluators.

Do you know how NPB players have their salaries determined by these evaluation guys in the front office? They are called *satei tantou* in Japanese, which basically means "the guys in charge of assessments." The satei tantou watch every single game. They travel with the team. They sit behind home plate, or maybe up in the stands, and evaluate the players' performance, like their defense, how clutch they were, and their contribution to each game. For example, if a guy hits a grand slam but the score was already 10–1, he might get a low contribution point. Each team has a different measuring system. At the end of the year, when they do salary negotiations, the front office shows each player his score. The score determines his raise or salary reduction. This doesn't apply to foreign players or big-time veterans, but it applies to pretty much everybody else. Players were starting to bring their sabermetric numbers to the negotiations, so the evaluation guys would come to us and ask about the numbers—if they were the real stuff, you know? We might tell him, "According to your scoring, this guy will be getting a pay cut, but actually he contributed so much that you should give him a pay raise." So, I was doing all kinds of different things my first year and my second year as well. The only difference was in my second year I was traveling with the big-league team as an interpreter.

By late 2008 the BayStars were falling apart. The ownership wanted to sell the team, and I was unsure about the future of the organization. An interpreting job with the Tigers came up. As a chance to work for the Hanshin Tigers or Yomiuri Giants doesn't happen very often, I applied for it and fortunately, I got it. I joined the Tigers in January 2009 and was assigned to interpret for Jeff Williams. He was a legend for the Tigers. I was very excited, and as it turned out, I learned so much from him. He taught me about life, taught me about how to take care of families. He had so much influence on me.

I interpreted for five years, then I moved into international scouting. I wanted to implement the idea of sabermetrics in scouting. I wanted to combine the two. There was nobody who had that concept with the Tigers organization back then, so I was paving the way. While scouting, I was listing candidates to sign based on their sabermetrics. I was basically telling everybody, the general manager, the scouting director, "Hey, this guy's worth signing, because look at these numbers. They're amazing." I tried to show them as many examples as possible. I told them, "This is what's going on in the States. You have to look at their tendencies. You can't just sign players off the top of your head, or after the one game you went to see when he went 4 for 4. You have to look at these guys through their playing numbers."

Well, back then you couldn't get batted-ball information at all, like exit velocity or launch angle. The most important analytic I was using for pitchers was strikeout to walk ratio, and then swing and miss, also called whiff (swing and miss per swings) and called strikes plus whiffs (CSW). If a guy had a bad strikeout to walk ratio in AAA, I didn't want to make a push to sign him even if he was throwing a 100-mile-per-hour fastball. Finding the strike zone, attacking the zone, and being able to get outs for a pitcher was what I was looking for. I was also looking at a metric called tRA, which measured a pitcher's effectiveness independent of his team's defense, and, of course, WAR (wins above replacement).

I also tried to look at a potential player's personality. Would he be able to play in Japan? A foreign player's mental makeup is probably more important—way more important—than his sabermetrics. That information was hard to get, but I talked with scouts, MLB front office personnel, and coaches and asked them, "Hey, have you heard anything about this guy?"

In 2015 the Hiroshima Carp signed Kris Johnson, a pitcher who ended up winning the Sawamura Award in 2016. I didn't think he would have success in Japan because when I looked at his sabermetric numbers, he wasn't really a standout. His numbers weren't too impressive. But at the time, there was this technology called PITCHf/x that tracked the speed and movement of pitches. I started digging into the information and found out that Kris Johnson sabermetrically might not be that great, but the quality of each pitch, like how much his changeup moved compared to his fastball and things like that, made him a good player for NPB. So, I started to feel that maybe sabermetrics was just one set of criteria, and you have to look at something else as well to correctly evaluate which players would have success in NPB. That was my starting point. Then I started learning about all kinds of things, like vertical movement and horizontal movement as well as pitchers' release points.

With sabermetrics information only, you can't really envision future performance, as it's based on past results. You can see consistency and try to project two or three years in the future. You could still do that, but I realized that analytics based on a tracking technology is more accurate, because you can look at every single pitch. For example, spin efficiency is how much of the spin contributes to the movement. If you're only having 85 percent spin efficiency, the ball doesn't carry as much. If you're having

Toshihiro Nagata. Courtesy of Toshihiro Nagata.

100 percent with the same spin rate of 2400 RPM, then you get more carry, you get more vertical rise, like a hop, which leads to more swings and misses. You can look at the quality of each pitch: each breaking ball, each forkball—the whole repertoire.

There was this new technology at the time called Trackman. Trackman is a radar system, designed to track missiles in the military. Several of the other Central League teams were already using it. I spent a year explaining to everybody in the organization, including all the front office higher-up personnel, the manager, coaches, and players, what Trackman is all about before we got the system, so there would not be any pushback. We had a problem because the old netting of Koshien's backstop interfered with the radar, but the stadium officials finally agreed to replace the net. I then traveled to Trackman in the United States and to the MLB league office in New York and talked with them about what kind of numbers Trackman spits out and what they meant, and about how the numbers should be analyzed. When I returned, I was in charge of installing Trackman at Koshien Stadium.

Because I had cautiously explained the value of Trackman before we installed it, the team embraced the information right away. The new analytics did not improve performances at first, but they helped in the long run, and Hanshin has been a contender since 2019. One of our pitchers, named Koyo Aoyagi, had problems with his control and the number of walks. He was afraid of attacking the zone. But we started doing his analysis a lot, and I kept praising him about the quality of his pitches and telling him, "Just pound the strike zone." After knowing his stuff is one of a kind, he started to attack the strike zone and became one of the best pitchers in NPB.

After the 2018 season the Yakult Swallows were looking to establish an analytics department. My current boss on the Swallows knew that I was doing analytics for the Tigers and that I was also involved with the scouting, so he approached me. I was enjoying the job and responsibility with the Tigers, but I was starting to realize that I wasn't really spending time with my family. I was thirty-five years old, and this might be the last chance for me to move to a different organization. I went to college in Tokyo and really liked the city, so I wanted to go back and live there with my family. It was a super tough decision for me, but I moved to the Swallows in the spring of 2019.

On the Swallows, we went from last place in 2020 to the Japan champion in 2021, and then we won the Central League championship again in 2022. People say that the 2021 Japan championship was largely because of our analytics. We were the first team in Japan to use Hawk-Eye technology. As a radar system, Trackman only calculates or kind of estimates the numbers, whereas Hawk-Eye is an optical system with many different cameras throughout the stadium. We have one in front of the scoreboard, one behind the backstop, two on the first base side, two on the third base side, and two in the outfield close to the foul lines. We have eight cameras now, although I think some MLB teams operate as many as sixteen cameras. So, it's way more accurate than Trackman. You also get to measure a lot of different things, like the gyro movement of a pitch, and for hitters you can measure swing speed and attack angle, and you can examine biomechanics with stick figures for each player on the field. Yeah, you get a lot of different stuff with Hawk-Eye.

So, everybody else in NPB had Trackman, but we moved from Trackman to Hawk-Eye, and we went from sixth place to the first place and took the Japan championship. I'm very happy when some people say that was the reason why the Swallows won. But I don't know; I don't believe it. I think the timing was right. The scouting did a great job, although analytically we helped out a lot on who to sign and which foreign players to sign and what we should do in player development. Also, we hired a new pitching coach in 2021. His name is Tomohito Ito, a legendary pitcher back in the 1990s. With him, we analyzed every single pitcher and what we should do, like tweak his off-speed stuff or add this pitch to his repertoire. It's called *pitch design* now.

We worked with every pitcher, and our pitching got so much better. After every outing, Scott McGough, now with the Arizona Diamondbacks, came to my room and asked, "Hey, how was it? What should I do to improve?" Soon all the young pitchers started coming to our room after the game, or the next day before practice, and we tried to find things that they could improve. That definitely contributed to the 2021–2022 success of the team. Of course, Munetaka Murakami emerged as a star. Players being developed in the minors started having success in the majors, and two of our foreign players, José Osuna and Domingo Santana, did awesome jobs. Before signing them, we looked at them analytically, and we recommended to international scouting that these guys should be solid. There wouldn't be too much risk of them failing. And as it turned out, they were great. The whole team had a great year. After our success, everybody in NPB started to shift from Trackman to Hawk-Eye.

The Swallows currently have four analysts: one for the minor leagues, two for the major leagues, and one that roams between the major leagues and minors. On a typical game day, I go to the ballpark around 12:30 in the afternoon and start collecting the data from the game on the night before. Then, I try to prepare the data for the pitchers, coaches, and manager before they come to my room to ask me questions about how the players did. The pitching coaches might ask me about a certain pitcher who had a really good start or one who got roughed up and gave up some runs. They will want to know analytically what he was doing. I try to collect as much information as I can from the Hawk-Eye and our internal system. And then, I make visuals, graph the numbers, and even make overlapping videos showing how the mechanics compare to another day. For example, if Munetaka Murakami comes in when he's struggling, I make side-by-side videos and overlay videos of his mechanics now and when he was hitting home runs.

I try to prepare as much as I can until people start coming to my room after practice to hang out and talk. I always try to give them hints. I don't want to force them to change, but I tell them, "This is what I found. What do you think?" I feel that it's important to show the players how to make their performance better.

Obviously, I stay through the game. I take notes on each pitch our pitcher throws. You know, this pitch was just great. This one was terrible. This pitch got hit—was it location, or was it pitch quality? I do that for each pitch as numbers spit out of Hawk-Eye, like velocity, spin rate, vertical break, horizontal break, vertical release angle, horizontal release angle, vertical approach angle to the plate, horizontal approach angle to the plate, release height. All this information comes out for every single pitch—boom, boom, boom, on the screen in front of me. So, I look at it and watch the game and take notes. After the game, pitchers who want to know right away come charging into my room with their uniforms still on to ask, "Hey, how was my stuff today?" Sometimes, there's a line of players waiting in front of the room. After I talk with the last guy, it's usually 11:00 to 11:30 p.m., and I get home around 12:30 to 1:00 a.m. When the team goes on the road, I get to work remotely. A younger analyst travels with the team. Except if the games are at Tokyo Dome or Yokohama Stadium, I go to those games. Well, that's pretty much my daily routine during the season.

There is a tremendous difference between Hanshin and Yakult. The Swallows are different from other teams because we are very close to the manager. We have such a small clubhouse and a small number of staff that, in a way, the Swallows are like a family. The Swallows manager Shingo Takatsu comes to my office every day before he gets on the field, to just chat and learn as much as he can. It's a daily routine for him. I don't know if this happens on other teams in Japan because talking with the manager is a really sacred thing in some organizations, especially with Hanshin. I don't think there is much communication directly from the analyst to the manager or analyst to the pitching coach or even from analyst to the players because some teams are very careful about what the analysts tell the players. Sometimes on other teams, the office personnel want to sit in to keep up with the information. That's a problem because the players can't open up. They can't tell you what they have in mind because they don't want to expose bad information to the higher-ups in the front office. They think that their salary might go down. So, I think it's a good setup for the Swallows that we are in such a small clubhouse and very close to each other.

We are one of the few teams that puts defensive shifts on aggressively, because our infield coach has a good relationship with our skipper and has convinced him that numbers show why we should do it. Other teams are probably reluctant to do it because once they put on the shift and a routine ground ball becomes a hit, the pitcher and pitching coaches will get mad. So, they don't want to take the risk of getting in trouble with somebody or making people mad. I think we are more laid-back because our infield coach communicates with the manager on a daily basis and they have a good relationship. The philosophy of the organization is definitely different from other NPB teams.

In the recent years, Japanese managers have embraced analytics because they realize if they don't keep up with the information their jobs would be in jeopardy. All of the NPB teams have analytics departments now, and they all use Hawk-Eye technology. But in terms of analytics, NPB is at least two years behind MLB. Budget is the huge difference between MLB and NPB. How much an analytics department can spend is the biggest obstacle for us. For example, our Hawk-Eye technologies are limited compared to MLB. They are doing so many crazy things, but we can't do those yet because of the budget and the setups in the stadiums. The MLB teams are smarter. They spend more on analytics to make all the players better even at each level of the Minor Leagues. That's a huge problem that we have to deal with, but it's also something that I'm hoping will change in the next five years.

14 / Ichiro Kitano, Trainer

A graduate of Plymouth State University in New Hampshire, Ichiro Kitano worked as an athletic trainer for the Philadelphia Phillies for ten years before spending the past decade as a strength and conditioning coach for the Chunichi Dragons.

◆

I played baseball in Japan when I was a kid, and I wanted to be a professional baseball player. I played until my sophomore year in college. At the end of college, a friend of mine had an interest in strength and conditioning, and he mentioned studying abroad. I thought, *That's kind of nice*, so I decided to go to the States to study strength and conditioning. But I ended up becoming an athletic trainer, which focuses on injury prevention and rehab, instead. When I became certified, I wanted to work for a baseball team, so I took an opportunity to do internship at Brown University for one year. I was able to work with baseball and women's volleyball teams while I was there.

Right before I started working at Brown, I had an internship with the Phillies for one week. So, I had a connection with them. After Brown, I joined the Phillies and was full-time with them for ten years. It was basically my dream job. I worked in the Minor Leagues for six years, and for the last four years I was on the big league team. My title on the big league club was a manual therapy specialist; basically, most of my work was doing massage therapies. I was the only Japanese in the organization at that time, so manager Charlie Manuel, whenever he remembered an experience from when he played in Japan, would ask me, "What do Japanese people think about this?" and stuff like that. He was a funny guy, kind of goofy. He had a good time in Japan, so he would ask me questions and talk to me.

Following my career in the States, I wanted to go back to Japan and work in Japanese baseball. In the States when you are trying to get a job, age doesn't matter, gender doesn't matter. But in Japan, age and gender and other stuff matters. So, if I wanted to go back, I had to do it while I was still young. Some organizations have an age limit. You have to be below thirty-five or whatever. When I got to the big leagues, I was thirty-four or so, and I spent four years there, so I had passed thirty-five. But I met one of the coaches with the Dragons while I was working for winter league in the Dominican Republic, and he didn't have any problem with my age, so I decided to leave the Phillies to come back to Japan to work for Chunichi.

My title for the first eight years with Chunichi was a strength and conditioning coach, but basically, I worked with the rehab guys, getting the players back on the field. I helped them with exercises and stretching and making recovery plans. The recovery methods in Japan were, and still are, old school. Most of the new methods and equipment come from the States or Europe, and we are still trying to purchase the devices. For example, we don't even have a cold tub. We have a hot tub, but we don't have a cold tub, so we can't do contrast. We are basically doing massage therapy and other traditional approaches. Acupuncture is big. Personally, I don't like it because I just don't like sticking needles anywhere in my body. But it releases tension in fascia, muscle, and tendons, so we use acupuncture a lot.

In Japan we don't just practice in one area. There are no borders; everybody works together: chiropractors, physical therapists, massage therapists, acupuncturists, athletic trainers, or whoever. Sometimes I even hit fungoes and play catch with the players and stuff like that. Also, any of us can be in the dugout during the games. The Dragons had five or six, but usually five, strength and conditioning coaches and eight or nine trainers, including massage therapists, acupuncturists, and chiropractors. In total, we had as many as fifteen people in the group but usually fewer than that. So, the Dragons' staff was a lot larger than an American staff. When I was in the Minor Leagues—more than fifteen years ago, so now it's a little different—a team had only one trainer and the strength guy, so basically two guys on the team, and then the big league club had a head trainer, an assistant trainer, myself, and the strength and conditioning guy.

When I returned to Japan, one of the first differences I saw was in spring training. In Japan, they put in long hours during spring training. Everybody gets together and trains together, whether it's baseball related, like hitting, fielding and throwing, or the strength and conditioning side of it. In the States, spring training hours are shorter because they are basically just preparing for the games. So, they do—I'm not saying the minimum—but they just do what they have to do. They don't do more. In Japan, it's always more, more, more, more. At spring training in the States, everybody gets done at one o'clock or two o'clock if they don't have a game. But in Japan, we start around 9:00 or 10:00 a.m., and if we don't have a game, we train until 5:00 or 6:00. The conditioning is also different. In the States, when the players come to spring training, they're physically ready. In Japan, they are too, but the teams make them do more conditioning, especially cardiovascular, like sprinting work and explosiveness drills, and stuff like that. It depends on the players and their positions. Pitchers run more than position players. Japanese players know that running is very important, so if we say, "Do this, do that," they are just willing to do it. In the past, the players did a lot of long-distance running; now we don't do that as much. But they have a good attitude about running. In the opposite way, American players tend not to run and usually don't want to.

Most of the time, we stretch and work out as a group in Japan. Culturewise, we like to do things as a group, so group training is easy. Although sometimes, players will want one-on-one, individual training, especially if they have a lot of specific questions about how to fix problems and improve themselves. In the States, it's easier to train one-on-one because the players are more individualized. That's Western culture. American players find it quite hard to do things as a group. For example, during stretching, they're talking to someone, facing the other way, and doing other stuff, and you have to say, "Pay attention please!" So, I think it's best to work one-on-one with them.

Back when I worked in the States, the Major Leaguers didn't do much stretching, especially not in a group. In the Minor Leagues at spring training, they did a group stretch, but not like we do here in Japan. When I was with the Phillies, one of the coaches had pitched for Hiroshima. The Carp did a lot of stretching before practice, like hour-long stretching. We don't do it that way anymore. We've shortened it to about twenty minutes as a group. Our foreign players with big league experience still say that's way too long. Over the last two years, I've started doing a lot more mobility work with the players. We still stretch, but now we do mobility, targeting the spine, thoracic area, hips, hamstrings, or whatever, as it reduces the risk of injuries and enhances performance.

Ichiro Kitano. Courtesy of Ichiro Kitano.

When I got to the Dragons, the strength and conditioning coach we had back then did a lot of conditioning on the field, and that kept them healthy and strong. Traditionally in Japanese baseball culture, especially in high school and junior high, we did everything on the field: stretching, long-distance running, interval training, sprinting, everything. The Dragons were doing well, so that culture lasted a long time. We had a weight room, but we didn't have guys coming in. We just had a bunch of old machines and stuff like that. We didn't have a culture of weight lifting. Well, that coach left, and people changed, and the culture began to change a bit. When I got the job as a strength and conditioning coach, I said, "Throw these old machines away, alright? They don't help the players." We threw them out, and now we have more room for weights. At first, the players were not accustomed to heavy lifting. They would come into the weight room, kind of stretch and leave. I'm like, "Dude, you got to work out, man!" So, I introduced some exercises and grabbed a couple guys and showed them some lifting—you know, kind of gradually. And gradually the group got bigger. Now they're doing heavy squats, dead lifts, bench presses. They now know that it's one way to keep healthy and keep them strong, so they do it as conditioning on a daily basis.

On the minor league team with the Dragons, their goal is not just to get stronger but to get on the top team. Some guys are not as strong, and some guys don't know how to lift, so we have to educate them and guide them in the lifting and getting stronger. That's probably the first step. Then they have to enhance their performance. I'm not just there to teach them how to lift, I need to help them play baseball better. So, we have drills connecting lifting and baseball to help them become better pitchers or position players. In the States, the players in the Minor Leagues already know how to lift from college or high school.

NPB and MLB players get the same type of injuries. But I would say there are more muscle issues in the States because there's a lack of stretching and lack of mobility. They're not flexible enough, and they produce more force and explosiveness when they play which leads to injuries. I was talking to one of the trainers yesterday about the number of Tommy John surgeries that we've had in the last ten years. We think it was only four or five. That's it. So, we're doing well. But in the States, we usually had like five or six, maybe at most ten, a year.[1] So the number of Tommy John surgeries here is much less. There are some reasons for that. In the States, if you have a grade-two ligament strain, sometimes you'll get the Tommy John surgery because you'll get stronger after you spend a year rehabbing. Also, a lot of doctors do the Tommy John surgery in the States. In Japan, we don't have as many doctors who do it. We only have one or two in the country. So, if you have a grade two, we don't like to do the surgery; we do rehab until they get better. If you have a grade three, then you have to get it done, but overall, we are more conservative about getting the surgery. Our pitchers throw more, but I would say mechanically they're better than most MLB pitchers because we're not as strong. If you are strong enough, you can throw hard, and you don't have to work as much on the mechanics to produce velocity. But here, the guys are not as strong as American or Latin guys, so we have to work on the mechanics to get better, which leads to fewer injuries.

In general, we also have fewer oblique injuries than in MLB. But it depends on the year. We had a lot of oblique issues after COVID-19. A lot of the guys stopped working out and playing during the pandemic, so when we restarted the season in June and the players went right into throwing hard and swinging hard, there were more injuries. But these days, we don't have many because of mobility exercises and stretching. If you work on mobility in the thoracic region, obliques, and hips, we can reduce oblique injuries.

Also, there are mechanical differences. Big league players focus on hitting homers. In Japan, not as much, not just because we are not as strong but because our mechanics are different. For example, Aaron Judge, Bryce Harper, Mike Trout, and Shohei Ohtani, players who hit a lot of homers, hit in a certain way. They swing upward, trying to get the launch angle that will lead to a home run. If you swing up, you open up the obliques, so you'll probably end up having more injuries. In Japan, we try to hit down, not up. If you shorten and swing down, you're not going to have a lot of oblique issues. But with the methods coming in from States, everybody is watching the drills on YouTube or Instagram, or whatever, players are learning to swing the MLB way, for power. So, we might see more oblique injuries in the future. That's why we are trying to do more stretching, mobility, and other core exercises to get ahead of that problem.

As I've said, in the States, the players are strong. They hit homers and they throw hard, but Japanese guys are a little shorter and smaller. I'm not saying weak, but not as strong as American players. So, we practice more. They don't practice as much. When I was in high school, there was no limit on the amount of practice and training time. Japanese amateurs and pros just practiced a lot and trained a lot. Now we're smart enough to stop when the players look tired; otherwise, they take longer to recover and might get injured. For example, they used to do the thousand ground ball drill, where a coach would hit one thousand ground balls at a player until he drops. We still do it in spring training, but now it's just a name. I don't know how many ground balls they actually take; it's still a lot, but probably just four hundred to five hundred. It makes them better through repetition. Our players still do a lot of running and throwing and hitting. Japanese baseball culture still emphasizes more and more and more. I'm not saying the Japanese way is better; it's just a good way. Personally, I like somewhere in between the Japanese and American approach, a kind of blend of everything. That's probably the best way to reduce injuries.

In my first eight years with the Dragons, I was a strength and conditioning coach but worked as a rehab coordinator. Now I'm head strength and conditioning coach for the minor league team. I deal with healthy players now, so basically my goal is to keep them healthy. During my career as a rehab coordinator, I was thinking about how to reduce the number of injuries. I had some ideas regarding the upper extremity injuries and muscle issues in lower extremity. As soon as I became the head coach, I designed a program with a blend of exercises and techniques and implemented it. It seems to be working now; we have had fewer injuries during the last two years. Reducing the number of injuries is not the only goal for us. We try to create the culture. It takes years to create the culture of weight lifting. Once they know that weight lifting will help them hit with power or throw harder, they will continue to do so. We try to have a group of those players. If they perform well and get called up to the top team, other players will be impacted by them. Then the culture will continue by itself. I work toward accomplishing these goals. It is fun but stressful sometimes, but this is what it is. I love working in baseball.

15 / Ken Iwamoto, Interpreter

A graduate of Oregon State University, Ken Iwamoto worked as an interpreter for the New York Mets from 1998 to 2002 before joining the Nippon Ham Fighters in 2003 as an interpreter for manager Trey Hillman. Iwamoto has been a member for the Fighters' front office since 2008.

◆

All the kids in Japan dream about being a professional baseball player. I played baseball in high school, and I injured my knee. I realized that my skills were not good enough to become a professional, so I quit baseball. But I couldn't give up my dream. I decided to work for a professional baseball team, just not as a player. I wanted to be an athletic trainer. After I graduated from high school, I went to the United States to study exercise sports science. I couldn't speak English at all at that time, so I studied the language for about eight months in Tokyo. I went to the University of Kentucky in 1992 as a full-time student for two-and-a-half years before I transferred to Oregon State.

When I was about to graduate from Oregon State, I applied for internships with MLB teams, but I couldn't find one. Then the Houston Astros said they were looking for a trainer who could speak two languages. I could speak English and Japanese, so I applied for that, but I got a phone call from them saying that they were looking for someone who could speak Spanish and English. I had no chance, but then I said, "Hey, I don't need money. I just want to have a chance to work for a professional baseball team. If I can get one meal a day, and if I can sleep under a ceiling somewhere, away from rain, I'm okay." That's what I told them. A few days later they called me and said you can come and join us. So, I went to Florida to join the Houston Astros rookie-ball team for one season.

After I finished the intern job with the Astros, Jim Duquette, who was the Minor League director at that time, told me that the Mets were going to sign a Japanese high school player and asked if I would be interested in being an interpreter for him. So, I joined the Mets as an intern in 1998. I got like $500 per month. My initial job was an interpreter and trainer. But I did everything. During the daytime, I went to rookie ball, and at night when they had a home game at Port Saint Lucie, I went there and did everything they asked. I would put a mask on and sing the Kit Kat song in front of a lot of people. I sold ice cones. I pulled on the tarps for the rainy days. Yeah, I just did everything. I stayed with the Mets for five years. When Tsuyoshi Shinjo came in 2001, I became his interpreter.

Shinjo was the first Japanese position player in National League history. So, at that time, there were not many Japanese staff members or bilingual interpreters around. I was the only Japanese staff in the Mets organization, besides a scout in Japan.

I came to the clubhouse earlier than Shinjo and did the small stuff, all the preparation. Sometimes I helped out the clubhouse guys set up the locker rooms. After Shinjo came in, I just interpreted and helped him communicate with the coaches and manager. Typically, position players play every day, so there's something going on every day, and being their interpreter is quite busy. The manager at that time was Bobby Valentine. Bobby had already been to Japan and could speak passable Japanese. That was really helpful, especially for Shinjo. Bobby also knew the Japanese cultural background and the differences. That was a huge help for Shinjo adapting to the new culture and new atmosphere and new type of baseball. Bobby also assigned me to do some of the analytical jobs. I entered all the strikes and balls and types of pitches into the computer program. So, there was something going on all the time.

The media in New York is not easy. Sometimes, they [reporters] try to pick up small things and make them big news. So, I was really careful which words or phrases I chose. The most important thing is to know what Shinjo really wanted to say, not the direct meaning or exact phrases. Do you remember Ralph Kiner's *Kiner's Korner*? One day, Shinjo hit a game-ending single against the Expos, and then right after the game, Shinjo was on the show. It was a live show at that time. Shinjo was asked about Chan Ho Park, and he said, "I don't know him." They had played against each other, and Shinjo should know about him. I mean, he was supposed to know about Chan Ho Park because he was a legendary Korean pitcher and he had played in the United States for many years. But he said, "I don't know about Chan Ho." So, I translated it as, "You know, it was the first time for me to face Chan Ho Park," or something like that. As an interpreter, I did those small things, like try to respect people. We didn't want to hurt anybody's feelings.

I took Shinjo back every night to his apartment after the game. When he went out to eat, or when he was spending time with his teammates, I was always there. When he got his driver's license in New York, I went to the Department of Transportation and translated everything for the test. He had no idea about the exams, so I translated all the questions for him. I was always with Shinjo.

Sometimes I felt like part of the team, but sometimes I felt like I wasn't there. It all depended on the players. In my Minor League days, the people around me accepted me very well. I had a great time with people in the Minor League system, but the Major Leagues were kind of different. There were so many different types of players. Some of the guys were really nice, but some of the guys were just focusing on themselves and did not really care about interpreters, which I understood, so it was not a problem for me.

Shinjo got traded to the San Francisco Giants after the 2001 season, but I stayed with the Mets. Satoru Komiyama, who's now the head coach for the Waseda University baseball team, came, and I became his interpreter for the 2002 season.

In 2002 I read in a newspaper that the Nippon Ham Fighters were going to move their franchise to Hokkaido, which is my hometown. Ever since I was a little kid, a lot of people dreamed of having a professional baseball team in Hokkaido. So, it was shocking, very exciting, news for me. The very next day, I sent a resume to the Fighters and said, "I'd like to be a part of the team. I would accept any kind of job." I didn't ask to be an interpreter. A month later, a guy named Toshi Shimada called me on my cell phone and said, "Are you interested in working for us?"

After the 2002 season, I went back to Japan to do the interview with the Fighters, and Toshi Shimada told me that they were going to hire an American manager. He asked, "Are you interested in being one of the candidates for his interpreter?"

I said, "Absolutely!"

They hired Trey Hillman. Trey came over for the Fighters fall camp in November and interviewed me, and I got the job.

Ken Iwamoto.
Courtesy of
Ken Iwamoto.

I started working with Trey in January 2003. That was the very last year that the Fighters had a franchise in Tokyo. They decided to move to Hokkaido the next year. So, in January, Trey went to Hokkaido to see all the governors and some key guys, and be on TV and radio shows. So, I went with him. Trey impressed everyone with his passion for the team and building the fanbase in the new location.

The biggest difference in interpreting for Trey and Shinjo was that Trey had his family in Japan, so I tried not to spend too much time with him outside of the ballparks because I didn't want to bother his family time. Whenever he needed me, I was there, but we were not eating together every day or spending all our time together. That was a huge difference. Trey was not demanding. He didn't rely on people too much, in a good way, you know? So, the total time that I spent with Trey and Shinjo was different. Also, my mother tongue is Japanese, so translating from English to Japanese is way easier. It's the opposite that's always tough, translating from Japanese to English. Languagewise, that was a huge difference. And then as an interpreter in New York you can't make a mistake. There was a lot of pressure. That's another huge difference between interpreting in Japan and in the United States. I also had to adjust myself to American culture. It was a lot of fun. I really enjoyed it, but, pressurewise, being an interpreter in the United States was tougher.

I was the interpreter for Trey mostly, but sometimes I helped out the American coaches as well. Two or sometimes three other interpreters were just for the players. Everybody was kind of busy. We had to multitask. Now we have seven or eight interpreters on the Fighters.

When I went back to Japan and became a Fighter, I saw a lot of differences between Japanese and Major League Baseball. The practices were obviously longer. Trey was our manager, so the Fighters were way better than the other clubs. There are also a lot of rules and restrictions in Japanese baseball. It is detail oriented. They care about the small things. Everything is a group thing—team harmony is the most important thing, not the individual.

After I joined the Fighters, there were things that I needed to care about besides baseball, like people's relationships and relationships with the ownership group. We are under the umbrella of a big company. We are the part of the Nippon Ham group. But the New York Mets is the New York Mets, a baseball club, right? There, I felt like I was working for the baseball team. That was another big difference between MLB and Japanese baseball. I really felt that at Nippon Ham, baseball was just part of the company. That was a huge difference. The Fighters are a way better organization now, but at the time MLB teams seemed to be more sophisticated than the Fighters. There were so many areas where they needed to make improvements. The club wasn't very organized. There wasn't a clear vision, no specific goals or direction. We were just playing baseball every year. That's why we hadn't won for forty-four years.

Under Toshi Shimada, Trey, and Hiroshi Yoshimura, the president of baseball operations who joined the club in 2005, we changed dramatically. We became systematic and more organized, and our player development system became way better. Hiroji Okoso, from our ownership group, was a big part of it too. He was fifty or fifty-one around that time, so he was a young owner, but he had a clear vision of how we should build the baseball team for Nippon Ham. Those four guys worked really closely to the build a real baseball team. That was probably the start of the current Fighters.

We are not one of the richest teams in Japan. Everybody knows that. So, we have put a lot of emphasis on player development and scouting, because our budgets are limited. And we really started thinking about how we could win. We had a clear vision of scouting and player development, but then also we had this phrase that we shared—I mean everybody shared it, including players. It was Fan Service First. We tried so many different things, many new things that the other clubs never did before. For example, on Opening Day the players greeted the fans at the entrances to the stadium. Another time, Trey held an autograph session at JR Sapporo Station. Over three thousand people showed up, and he signed for all them. He had to take a pain killer for his wrist to recover!

After Trey left, they gave me a public relations job, so I was still with the team. At that time, there was no one doing international scouting, so they assigned me to be a part of the international department. I did both PR and the international group for the first season after Trey left in 2008. But the international part got too busy, so I gave up the PR job after just one season. From 2009 on, I became the team director. I'm with the team all the time; I travel with them. I'm kind of in between the front office and the players association. I listen to what players are requesting or thinking, and I also send messages from the front office to the players association so that we can keep up a good relationship. I also report what's going on in the team and in the clubhouse to the GM. And then I send messages from the front office to the players too. That was probably pretty much the main job for me. Now I'm more like an assistant GM because I work closely with the president of baseball operations and the GM.

Our philosophy is to try to get the player who is number one in the market for each draft. Shohei Ohtani was obviously the number one player by far in 2012. You can't even compare him to other guys. So, we decided to take him, although he had made it pretty clear that he didn't want to go to an NPB team and had decided to go to the United States. So, we were the only ones who drafted him. After we drafted him, our scouting director and our president tried to see him, but they couldn't; only his parents showed up. But after we mentioned the two-way-player thing, he was really interested. Hideki Kuriyama, the WBC skipper, was our manager then. He went to Iwate Prefecture to see Ohtani, and it was probably the first time for Ohtani showed up to talk to us directly. We discussed being a two-way player. Probably the only reason he decided to come to the Fighters was because he always liked a challenge—you know, doing things that people believed impossible. The two-way-player thing, nobody believed that he could do it. I think he really liked that challenge. He's the kind of guy who's always thinking about baseball. He's not interested in going out and having fun and drinking. He just doesn't have any interest in having fun outside of baseball. He is pretty much the same as he was the first time I met him. He still just focuses on baseball. He's a very nice kid. Even when he was seventeen, he used beautiful Japanese phrases. He was just a genuinely nice person, and that has never changed. He always makes people around him feel comfortable. I don't know any single person that doesn't like Shohei.

Believe it or not, nobody thought, *Let's do this with Shohei to make money*. Nobody said that—nobody. We didn't really think about the business of using Shohei at all. Yoshimura, Masao Yamata, the GM, and Kuriyama were all thinking about how we should make Shohei's dream come true. That was the only interest. We knew that he wanted to go to the States, and after he went to the States, we probably would make some money because of the buyout fee. But, believe or not, nobody talked about it. That came after. The only interest from the Fighters at that time was to win and get Shohei to MLB safely, without injury or distractions. So yeah, that was the only thing. That is the truth. The ownership group didn't talk about money at all. They never asked, "How much can we get for Shohei from posting?" It's more like he was for everybody, not only for the Fighters. He was a treasure of Japanese baseball.

Part 5 / **The Front Office**

16 / Marty Kuehnert, General Manager

After graduating from Stanford University in 1968, Marty Kuehnert was involved in professional sports for fifty-five years as a general manager, marketing director, advisor, journalist, author, and agent. He was the president of International Sports Management & Consultants (ISMAC) from 1980 to 2024 and a visiting professor at Tohoku University from 2006 to 2024. He was also the author of seven Japanese-language books on baseball. Marty became ill a few weeks after this interview and died in November 2024.

◆

I first came to Japan on an exchange program when I was at Stanford University. After I graduated, I worked as an interpreter and guide at the 1970 World Expo in Osaka, where I became friendly with Cappy Harada. Cappy was a real mover and shaker. He was an intermediary between Japanese and American baseball for decades. I had returned to the United States in 1972 when Cappy called me and said that his friend, Nagayoshi Nakamura, had bought the Lodi franchise in the California League, and asked if I would like to be the GM of the club. During my second year at Lodi, we won the Cal League championship, and I was named Executive of the Year, but Mr. Nakamura said he was no longer interested in owning a Single A team in the United States. So, he gave me the option to buy the team for just $6,000 or go to Japan and work for him. He was buying the Nishitetsu Lions and renaming them the Taiheiyo Club Lions. I opted to go to Japan.

I became the Lions' director of sales and promotions in 1974. Since I'd been a GM for two years in the States, I was able to bring in some new ideas. I introduced Japan's first "real" mascot. I bought an actual lion. We had a naming contest and named him Rara-chan. He was about two months old when we got him. I found it was easy to buy a lion, but difficult to get rid of one. He came in a crate, and we were scared to death to open it. We called the zoo, and some guy came down, and he looked at the crate and said, "It's in this little crate?" He just took off the lid and grabbed it like you'd grab a cat, by the back of its neck, and put it on the ground and said, "Here's your lion." When they're a few months old they're very manageable. But Rara-chan got bigger and bigger and bigger and bigger. We hired a veterinary student to take care of him, and we had a cage built at Heiwadai Stadium. He would take Rara-chan out on a leash right before the games, and he was very popular. But by the end of the season, Rara-chan was too big to handle, and then I thought, *Well, how do I get rid of this lion?* The Fukuoka Zoo didn't want him, and all the zoos have got lions—apparently they breed very rapidly—so we couldn't find any takers. Finally, Mr. Nakamura, who had been the first secretary to Prime Minister Nobusuke Kishi, asked for help, and the prime minister put the screws on the Yamaguchi Zoo to take Rara-chan off our hands.

One of the things I did when I got to Fukuoka was ask the Lions' salespeople, "What is your worst-attended night?"

They weren't even sure; they had to go calculate it. But it came back that Wednesday was the least-attended night.

I said, "Okay, let's make Wednesdays Ladies Night—let all the ladies in free."

And they said, "Free?!"

So, I said, "Okay, 100 yen or something, make it almost free. If you've got 25,000 empty seats, why not fill them up? And if you have a lot of ladies coming, you're going to draw guys as well."

Since then, all the clubs have gone out of their way to get as many ladies to the ballpark as possible. For example, with Rakuten from 2005 to 2008, I did an afternoon tea for ladies to learn about baseball. They would have tea and cakes with me, and I would explain the game and tell them funny baseball stories.

When I joined the Lions' front office, all the media wanted to talk to me because I was a foreigner. It actually caused friction because the general manager and president weren't happy that the media wanted to get answers from me and not from them. I had to be sensitive about that and tell the media, "That's not an appropriate question for me; you need to talk to the president, or you need to talk to the GM." If you're a foreigner here, then the media wants you all the more. They find the differences in culture and how you're adapting, and what kind of Japanese food you like, a big deal.

The media is also tougher here, because there are six or seven national sports newspapers. There's a lot of pressure on them to come up with a new story every day, so they cover the players like hawks. When Randy Bass was a Triple Crown winner, the Hanshin-crazy fans couldn't get enough of him. He came home one day, and when he opened the door, there was a photographer standing on top of his steps, taking pictures in his house! The reporters go to real extremes to get stories. You wake up in the morning and come out of your house, and there's a reporter there. This continually happens in Japan. There's not much of a private life when you're an athlete, especially if you're a popular athlete. The media is going to be all over you.

Daisuke Matsuzaka found out the hard way that the press is always going to be there. When he was just eighteen, after he lost his license for speeding, he drove a car belonging to the Seibu Lions to his girlfriend's house, parked it illegally, and got a ticket. So, the Lions public relations manager Akira Kuroiwa went to the police and said that he had driven the car, so that Matsuzaka wouldn't get in trouble. Unfortunately for him, a reporter from one of the scandal magazines was out front taking pictures. He had photographed the whole thing: when Matsuzaka had gone in to see his girlfriend, when Kuroiwa arrived, and so forth. So it became a huge scandal. Kuroiwa had to resign. The president of the Seibu ball club resigned, and Matsuzaka lost ten commercials worth about $10 million. That was an expensive night of sex!

Many of the ballplayers kind of go crazy in their first year as pros, because as high schoolers they've been under the thumb of the coach for so long. I think there are lots of virgin boys who come out of high school because they've been playing baseball from morning to night. They're going 365 days a year, so they have no chance to go out and do anything. But as soon as they become a pro, they may have half days off or a full day off, and then they've got all these women around them who are willing and able. It's easy, and they go crazy for sure.

I only stayed one year with the Lions. I made a lot of suggestions, like improving the bathrooms and the concessions, but Mr. Nakamura never went for most of them. I realized that Mr. Nakamura wasn't interested in making baseball a career. He only bought the team to flip it and make money. He eventually sold it to wealthiest man in Japan at the time: Yoshiaki Tsutsumi, who owned the Seibu Railway Group. So, I moved to Descente, the sportswear company, in 1975 and worked for them for five years. After that, I founded a sports bar called the Attic in Kobe, became a sportswriter, did baseball broadcasting, wrote books, and founded a sports agency.

When I was going to the United States in the 1980s, I saw the sports-card industry skyrocketing. There probably was a card shop on every corner—not a Starbucks, but a card shop. It was just incredible how new card companies were coming up left and right, and I think there must have been like a hundred magazines covering the card industry. I would come back to Japan, and Ikuo "Ike" Ikeda, the president of *Baseball Magazine*, and I would eat and drink and talk. I said, "If even a small percentage of the sports-card business would start and grow in Japan, I think it would be a good business to be in." At that time, there were a few companies in Japan that were producing cards, mostly as give aways with other products. For example, Calbee was giving away a card in their bags of potato chips. But none of the companies had put ever put out a complete set with a card for every player on the top team. We talked about it for a couple of years and decided in the late 1980s to go ahead and do it. So, we formed the BBM Card Company.

We cranked it up in 1990 and came out with the first set in 1991. It did pretty well, but it didn't take off nearly as much as I thought it would. The card industry here has never blossomed for a couple of reasons. Japanese houses are so small that they don't have room to store one hundred thousand cards. So, I think the compactness of things in Japan hinders the hobby to some degree. You also don't find the Japanese going crazy from a nostalgia standpoint. In the States, you go back with the Honus Wagner card. There were baseball players playing here when Honus Wagner was playing, but who cares? For example, Old-Timers Games here never took off, except for the Suntory Malts game that they do every summer. There have been other attempts to have Old-Timers Games, and they have all flopped. People don't care about coming out to watch a Futoshi Nakanishi (a great of the 1950s).

My favorite player, who I think may be the best player to have ever played in this country, was Yutaka Fukumoto, the center fielder for the [Hankyu] Braves. He has 200 home runs as a leadoff hitter, and he was the main reason why Hankyu won three consecutive Japan Series. If he got on base, he was going to score. To me he was the best player that's ever been.

But do people go gaga over him? No. Will people pay a lot for a Fukumoto baseball card? No. There's a different attitude toward collecting in Japan. Fans and collectors are just interested in the current stars. It's all about now. It's amazing for a country that seems to revere its past. I guess baseball is not old enough. It's got to be thousands of years old before they pay any attention to it.

One of the problems here is that there's not actually a big sports culture. Japanese usually follow just one sport because in junior high school when they join the club system, they have to choose one. I wrote a book about how there are no scholar athletes in this country, which is really true. You can't do two things here. They think you can only do one thing well. So, if you join the tennis team in junior high, you may play in high school, but if you're not good enough to make the team, sports are finished for you because it's too late to start another. When they get older, they usually only follow the sport they played. So, there are few Japanese who are fans of multiple sports.

In the spring of 2004 I met Hiroshi Mikitani, the owner of the technology company Rakuten. Mikitani was complaining about how difficult it was to run his soccer team in Kobe. At that time, I was teaching sports management at Waseda University, so we got together for dinner to talk about it. After dinner, he asked if I would consider working for his soccer team. I don't care for soccer—it is not my game—so I told him in a nice way that I really appreciated the consideration, but no. Then I joked, that if this were a baseball team we were talking about, it would be a different story. He said that he understood, and off he went. In late September, it came out that the Orix BlueWave and the Kintetsu Buffaloes were going to merge and that there was going to be an expansion team, the first since 1950. Mr. Mikitani called me and said, "I'm going to get that team, so let's get together and talk about it." We met for breakfast, and a few days later I was offered the job of general manager.

The position of general manager is different in NPB than in the Major Leagues. An MLB team is divided between business and baseball. On one side are the business operations. That group has a president, a vice president, the people who run the tickets, everything that has to do with business. On the other side are all the baseball operations. Instead of a president, it starts with a general manager, his assistants, the scouts, all the trainers, and the people running the ball club. In Japan they don't have this. There's no clear delineation between the two. You have an organization that starts with the president, or the owner, and then all the names and titles will be mixed together. Some people perform more than one function. It's confusing. You don't know from organization to organization who's doing what. Many teams here in Japan don't even have a guy called the general manager. He's called *daihyo*, the representative director of the parent company. Sometimes their business card will say *daihyo* in Japanese, and if you turn over the card and they have an English equivalent for it, they'll put general manager so that somebody in the States will understand what they do.

I've been watching Japanese baseball for almost fifty years, and in the old days, it was really the Dark Ages. It used to be that when you went into a team's office, it was full of guys smoking and reading sports newspapers. It was not very businesslike. Almost all the people working in the front office were former players, usually brown-nosed kind of guys, or guys who were kicked down from the parent company. This had a lot to do with the teams being set up as PR tools for their corporations. The corporations sent people they didn't want anymore in the main office to the ball clubs. There's a thing called *madogiwazoku*, or "the man by the window." There are two ways of getting rid of a guy in Japan when you want him to move on. One is to give him a little room, maybe in the basement, with no windows. But you also can put him in a very prominent spot in an office where everybody else is working but give him a desk by the window and nothing to do. So, he sees everyone else working, and he starts to get embarrassed because he's not contributing. I've said that the people who ran baseball teams here in the past have been that madogiwazoku guy. They leave the parent companies and come to the ball clubs in a revolving door that takes about two years to go through. A guy learns a little bit about baseball in the two years that he's there, but then he leaves, and another guy comes in from the parent company, who doesn't know anything about baseball. With some organizations it's a reward. When you did a good job for years with the parent company, they'll let you run the ball club for your last two years. So, in general, the people who used to run the teams here didn't know a lot about the game. It's one of the reasons that baseball had not been financially successful here. Around 2005 the only two teams that made any money were the Giants and the Tigers. No team in the Pacific League made

Trevor Raichura, Randy Bass, and Marty Kuehnert. Courtesy of Trevor Raichura.

any money, and that had been the case for decades. It has changed in the last five to ten years. The organizations have gotten much better. Today when you look at organizations, you see a lot of businessmen working in the front offices. I'd say almost half the teams are making money now. Look at Yokohama. DeNA came in and turned that club around completely.

Here, what the general manager (if there is one) does depends upon the team. When I was a general manager at the single A level in the States, I did everything, from cleaning out the locker rooms to washing down the concession stands. I felt that when I became the general manager for Rakuten, once again I did a little bit of everything. I also quickly learned that I was a general manager who was not expected to have complete power. Initially, I was very involved in making the decisions about who we were going to sign, but soon after the club got set, the representative director took over the baseball operations, and I was giving speeches to all the Rotary clubs and all the junior high schools. I was the face of the ball club. I was doing the TV shows and those kinds of things, but it wasn't like being a GM in the States. I was more of a PR guy than a baseball guy.

When I got the job, the priority was getting a staff. We made Yasushi Tao our manager because he was still young, was very energetic, and had been a good player. Then we had to select the coaches and scouts and the staff. When we advertised for our thirty front-office spots, we got eight thousand applicants. We didn't choose many baseball guys; we chose more businesspeople, guys from outside the game.

Then we started looking at how we would draft. In the States, they have an expansion draft, where you can choose a couple players from each team. Here, they gave us a dispersion draft, where we were able to get the leftover players from the two worst teams in the Pacific League. You want to talk about unfair draft? That was an unfair draft. Here we had Orix and Kintetsu, they were fifth and sixth in the league and didn't have much talent. We had to start with guys who were completely left over, because the new combined team, now called the Orix Buffaloes, was able to keep the top twenty-five guys. By the time that we were able to choose, there was nobody left that we really wanted. The only saving grace for us was that Hisashi Iwakuma had a beef with Kintetsu and he didn't want to stay there. And the same for Koichi Isobe. He had been the captain of Kintetsu, and he had spoken up against getting rid of a team. He was very vociferous about it. As the Buffaloes didn't want Isobe, we were able to get him. He was still a good player, and certainly Iwakuma was the gold mine. So we got two good players, and other than that we got the dregs.

Then on top of that, our owner, Mr. Mikitani, further tied my hands by saying, "Let's build this team from the ground up with young players, so don't spend over $500,000 for a foreign player." I told him, "Mr. Mikitani, we're not going to compete if we can only spend $500,000 for foreign players. That's not the market now." The two guys I wanted were

Roberto Petagine and Andy Sheets. I offered Petagine $500,000, and his agent laughed. And I talked to Andy Sheet's agent, and he laughed at the $500,000 too. He signed for about $4 million with the Tigers. I figured that if I signed those two guys, I had 70 home runs in my lineup, and that was something to build on, since we got so little in the dispersion draft. You'd think that if you wanted to make a splash when you start out, you would spend some money.

After the dispersion draft, we had the amateur draft in November 2004. Overall, I don't like the NPB's draft system. Right now, they've got a lottery in the first round. I think the waiver system, where you give the last-place team an opportunity to draft first, tends to balance out the talent. But the teams that are really strong, really good, don't want a waiver situation where the best team is going to get the last pick. Even if they finish first, they still want a chance to get the No. 1 draft choice. If you look back at the history of the draft, it's changed many times at Yomiuri's insistence. Whenever the Giants can't get the players they want, they change the draft system. Unfortunately, Japanese baseball still does what the Yomiuri Giants want to be done.

In the NPB draft, any team can nominate the player that they want in the first round. If nobody else choses that player, they get him. But let's say four of the twelve teams choose the same guy; they then put the four teams' names in box, and they draw the winner. The basic thing is that you should never have this situation, a lottery for the top players. That's the crazy part. The draft system was designed to level the playing field, to give the small-market, the low-money, teams, a chance to get the top player. But that doesn't happen here in Japan. It's not the small-market teams that have a better chance of getting a good player. So, the draft doesn't help level the playing field. It's very unfair. The idea doesn't make much sense.

All the draftees get the same $1 million signing bonus, the same $500,000 in "incentives," and a $150,000 salary. (I'm doing this with the 2004 exchange rate at ¥100 to the dollar.) So, it always comes to $1.65 million; everybody gets $1.65 million. But there's money under the table, as well. People may say that it didn't happen, or it doesn't happen, but it does. The top picks routinely get extra unreported bonuses, often worth millions of dollars. For example, when Yoshinobu Takahashi signed with the Giants, it was rumored that a lot of his dad's company's debt was paid off. I think that's a true story.

In 2004 we drafted Yasuhiro Ichiba first, and we were able to get him without paying any money under the table. We had been told through intermediaries that he wanted the standard under-table price of $5 million to sign with us. But he became tainted goods. The Giants, Tigers, and BayStars were caught giving him bribes disguised as meal money when he was still a college player. All three of the teams thought by giving him these payments that he was going to choose their team and tell the other teams not to draft him. All three of the clubs' presidents stepped down to take responsibility for the shenanigans. In the end, Ichiba was delighted to sign with us because he thought that nobody else would sign him. We thought that we were getting a bargain because we didn't have to pay that $5 million under the table, which we didn't have or didn't want to spend. So, we drafted Ichiba, and we passed on a guy by the name of Yu Darvish! That was the biggest disaster of my general managership. Darvish didn't have a spectacular first year—he was 5-5—but Ichiba didn't win his first game until September, and, of course, Darvish became a star.

When the 2005 season started, we won our first game and then lost twenty-two games in March and April. We were the slowest team ever to get to 10 wins, going 9-37 before winning on May 24. Well, Mr. Mikitani is like George Steinbrenner on steroids. To say that he is impatient is putting it mildly. One of his expressions for his company, Rakuten, is "speed, speed, speed." I think Mikitani-san thought that with his business acumen, he could change things right away and that we could do amazing things in spite of not having the horses to run with. Somehow, I was supposed to take these players and magically make them win. At the end of May, he demoted me, the head coach, and the hitting coach. I became an advisor to the president of the ballclub.

Our manager, Yasushi Tao, lasted the season, and then Mikitani hired Katsuya Nomura to manage in 2006. In Japan, there's a big difference between the power that certain managers have and that others don't. When Nomura and Senichi Hoshino were given the reins at Rakuten, they were given a lot of power. They could sign and trade players and set team strategy. They acted a lot like a GM does in the States. When Hoshino left the Dragons and took over the Tigers job, they allowed him to bring in all his own coaches and gave him $30 million to spend on whatever players he wanted. Compare that to what Marty Brown got when he became our manager in 2007. Marty

Brown got nothing. Even Hiromoto "Dave" Okubo, who managed in 2015, was not given a lot of authority. Some managers are so strong—and I think Nomura and Hoshino are two of the prime examples—that front offices are so scared of them that they won't tell them what to do.

Another thing about Japanese managers, and Japanese sports in general, is the corporal punishment, called *taibatsu*, that is given out. Probably the most infamous guy for hitting players was Hoshino. I've always called Hoshino a Jekyll and Hyde, because when he's on Japanese Broadcasting Corporation (NHK) in his suit, he's the perfect gentleman. But when he puts on a uniform, the players get scared. He was infamous when he was Chunichi's manager for beating the crap out of his players. One day, Hoshino called a young pitcher into his office after the kid had given up a couple of hits that cost him the game. When the kid walked out of the office, there was blood pouring out of his mouth and he had to go to the hospital and get stitches. After Alonzo Powell realized the seriousness of the injury, he walked into Hoshino's office and said, "If you hit one of my teammates again like that, they're going to have to call an ambulance for you." And you know what happened? A couple days later, Alonzo got traded to the Hanshin Tigers. He had won the batting title the year before! That's how much power Hoshino had. Another time, Hoshino got upset with a player, so he brought some of the team under the stands and had the kid get on his knees. Then he started slapping him across the face. First with the right hand on one cheek and then with the left hand the other cheek. He kept doing that for minutes. The kid was basically sobbing and started bleeding. One of the American players was watching and felt that he should go to the police to report it as criminal. But the other players said, "Don't do that. You'll just get yourself into trouble." So, there is a different dynamic, certainly. You could be a manager at the minor league level now and hit a player. I can guarantee that it still goes on. It doesn't go on to the degree that it did in the old days when every manager thought that part of his duty was to hit the players. It has decreased, but it's not disappeared.

I get asked about the future of Japanese baseball quite often. It's always difficult to answer, but the main thing I can say is that the players have gotten so much better over the years that I've been here. Forty or fifty years ago, I didn't see many guys who I thought could play in the Major Leagues. And now every team has some players who can play in the big leagues. In the old days, I think a lot of the players weren't sure of themselves. They weren't sure that they could make it in the Majors and didn't want to go and embarrass themselves. But now when they see all the players who are being successful, more of them are thinking that *if he can do it, then I can do it too*. So, I think more Japanese players are going to want to go to the States in the future.

In my first general managers' and presidents' meeting in 2005, I made a couple of suggestions, and one of them was that all twelve teams work together on marketing. And that was 2005, twenty years ago. You know what still hasn't happened? The best they could do is get the Pacific League marketing together. But you can't really market Japanese baseball internationally with only half the teams participating. They just don't have their act together.

One of the problems with NPB is the lack of good management and leadership. I've written articles about the average age of the commissioner when he starts. It is like eighty-one or something. If you're going to start the job at eighty-one, how much are you going to learn, and how much are you going to be able to do? Whereas if you look at the commissioners of sports in the States, they are decades younger, twenty to thirty years younger on the average, than the people who run sports here in Japan. And these old guys here have no experience! What a contrast! So where does it go from here? NPB really needs somebody dynamic to control baseball here and really do some major things with it, whether it be a real World Series or whether it be a league that involves teams in Asia against teams from other parts of the world. I think a lot of things could be done, but it's going to take a young, dynamic person. And that's one of the problems here in Japan. People see a guy who is fifty-five years old, and they think that he's just a young whippersnapper who doesn't know anything yet. So, I don't have any great hopes for big changes soon. If they get a commissioner who really understands business and really understands the game on both sides of the ocean and understands the big picture, then maybe things could move forward. But unfortunately, the people who are put in charge here are not that type of person.

17 / Tomoko Namba, Team Owner

After receiving her MBA from Harvard Business School, Tomoko Namba became a partner at McKinsey & Company before she founded DeNA, one of Japan's largest mobile-technology companies. She became the first woman to own an NPB team when she took control of the BayStars in 2015. Six months after this interview, the BayStars won their first Japan Series under DeNA's ownership.

◆

As the owner of the Yokohama DeNA BayStars, my passion for baseball runs deep. I often enjoy watching games from a regular seat in the stands, where I find immense pleasure in cheering along with our fans, enjoying a beer under the bright blue sky. The atmosphere is electric, and I love singing along and high-fiving with everyone.

My love for baseball dates back to my childhood, when it was the only professional sport available. Growing up in Niigata, I could only watch Giants games on TV. In those days, everyone was either a Giants fan or simply anti-Giants. The first professional NPB game I attended was between the Nankai Hawks and the Lotte Orions from the Pacific League. This was a monumental event in my life because professional baseball games were a rare occurrence in rural areas. It was something special, a spectacle usually confined to television.

I vividly remember the excitement when a game was scheduled in Niigata. My father asked if I wanted to go, and my sister and I eagerly agreed. On the day of the game, my mother, dressed in her best clothes, looked noticeably different and was the most excited among us. However, my father hadn't anticipated her enthusiasm and had only secured three tickets. True to her traditional Japanese values, my mother gracefully bowed out, joking she had forgotten to wash the dishes, and returned home.

This memory is etched in my mind, a bittersweet yet cherished moment. Although we felt sorry for my mother, we thoroughly enjoyed the game and shared every detail with her upon our return. Her excitement to hear about the game made the experience even more memorable.

I founded DeNA, but after twelve years, my husband fell seriously ill, and I decided to step down to care for him. We faced this challenge together. During this time, the new management team expressed interest in acquiring a baseball team. Initially, I was against the idea, arguing that it was a significant departure from our core business and that we lacked experience in this field. However, they saw it as a rare and prestigious opportunity, given the limited number of teams. After thorough discussions and addressing my concerns about profitability and operational knowledge, they presented well-prepared answers and convinced me to consider the acquisition.

DeNA was relatively new and not widely recognized at the time. While we excelled at college-campus recruiting, parents were often unfamiliar with DeNA, leading to questions like, "What is DeNA?" and "The founder is female?" To establish a stronger reputation and improve our branding, acquiring a baseball team seemed advantageous. It would increase DeNA's visibility and prestige. Additionally, the management team had a genuine passion for baseball. Trusting their preparation and vision, I agreed to pursue the acquisition of the Yokohama BayStars.

I was not the initial owner of the team, as I was absent at the time. Makoto Haruta, who became the chairman of DeNA after I stepped down, served as the first owner. He had a deep understanding of baseball. I later returned to DeNA full-time, and I assumed the role of owner in January 2015, becoming the first female owner in the NPB. While this made headlines, it didn't hold much personal significance for me, as I've often been the first woman to achieve a number of milestones in my career.

Historically, professional baseball was seen as a philanthropic endeavor or a means to boost employee morale, often operating at a loss. Ownership changes typically occurred when the parent company could no longer sustain these losses. We aimed to shift this paradigm by leveraging our business acumen to make the BayStars a successful enterprise. Achieving profitability ensures the team's stability, irrespective of DeNA's business performance, and eliminates the possible need to sell the team down the line. This financial stability is crucial for providing a consistent environment for players and coaches.

By demonstrating how to make the BayStars profitable, we also contributed to the sports industry as a whole. For the sports industry to grow, the sport itself must be profitable, creating a virtuous cycle of expanding growth. If baseball teams cannot achieve profitability, there is little hope for other professional sports like basketball or soccer, as baseball is the biggest professional sport in Japan. Increasing the business scale of the NPB is crucial, requiring collective efforts from all twelve teams. In this regard, there is much we can learn from the United States. While the level of baseball here is very high, the business scale is vastly different. We cannot pay star players the same salaries as in the United States due to our business size.

Running a baseball business is relatively straightforward, with revenue streams from tickets, concessions, merchandise, broadcasting, and sponsorships—all interlinked with attendance. When we acquired the BayStars, attendance was abysmal. We understood it would take time to improve the team's strength, so our immediate focus was on other ways to engage fans and make it exciting and fun to be in the stadium, even if the team lost.

That was a major reason why we appointed Kiyoshi Nakahata as our first manager. He is an iconic and energetic figure who was also an entertainer, and his charisma and engagement with fans and media created a lively atmosphere. Nakahata-san's popularity helped draw more fans, and his enthusiastic fan interactions inspired the players to do the same. This decision was strategic, and Nakahata-san's presence indeed immediately boosted fan engagement.

As the number of fans increased, we introduced various attractions and special packages, such as ¥1 million tickets that included perks like getting to ride in a limousine and helicopter tours, and a full ticket refund if you were dissatisfied with the game. These innovative offerings, along with our targeted marketing efforts, significantly increased attendance.

We also introduced innovations in how the time between innings was utilized. While most attendees typically get up to go buy food or beverages or use the restroom, we decided to challenge that norm. Instead, we aimed to provide entertainment during these intervals to make them livelier and more engaging for the audience.

We also brainstormed ways to bring content to our fans beyond the games and the stadium. One notable project was the creation of a documentary video that highlighted key moments from the season. This allowed fans to relive exciting moments even after the season had ended, helping to keep them engaged and building anticipation for the upcoming season.

The team also did not have a solid marketing strategy. Leveraging DeNA's strong marketing capabilities, we identified our target segments and tailored everything—from seating to concessions—to their preferences. Through marketing analysis, we identified the primary target segment as business professionals in their thirties who would attend games with colleagues or partners. We aligned our marketing strategy to effectively go after this target segment. The entire staff took part in distributing flyers, with Yota Kimura, the current president of the BayStars who incidentally majored in rocket science at the University of Tokyo, personally handing them out at train stations during commuting hours. We placed advertisements in business magazines and online. Additionally, we aimed to make the stadium a popular dating spot for young professionals. One of my initial directives was to improve the women's restrooms, as I recognized that cleanliness is crucial for attracting female fans. Ensuring comfortable facilities for women was a key aspect of our strategy.

Of course, all of these initiatives contributed to improving our performance, but the best possible delight we can provide to our fans is victory on the field. Throughout this time, we steadily invested to strengthen the team. All these efforts were part of our push to do everything we could to improve the team's business performance. Before we bought the BayStars, they were losing more than $20 million every year. We reduced these losses to $2–3 million per year. However, we still couldn't make a profit because we had to share the revenue with the Yokohama Stadium Company. The stadium is very important to us since it hosts our games and other events. We often had to ask them to change the setup for these events. Also, we were always negotiating how much of the revenue we had to share, which was not a good situation. Since the stadium is so important to our business, we waited for the chance to buy the stadium company.

There was one individual in the stadium company who fully understood our vision. He recognized that it would benefit the fans, businesses, and local municipal government if we controlled the stadium. With our aggressive approach, we could transform it into a versatile business venue, hosting not only baseball games but also concerts and other events. Thus,

Tomoko Namba. Courtesy of Tomoko Namba and the Yokohama DeNA BayStars.

in 2016, we successfully acquired the stadium company through a friendly takeover. With ownership, we took control of the concessions. As a foodie, I prioritized enhancing the quality of the ballpark food. We have our own tenants for food services, and we also introduced our own brand, including our own beer. While we outsource the food preparation, it is done according to our specifications to ensure high quality. We have two types of tenants: those who use our space and those who operate independently. This dual approach allows us to maintain excellent food standards. After gaining control of the stadium, we turned a profit immediately in that same year.

As the owner, my focus is on the big picture and the future goal for the team. My primary responsibilities include setting the overall budget framework and making key personnel decisions, such as appointing the manager and GM. Beyond that, the team's management operates independently. I consciously refrain from intervening or even asking questions about player decisions, as I once inadvertently influenced the manager's choices by merely asking about a player's usage. To avoid such issues, I leave baseball operations entirely to the professionals. However, as a fan, it can be challenging! In private, I often express my thoughts to my family and friends, but I never interfere with the manager's or GM's decisions. On the business side, I actively suggest improvements, such as enhancing the food in the suites or the types of merchandise we should offer. These are merely fan suggestions, and it's up to the team whether to implement them.

In managing my company, my philosophy is to delegate responsibilities and encourage independent thinking rather than issuing direct orders. While there are times when decisions must be made and directives given, it's crucial for team members to understand the reasoning behind them. This approach ensures that if they need to make decisions independently, they do so with a deep understanding of the rationale. At DeNA, we maintain a flat organizational structure, fostering open discussions without hierarchical barriers. This management style contrasts with the more directive, hierarchical approach typical of sports teams. Our team embraces a more liberal approach, involving coaches and players in discussions. That being said, we haven't yet proven this method effective, seeing as we haven't won a championship, so we remain open to adapting our strategies.

I was surprised at how challenging it is to win a championship. There are only six teams in the Central League, yet we haven't won since 1998. I've heard about the celebrations in Yokohama when the team won in 1998—I heard that the entire city was in festive chaos, with shops giving away products for free and four hundred thousand people attending the parade. Some people got on top of cars. I dream of witnessing such excitement, with my team at the center. Unlike movies, where the excitement comes from someone else's creation, sports offer a unique thrill because the players are competing for themselves. The DeNA BayStars hold a special place in the hearts of the people of Yokohama. No matter where I am, I'll be heading to Yokohama when we win.

One of the reasons for owning a baseball team is to contribute to society. To achieve this, the team must be profitable. Our success directly benefits the surrounding community. The team is an icon for the people of Yokohama, and when the BayStars perform well, it brings happiness and smiles to everyone. Although Yokohama is adjacent to Tokyo, it is not merely an extension of the metropolis; Yokohama stands proudly as its own city with a strong sense of civic pride.

Beyond baseball, the stadium also plays a vital role in supporting the community. With only seventy home games a year, there are over 290 days without professional baseball. As owners, we are responsible for making the stadium a lively place during these off days by hosting concerts and other events. Additionally, we support local businesses by attracting visitors to the stadium, who then explore nearby areas like Yokohama Chinatown and other local attractions. Increasing foot traffic at the stadium helps boost the local economy. In many ways, owning the team allows us to contribute significantly to society.

We also look beyond the stadium. Right in between Yokohama Stadium and nearby Kannai Station is the old city hall district of the City of Yokohama, which we are in the process of redeveloping. This site is an excellent location for driving activity and engagement in the community. Having the opportunity to develop such a prime site in the heart of Yokohama, next to our stadium, and engage with fans is rare, rivaling the significance of the opening of the port of Yokohama to the West back in the 1800s. We are planning a number of new initiatives to attract people to the area on both game and nongame days by leveraging DeNA and BayStars content. Through these efforts, we aim to give back to the community. This is the key role that DeNA strives to fill.

In the broader region, I applaud MLB's efforts to expand into the Asian market. It is a welcome development because baseball, despite being a great sport, is relatively local, primarily played in a few Asian countries like Taiwan, Japan, and Korea. MLB's substantial financial power entering the Asian market can bring attention to baseball in other Asian countries, allowing more people to experience it and get excited about the sport. Expanding the market benefits everyone in the industry. In the future, we aim to play baseball games internationally and to attract world baseball fans. Hosting international games, such as MLB or WBC events, in Japan can bring many fans from Asian countries, which will help to extend the market for baseball.

I hope there will be a true World Series someday. The level of baseball in Japan is quite high, and international teams would enjoy playing here. However, the significant financial gap between Japanese baseball and leagues like MLB is a fundamental issue that needs to be addressed. Due to this disparity, we often lose our best players to the United States. While it is each individual player's decision to pursue his dreams on the biggest stage, I don't think it should have to be this way. Japan has the potential to be an attractive and competitive destination for top talent. I deeply love Japanese baseball and envision a future where American star players might come to Japan for higher compensation and a more enjoyable experience. Baseball was introduced from the United States, so catching up is challenging; still, that remains the dream.

18 / Shun Kakazu, Assistant General Manager

A graduate of Harvard University, Shun Kakazu has worked in the front offices of both NPB and MLB teams since 2006. He is currently an assistant GM for the Fukuoka SoftBank Hawks.

◆

I was raised in Tokyo, mostly, but because of my dad's job I lived in Bangkok for three years and went to high school in Sydney, Australia, for one year. I majored in film at Harvard and really enjoyed it, but when I started looking into jobs in the film industry, everybody was discouraging me. They were like, "It's a tough job. It has long hours. It doesn't pay much." I was reading *Moneyball* at that time. I found it fascinating that somebody like me, who had very limited experience playing baseball—I was in Little League and that was it—could work in the game and then run a baseball team. That opened up my eyes. I thought, *Maybe working for a baseball team might be fun*, and I started looking into it.

I wanted to start my career in MLB, but it's common to wait two years just to get an internship, and I'm a Japanese citizen, not a U.S. citizen, so it was more difficult. I finally got interviews to be an interpreter for Japanese players, but it was really tough for me to get a visa. In 2005 the talk of Japanese baseball was this American manager named Bobby Valentine, who had a new way of managing and approaching fan service. Even though I was only looking at MLB, I thought that maybe his Chiba Lotte Marines would be a good team to work for. A friend of a friend helped me connect with Bobby. He happened to be back home at Stamford, Connecticut, for the offseason, and I was in New York looking for a job. He said, "I'm going to New York to get my visa renewed at the Japanese consulate, so why don't you meet me there?" I waited in the lobby, and after he was done with the visa, we got into his car on the street and started talking, and he highly recommended me to the club.

The Marines were one of the first teams to actively hire people who wanted to work in sports, and baseball in particular, as opposed to people coming from the parent company who might not necessarily be interested in baseball. At that time, for most of the teams in Japan the managers were like general managers, so Bobby was in effect the general manager. He had an interpreter on the field but was looking for somebody to help him in the front office. I did a little bit of everything; whatever Bobby wanted me to do, I did. I was also a liaison between him and the scouting department. With Bobby's direction, I implemented scouting standards based on how MLB teams value players and gathered all the reports from the scouts to build a database.

I think Bobby was one of the best managers both in Japan and in the States. First of all, he was very game savvy. He was a good manager in terms of strategies, and he was one of the first to focus more on statistics and the data, but also he knew what limitations data has. He was good at making the balance between the analytics and instinct. Also, he was very good with communication. He was always talking to the coaches and the players. He let the veteran players just do their work and respected their routines—all they had to do was perform on the field. He also was very good at communicating with the minor league manager and team. Everybody in the farm system knew that if you were playing well in the minor leagues, in a week or two you could get called up to the major league and start in the games, whether you were a pitcher or a position player. So, there was this good vibe between the major league and farm league. Part of it was that Bobby changed the lineup all the time. Like every single day, it was a different lineup.

In 2009 I moved to the San Francisco Giants. The Giants wanted somebody in Japan to scout not only Japanese players but also American players doing well in NPB. Signing American players returning from Japan was a trend that started about that time. Colby Lewis went from Hiroshima to the Texas Rangers, where he played really well. And we would later sign Ryan Vogelsong, who played in NPB from 2007 to 2009.

When we were evaluating Japanese players, we mostly looked at their baseball skills to see whether they could perform on the field. All the other stuff, the personal stuff, was very important, and we did a lot of homework on that, but it is really hard to predict what will happen. I remember that there were three shortstops in Japan who wanted to move to the States: Tsuyoshi Nishioka, Munenori Kawasaki, and Hiroyuki Nakajima. The Giants, and other teams, were actively pursuing all three guys. In terms of mental makeup, the least favorite for us was Kawasaki because he kept saying, "I'm not interested in MLB. I'm only interested in playing with Ichiro Suzuki, my idol."

All the teams were like, "Well, that's very concerning. Your motivation to go to the States is just that?"

Nakajima, on the other hand, was very, very interested in going abroad. He would go to Latin American countries on his own to watch baseball, and he would go to dinner with American players who were playing in Japan. So, he looked like the best fit to come to the Majors. Well, Kawasaki ended up becoming one of the most popular Japanese players in the Majors, and Nakajima didn't work out at all and went back to Japan. So, it's tough to predict the mental aspects. I'm not saying it's not important, but it's tough to judge human beings.

I spent three years with the Giants. I was turning thirty and still loved scouting, but I had some concerns about my career steps and my growth. That's when DeNA was buying the BayStars and looking to hire, so I went there. I became the assistant GM and also the director of International Operations at one point. I helped the general manager on scouting and player development and built a system to evaluate our own minor league players, manage their playing time, and help the young guys develop in the right way. I also spent a lot of time going abroad to scout foreign players.

In NPB we can sign as many foreign players as possible. There's no limit to that. However, we have a limit on the number of foreign players who can play on the top team. It's five now. It used to be four. And they cannot be five position players or five pitchers. People say that American baseball and Japanese baseball are different, so you could be playing really well in American baseball but not do well when you come to Japan. We're trying to figure out the formula for that, but, again, it's really tough. First of all, we're looking for players who are playing well in the States—nice and simple. They have to be playing well enough for us to get interested in them, but they shouldn't be playing too well, otherwise they will be going to the big leagues and will not be interested in coming to Japan. There are tons of players in MLB, so we sort through all the players who are playing well and might be interested in Japan. Then, we talk to their agents. There's a lot of traffic control of information. Basically, the groundwork is who's interested in Japan, who's doing well, and who doesn't have options and therefore could not be sent down to the Minor Leagues. Those things are the foundation of international scouting.

Once we narrowed it down, I did personal interviews. If they were free agents, I would approach them through their agents, have a coffee with them, and talk about Japanese baseball to see if they were interested in coming over. I think the meetings help, but they can also be misleading. Since it's a job interview, they can say whatever they want. So, they'll say all the right things. I'm not saying these meetings aren't important, but I also talk to scouts and watch them play. That tells me a lot more than an hour interview over coffee. A simple gesture on the mound, when somebody gets hit or whatever, that tells a lot.

In 2013 I read a small article in a Japanese newspaper—not a sports paper but a general newspaper—that the Cuban government would start sending professional athletes to foreign countries. I was scheduled to make a trip to the Dominican Republic in the offseason, so I thought that I might go to Cuba just to check out what was going on. I called up the Cuban Embassy in Tokyo and also talked to the Japanese Embassy in Cuba and then went to Cuba and met with the Cuban Sports Ministry. We were the first ones to get there after that announcement. They were like, "Thank you for coming over. Let's keep in touch. Hopefully we can send our players to your team." And that was it. We weren't looking at hiring somebody right away, so we went back to Japan thinking we would circle back after a year. Then a month later, they asked us if we would be interested in Yulieski Gurriel. We were like, "Heck yeah! He's the best player on the Cuban team." Even though our roster was almost full, we scrambled to get him. It was huge—one of the highlights of my career. Everybody was calling me, especially MLB guys, congratulating me and asking, "How did you make this happen?" They hadn't seen much of Cuba. But people in Japan have always had positive feelings toward Cuba. I think Castro was a huge admirer of Japan as a country and as a culture and of our baseball as well.

In 2015 I moved to the Boston Red Sox. They wanted me to head scouting, not just in Japan and Asia but also in Cuba because of my achievement there. Then right when I joined, MLB said not to go into the Cuban market yet,

Shun Kakazu, circa 2013.
Courtesy of Josh Rawitch.

because they hadn't figured things out with the Cuban Baseball Federation. We were just waiting for the go-ahead, and it ended up not happening at all. I worked for the Red Sox for about four years when the Fukuoka SoftBank Hawks asked me to come on board to help with baseball operations. Since SoftBank bought the Hawks, they have been trying to make the Hawks the No. 1 team in the world. I thought that was an interesting project, so I got on board. That was in 2019.

As an assistant general manager, I do a little bit of everything. I do scouting, which has been my specialty for almost twenty years. I'm also doing player development. We have four teams, three minor league teams and the major league team. We're the only team to do that. The second and third farm teams play industrial teams and independent teams mostly, in addition to college teams, but we can't play high school teams. We have many more players on our rosters than an MLB team because there are no limitations and no options or anything like that. With NPB players, as long as they're on the seventy-man roster, they can be called up to the top team, or sent down to the minors, as many times as necessary. There's only one limitation. Once you are sent down, you cannot come back up for ten days. So, I figure out the best ways to carry that system, like how many players do we need, how many coaches do we need, and how many games do we need to get the right amount of playing time, not too much, not too little—basically, building a system, whether it's on the internet or whether it's on the actual ground, to make sure that the baseball operations run efficiently. Also, I attend the Executive Committee of NPB. So, I join those meetings and make suggestions.

The Hawks' slogan and philosophy is to be No. 1 in the world. To be No. 1 in the world, our league has to be No. 1 in the world. And to do that, we have to get everybody involved and work as a league. That has been a little challenging. So, it's a long-term project, and we're doing it step by step. Our team's success is based on four things: player development, free agents, foreign players, and a winning culture. So, for player development, we're one of the only teams that has a second farm team, and we are the only team that has a third farm team. I think it helps us out tremendously just to have the infrastructure. As for foreign players, we've been looking for talent all over the world. We have players from Cuba, Dominican Republic, the United States, and Mexico. We don't currently have any Taiwanese players, but we did in the past. We even went to see players in Uganda, Africa. We heard that the Dodgers have an academy there, so we went to check them out, and then we actually held a tryout. Winning culture—I've worked on many different teams. I've seen the bad teams and good teams and teams that are turning worse. When you're winning, you keep winning. When you lose, your team gets sour, and you keep losing. I think keeping a winning attitude is something that cannot be neglected.

Obviously, if you want to win a world championship, you have to have one. Right now, there is no way of having a world championship, a true World Series, because the current World Series is the biggest stage that MLB has. So, they're not going to have something else on top of that to devalue the World Series, which makes sense. We could do an exhibition.

But that becomes an issue, more for us, to travel in March or in October to the States and find a team that would play us. That's too hard from our standpoint. Even though we want to be the world No. 1, nobody wants to lose tons of money.

Maybe we can start with Korea and Taiwan and then build up Asian baseball as a whole, then maybe do something down the road with MLB, whether it's in ten years or fifteen years. That could be one strategy. Before COVID, we had baseball clinics in Hong Kong, and we had something going on with China as well. We're trying to build that back up. Japanese baseball is already huge in Taiwan. In the spring of 2024 the Yomiuri Giants had a two-game series against the Taiwanese professional teams in Taipei and the games sold out about thirty minutes after they started selling tickets. So, it's a good market. I think there is a huge opportunity in those countries.

My career goal is to increase the value of NPB, or at least help it get more attention. I keep thinking about whether Japanese players going from NPB to MLB for huge contracts is good or bad. It's a very tough question, as I've been on both sides, Japanese baseball and American baseball. But I think it's good because it gives NPB more attention and it's good as a whole to have more people get interested in baseball. I think it is a little sad, though, that Ohtani was Ohtani when he played in Japan and Yamamoto was Yamamoto when he was in Japan, but because they were NPB players nobody cared, except for avid fans. Then they go to MLB and even casual fans start watching them. They are the same players. They were top notch, the best in the world, when they were in Japan. It's really our failure to appeal to the fans. We need to do a little more on the league level and to have a vision of what we want to do as NPB.

We still have a baseball-playing population, even though the population of Japan is decreasing. We still have a lot of good guys coming up. Each year it seems like there's one guy who goes to MLB, but there's another guy who comes up out of nowhere. We keep producing stars, right? So, I think we are fine and have a bright future. When I started working, the league was on the verge shrinking to ten teams, but in the last twenty years or so the Pacific League has grown a lot. So, I think the NPB's value has gone up overall. This is by far the second-best league in the world, and it's very close to the first one. There's a lot of potential. But we need a vision, and we also need strong leadership. That's going to be key.

I love that Japanese baseball has a strong history. My grandparents were baseball fans. My parents were fans. I have friends from all over Japan who are baseball fans. When we talk, we say things like, "Who's your favorite player?" or, "I love this guy from the '80s, you know, with the Hiroshima Carp." We kind of share the same memories. That's what I like about baseball.

I was watching TV last year, and there was a famous Houston Astros fan who comes to every game. He was asked why he likes baseball, and he said, "Everybody comes together at a baseball game. It doesn't matter where you're from or whether you're rich or poor. It doesn't matter. Everybody comes to baseball and comes together." I thought that was a very cool thing to say. And you know, I feel the same way about Japanese baseball. Because of my job in baseball, I get to go to Cuba. I get to go to the Dominican Republic, Taiwan, Korea, even Africa. And then, I get to make friends with people from all over the world.

19 / Jonathan Fine, Assistant General Manager

Jonathan Fine has been a practicing attorney specializing in sports business, economic development, and corporate law since 1993. He has been associated with the Hiroshima Toyo Carp since interning with the team in 1989. He is now the team's assistant general manager and attorney.

◆

While at college in the late 1980s, I studied Japanese and also worked for my local Minor League baseball team during the summers. I was about to graduate, and I knew that I wanted to go to law school at some point, but I also knew I didn't want to go right away. I did not study abroad during college, so I thought it would be interesting to marry up my interest in baseball and my interest in Japan. So, I contacted all twelve NPB clubs. This was preinternet, so I probably looked them up in an almanac, or something like that, and wrote them each a form letter that basically said, "I'm Jonathan Fine, I'm about to graduate from university. I studied a little bit of Japanese language, and I've worked for my local baseball team for a couple of summers. If you have something that you think I could do for a job, I'd love to come work."

I think I heard from a couple of teams by return reply letter, something along the lines of, "Thank you for your interest, but we really don't have anything." It was getting late in my senior year of college, and I had deferred law school, so I was getting a little nervous. Then, I got a call from an attorney in New York who introduced himself as the international representative for the Hiroshima Toyo Carp baseball team. They got my letter and wanted to know if I would come to New York for an interview. I said sure.

So, I got myself up to New York City. He was in the Pan Am Building right on top of Grand Central Station. I met him for lunch, and we had a nice chat. At the end of it he said, "Well, I've enjoyed speaking with you, and I'm going to recommend to the people in Hiroshima that they hire you."

I remember asking him, "Okay, that sounds great, but what's my job going to be?"

And he said, "I don't think they know exactly, but they're just intrigued by the idea of a young American coming over and working in their front office. They've never done anything like that before."

I went that summer. I was there for a year or so and worked in the front office. The Hiroshima club was at the time and remains to this day owned by the Matsuda family, which is also the family behind the Mazda Motor Corporation, which is headquartered in Hiroshima. The gentleman who hired me, the owner's son who was more or less running the team, had spent time in the United States and was very internationally minded. He thought that it would be interesting for his employees to have an American working side by side with them. He also thought it would be very interesting for me to have a similar experience. And it was life-changing for me. It was wonderful both personally and professionally, and it blossomed into what is now a thirty-five-year relationship. It's been extremely rewarding for me.

There was one, maybe two, people in the office who spoke English well enough to communicate easily with me; however, other than those two, everyone else who even could speak a little bit of English were given instructions not to speak with me in English. They could only speak to me in Japanese. At the time I found it very frustrating. As time went by, however, I came to understand the rationale. It was to improve my language skills as quickly as possible. And it did.

Not being able to speak the language fluently at first, I helped out where I could. If there were ticket stubs that needed to be counted, I did that. If there was food and beverage that needed to be stocked, I did it. If there were merchandise sales that needed to be accomplished or goods that needed to be moved back and forth somewhere, I did it. I did everything and anything I could to help.

I also helped with any communication that was necessary in English, such as talking to people back in the United States. At the time, we were building a baseball academy facility in the Dominican Republic. Since I had six or seven years of high school and middle school Spanish, I could get by in that language, so I helped with communication in Spanish as well.

I lived in the team dormitory. Today, most Japanese clubs still have team dormitories. The rookies and the younger players typically live in the dorm before they get places of their own. When I lived there, however, nearly all of the single guys lived in the dorm. My room was next to Kenjiro Nomura, who would become one of the best Carp players ever. To this day, we remain friends. On the other side of me was the director of our Dominican Academy, César Gerónimo, who played on the Cincinnati Reds in the 1970s. Those guys were like roommates. So as a big baseball fan and a twenty-two-year-old, it was a lot of fun for me.

It was difficult living in a new place and not really being able to communicate in the native language at first. But of course, I adapted and grew into my role. I made it clear from the outset that I was willing to do anything and everything they wanted me to do. I was rotated around various departments to learn about the various aspects of their baseball business.

There were around one hundred or so full-time employees in the front office. There was the ticket sales department, the marketing department, the PR department, food and beverage, and merchandise sales. Then, of course, you had the administrative support, an accounting department, an HR group, and so on and so forth. Here in America, you have those same basic departments. On the baseball side back then, you had the general manager and his group. They call it the "baseball formation group," the people who are in charge of putting the team together. Then you had your baseball field support staff: statisticians, analysts, and those sorts of things. And of course, there was the manager and coaching staff. Then we also had an international staff. Back then it was two people, now it's several more.

At that time, thirty-some years ago, the marketing practices in the United States and Japan might have been a little different, but not terribly different. It was still about selling tickets. It was about selling merchandise. It was about making the experience fun, affordable, and safe for families. It was about entertainment. It was about camaraderie, and it was about the game. That is very much what we still do today.

Back then, the Japanese stadiums were kind of cookie-cutter, and the fan experience was more uniform. One didn't have many options in terms of the food, where you sat, and what you did when you went to the game. You either had an outfield seat or an infield seat. You got your Asahi beer. You had your cheering stuff, and you participated in all the cheers, and you knew all the players. If you went with a group, it was about the group experience as much as it was seeing the baseball game. The ballpark experience

Jonathan Fine. Courtesy of Jonathan Fine

was, naturally, very Japanese as compared to the ballpark experience in the United States. That was new to me. Nowadays you still get that, but it's become somewhat Americanized in a lot of respects both on the field and off the field. Modern ballparks in Japan have American-style amenities, such as huge selections of food and beverage. Our ballpark in Hiroshima does a fantastic job with all kinds of different seating and dining options. In a lot of ways, our ballpark is unique in NPB. It is the only relatively new ballpark in Japan built in that throwback, asymmetrical style first popularized in the United States with Camden Yards. There are nooks and crannies, and there's all sorts of different seating options and food options. I'm a little bit biased, but I really do believe that it's a truly wonderful experience.

Hiroshima is not a big city as far as cities that have NPB teams. We have a thirty-two-thousand-seat stadium, but that's capacity, standing room filled to the brim. The average attendance in Hiroshima is close to thirty thousand. We pack them in. People go nuts for the Carp in Hiroshima. They love it even when the team is not terribly high up in the standings, partly because the ballpark experience is so enjoyable. When I see the marketing guys, the ticket sales guys, I tell them it's incredible. People love it.

The Carp are also known among NPB teams for being extremely savvy and successful at merchandising. The club's merchandising efforts capitalize on the whole kawaii culture, the whole sort of Hello Kittyization of the merchandise world. Can you get an authentic jersey? Of course. Can you get T-shirts? Of course. But we take that a step further. For example, if a player on our club gets a sayonara hit to win a game, we print limited-edition T-shirts the next day. They sell out very quickly. People love it. We do a lot of different kinds of things like that. There are just so many unique ways people can connect to our club through the merchandise. There's a concept called *Carp joshi*, or Carp girls. It's become somewhat of a fashion statement for young women to wear Carp gear. The marketing department has created all of this, and it's really fantastic. They work extremely hard at it, and they're very clever and come up with wonderful promotions, but part of the success is just the city of Hiroshima and local fans' attitude about their team. Hiroshima people are extremely proud of the team. The Matsuda family may be the owners, but they're really just the stewards of a community asset. The team belongs to the people of Hiroshima and always has.

After that year in Hiroshima, I went to law school, but I never lost the connection with the Carp. Even in law school, if they needed to contact an American company, I'd help to facilitate the communication. After I finished law school, the lawyer who interviewed me in New York retired, and I started working on player contracts and became the Carp's U.S.-based business representative and attorney.

When I first started working for the Carp, there were not a lot of the big, goofy mascots in Japan. The San Diego Chicken only dated to the late 1970s, so at that time most teams in the United States had only been using mascots for about fifteen years. Mr. Matsuda, the owner, thought that that implementation of such a mascot might be a fun idea and set the Carp apart from other NPB clubs. He was always trying to be ahead of the curve and do different things. Around 1994 we contacted a company in New Jersey that was preeminent in the mascot business. This company had designed a lot of the Muppets for Jim Henson's organization and had designed several famous mascots, including the Phillie Phanatic. If you look today at Slyly, our Carp mascot, there's a strong resemblance to the Phillie Phanatic. The design bears an even stronger resemblance to a retired mascot that had been created for the New Jersey Nets. Side by side, you'd be hard-pressed to tell the difference. So, as the team's attorney, I insisted that the company sign over those intellectual property rights to the Carp, because the design was so similar. So the Carp to this day, I think, still hold the rights to the design of the old New Jersey Nets mascot. Slyly has been a huge hit now for almost thirty years.

I've been practicing law for thirty years, in and out of firms or working on my own doing consulting and legal work in the sports world. I was the general counsel of the Carolina Hurricanes of the NHL just after the team moved to North Carolina in 1997. I started doing a lot of their work when they built a new arena in Raleigh. I worked on the naming-rights deal, and various arena-related contracts. Then, I became the general counsel of the Charlotte Hornets, the NBA team, for several years. These days, I work for mostly Minor League Baseball teams, helping with various contracts, ballpark development, and team sales. And of course, I work for the Carp.

The Carp work takes up a considerable chunk of my time. I'm officially assistant general manager—USA, although my title has either been nonexistent or fluctuated over the years. I facilitate communication and work on agreements between the Carp and American companies. A substantial part of my job entails working to sign North American—based players to go play for our club over in Japan. I work with our people in Japan and our U.S.-based scouts to identify the players we want to try to sign to play for our team the following season. We have now three U.S.-based scouts, all three of whom played for us and whom I signed to play for the Carp. The three of them will scout in person all of AAA baseball. Then the data they gather is shared with our general manager, the scouting department, the international group, and field staff in Japan. By the end of the season, we've more or less identified the players who we think will best help our club. Our scouts talk with their contacts throughout MLB and MiLB to learn about a potential player's makeup to determine if he has the temperament to successfully adapt to Japanese baseball. That's an important part of our evaluation process.

Shortly after some organizational meetings, which we all attend over in Japan, I try to sign the desired players. Sometimes that entails negotiating a buyout of those players' rights from a big league club if they're under contract. And I have to negotiate a player contract with the player's agent. Most of these are one-year contracts, especially for first-time-in-NPB players. Foreign-player contracts in NPB usually include a salary guarantee. I'm responsible for those negotiations, and I'm responsible for much of the related paperwork—for example, paperwork for the NPB league office and work visas. There's also an immigration process to be facilitated for players and their families.

The new foreign players all have questions about their, and their families', new lives on the other side of the planet where they don't speak the language. There is a lot of hand-holding at first, a lot of making sure a comfort level is achieved and all questions are answered. We try to visit with these guys during December or January, not only so that they can see the American staff and know that we're here to help them and to support them, but also just from a comfort-level standpoint. Because once they go to Japan, they hit the ground running, and it can be like drinking from a fire hose. I think we do a pretty good job of moderating their trepidation. Our American-based scouts go over to Japan and spend the first two weeks of spring training with them. The idea is to help the new players with expectations and to facilitate the integration process. Our coaching and managerial staff trust our scouts, as many of them played together on the Carp, and that helps facilitate the transition.

We decided a long time ago that when it came to our foreign players, we were going to be in the customer-service business. Knowing how intimidating the transition can be, we make their experience, and particularly their families' experience, as seamless and comfortable as possible. That starts with their trip over, making sure that it runs without a hitch, making sure that when they emerge from the customs area at the Tokyo airport they are more or less held by the hand all the way to Hiroshima and that their apartment is set up and ready for them. We've compiled a book over the years with all the information they need. This is where you get the American-branded groceries. This is where the English-speaking dentist is. This is where the three best English-language daycares are. We take great pains to take care of our foreign players and their families. I cannot recall an issue that has come up over the last fifteen years or so that we haven't figured out. I tell all of this to prospective players, and the agents know it too. I say, "Don't just take my word for it; your agent placed this guy with us several years ago—call him. In fact, have your wife talk to his wife." It even could be a player who frankly didn't have success with us on the field, who may have been with us for just a year, but I feel confident in every single instance because that's a selling point for us.

From a baseball-operations perspective, Japanese baseball has evolved over the past thirty years. Look at the Japanese athletes themselves. In general, they're bigger and stronger than they were thirty years ago. Many of the guys who come over to the United States to play are physically equal to the American professional players. That's not across the board, but more and more so. As the American game has grown and matured, so has the Japanese game. There is more strength, there is more speed, there is more power in the game, and thus strategies are employed take advantage of those physical attributes. Moreover, diet, training technique, technology (in terms of data and analytics)—all of that has transformed the Japanese game just like it has transformed the American game. It has always been said that NPB is the next best professional league in the world after MLB. I think that MLB is still ahead, but over the last thirty years, I've witnessed that gap shrink. Just look at the success so many Japanese players are having in America these days. I could point to Hiroki Kuroda and Kenta Maeda just from the Carp. Seiya Suzuki was a great hitter for us and now plays right field for the Cubs. And don't even get me started with Shohei Ohtani. Well, he's a bad example because he's literally better than everyone. When Japanese players make it over to Major League Baseball, there's not a lot of resentment from NPB, particularly among the fans. It's more, "Okay, it's your time. You're going to make us very proud. You're going to make NPB and the quality of our baseball look great when you succeed on the biggest stage."

I think that the level of our league will always be great. The game has grown. It's become more sophisticated. What makes Japanese baseball so interesting and fun is that it's not just a carbon copy, a sort of little brother of American baseball. The league still has a very Japanese approach. Nowadays in the United States professional leagues, they consistently swing for the fences. It's a home run or a strike out. That's how they're taught now. In Japan, it's still more of a make-contact, put-the-ball-into-play brand of baseball. There is still very much the Japanese collective and consensus approach—team first, train together, strength in numbers—and philosophy behind the game. That probably differs from team to team, but it's still a strong philosophy within our team, and we've been able to achieve a lot of success with it. I enjoy that a lot, watching the modernization of the game but maintaining it in a Japanese context, both culturally and baseballwise. It's a lot of fun.

Part 6 / The Business of Baseball

20 / Shigeo Araki, Marketing Director

In 2004 Shigeo Araki left his position as CEO of Deutsche Telekom, T-Systems Japan to follow his passion in sports marketing. He became the managing director of Business Operations of the Chiba Lotte Marines, director of the Board of Directors for Pacific League Marketing, and special counsel and corporate officer for Samurai Japan. Now, he is the CEO of Sports Marketing Laboratory.

◆

I joined the Chiba Lotte Marines in January 2005 after meeting the team's president, Eisu Hamamoto, at Tokyo University's Sports Management School. He wanted to revolutionize the way his club was operated. We got to talking, and he asked me if I wanted to help change the organization.

When I started, the team was not really doing anything in terms of business development. This was true not only of the Marines, but it was the overall mindset that was in place for all NPB teams. NPB teams are owned by parent companies, and these parent companies basically saw the team as an advertising tool and nothing more. They weren't actually viewing the clubs as a separate sports business in and of itself, so they didn't put any effort into marketing the teams.

Soon after I started, Bobby Valentine, who had become our new manager, came to Chiba before he had to head off to spring camp. The day before he left for the camp, I got an opportunity to meet him. We ended up talking for more than seven hours that day, and he handed me a list of things that we could do for the fans. That list had two hundred or more items on it! This was completely unheard of at that point in Japan. It really threw me off guard to have a list of things to do for the fans because it just wasn't the way that Japanese baseball operated at the time. But Bobby said to me—and this really changed my way of thinking—"In baseball, even if you win the pennant or win the championship, your team is still going to lose four times out of ten, which means that the fans are going to leave the stadium sad four of ten times. It's not all about wins and losses. Pro baseball is about making sure that fans leave the stadium happy ten times out of ten." As we talked on that day, we realized that one day of talking was not enough. So he asked me to come to the spring camp, which was pretty unusual to have someone like me being called down to a place where they're working out. Bobby and I would meet after practice, and we continued to have these talks about what we could do to improve baseball operations. Even when the season started, I often found myself in Bobby V's office before game time talking about baseball operations. There's no manager like him in all of baseball. No manager spent that much time thinking about business operations.

Our goal was to create an environment where the stadium would become the home base for the team and its fans, a kind of community space. It was often said that the Central League operated up in the air and the Pacific League down on the ground—meaning the Central League, with the Yomiuri Giants, controlled the broadcasting rights and could earn income from the broadcasts, whereas it was harder for the Pacific League to get broadcasting rights for games, so they had to rely on ticket sales for income. Therefore, we wanted to ensure that we had a firm foundation in place for the team and our fans.

To transform the Marines into a viable business, I developed the Clothing Size Strategy, where the initials of clothing sizes, SS, S, M, L, and LL, stand for different concepts. I'll start by explaining the SS size. SS stands for sponsors and supporters. Up until then, sponsors simply gave teams money. But we devised a strategy to work with sponsors as partners, rather than just asking them to provide money, to cooperate with the team to build up the area around the stadium and build up the community.

I'll jump right into the supporters part. The old mentality was that fans come to the stadium to watch the game. Rather than that, we wanted to see them more as participants, as members of the team. So, what does that mean? That means that they are cheering. That means that they are wearing uniforms. They are putting a number on their backs and becoming one of the members of the team and not just people who come to watch. The point here was not just to increase the number of fans in the stands or use that as the sole measuring stick of success; it was to increase the time they spent at the ballpark. We wanted them to come not just for the three-hour game, but rather come early and stay longer. So, we had fireworks displays after every night game, and sometimes after the games, we would let the kids on the field and allow them to run the bases. We also built up the area around the stadium so there were things for the fans to do before and after the games. We made it into a community space. There were food stands, and there were places to have events. In that way, the income for the team was not just coming from ticket sales but also from all the things that fans could participate in before and after the games.

We would not be able to put any of those things in place without having the rights to the stadium operations, so that is where the S for stadium comes in. At that time in Japan, cities or prefectures generally operated sports stadiums, as well as facilities like libraries, senior homes, prisons, and so forth. The city of Chiba operated our stadium and retained the income from concessions and fees. The Marines as a team were in the red, but the stadium was in the black. To revolutionize the franchise, the stadium needed to be held by the team, and the team business and stadium business needed to be integrated. We acquired the rights to operate the stadium in 2006 under the Designated Manager System, which had just been implemented in Japan in 2004. From that point, we had full control over the stadium's infrastructure and were able to integrate ticket sales with merchandise and food and beverage sales. In three years, we were able to increase our sales by 380 percent.

M stands for media, and that can be divided into two parts. One is mass media, and the other is in-house media, or team-owned media. Japan's media environment has a structure in which there are key stations in the metropolitan areas, and local stations in rural areas as affiliated stations. Because Chiba is part of the Kanto region, we fall into the same broadcasting area as the other teams in the Tokyo area, including the Yomiuri Giants. There was almost no promotion of the Chiba Lotte Marines within the area's key broadcasters, which meant that we weren't getting our information spread to the nation. We felt that we needed to do something to change that. What we could do is not only put a better product on the field, which still might not get the appropriate attention, but also give the mass media something to report about, give them stories to work with. For us that came in the form of having fan service like no other team. So, our strategy was to make the news not only based on game results but also on other things around the ballpark.

Shigeo Araki. Courtesy of Shigeo Araki.

Since no key stations in the metropolitan area were covering us, we had no choice but to do it ourselves. So we created a strong in-house media to disseminate team content. In 2005, our first year, we started Marines TV on the internet. We created a studio and produced all the content for the website ourselves. I took videos with my camera and wrote articles.

We made special programs that featured our players and gave the fans information that they couldn't get anywhere else. No other team in NPB at the time had anything like this. It was unique to us, so it gave our fans something special.

The *L* stands for local. But local means not only the fans but also the area around the stadium. There's something in Japan called *jokamachi*, which basically means the town, or the area, surrounding the castle. *Jo* is the word for castle, and it's similar to *kyujo*, the word in Japanese for stadium. We created this idea of the jokamachi, meaning the neighborhood where people live surrounding the stadium should be connected culturally to the stadium. Nearby, there is a huge apartment complex called Makuhari Bay Town, where over twenty thousand people live. So, we wanted to make that a part of our local community, to bring them into the team and make the area part of the team atmosphere. We wanted to have this atmosphere not only on game days but also 365 days a year. It just so happened that Bobby Valentine was living in this area, and then I moved into it, and we worked hard to build up that type of atmosphere through activities. For example, when we won the championship in 2006, we held a victory parade that started in the city's commercial area but ended in Bay Town.

Finally, LL—the first *L* is Lotte, the second one is league. So in terms of Lotte, in order to revolutionize the Marines as a business, the parent company Lotte needed to invest in the ballclub. The team, of course, was in the red. That was to be expected, as that was part of the plan at that time for teams to be used as advertising and tax write-offs. Lotte didn't really have a mindset to invest more money into a product that was not earning money. But before I joined Lotte, I worked for IBM, and I caught an interesting, mind-changing phrase from them, and that was "Sell Japan in IBM; sell IBM in Japan." I turned that into "Sell Lotte in Marines. Sell Marines in Lotte." So that meant working hard to create a connection between the parent company and the baseball team. When operating the Marines, we had to keep Lotte's interests in mind, but we also had to sell the Marines brand within the Lotte Corporation. I made sure that the parent organization and the team were engaging with one another. I met with the owner of Lotte every month to discuss business strategy, and I was successful in getting him to invest in the team.

So, the second *L* is league. Basically, all of the Pacific League teams were looking to change what they were doing. All the teams were aiming to localize and to center their communities at the stadium. But the more you localize your product, the harder it becomes to gain national attention and national sponsorship. So, the local movement was a good thing, but we also wanted to turn the Pacific League into a national product. If you look at the geographical locations of the franchises, the Central League is mainly located in the Tokyo area and central Japan, with the Carp out west in Hiroshima. On the other hand, the Pacific League is much more spread out. You have six dots, if you will, on the map for each of these six stadiums in the Pacific League. We thought that if we could find a way to connect those six dots from all the way up north in Hokkaido right down to the south in Fukuoka, then we would have something that could be nationalized, as those six dots reach all the way across the nation as opposed to the more condensed Central League. We also thought that if we cooperated as a six-team league and had one operation system, it would help us to cut costs. So, we formed the Pacific League Marketing group in 2007.

I left the Marines in 2009 and started my own company called Sports Marketing Laboratory, which enabled sports organizations to have a stronger business operations. Then in 2013, the NPB players association was unwilling to have the players join the WBC. Team Japan was not a business entity; it was just a team formed to play in the WBC, and that didn't go over well with the players because they were not compensated. So, Team Japan needed to be turned into a business that could compensate the players. Then, players would have an incentive to participate. The players association agreed that if this happened then they would play in the WBC. So NPB reached out to me and asked if I would create a strategy that would turn the team into a business.

At that time, professional baseball and amateur baseball in Japan were separate entities. There was nothing that connected the two. Amateur baseball included the under-twelve national team, the under-eighteen national team, and so on, which fell under the bracket of the World Baseball Softball Confederation (WBSC). But there was no connection between them and the professional baseball national team. Even the uniforms were separately designed. My strategy was to unite the marketing rights for amateur and professional baseball under the name Samurai Japan. So, the under-twelve team, the under-eighteen team, all of the youth and amateur teams that represented Japan, would be called Samurai Japan, all the way up to the pro level. Then young kids would aim to be part of Samurai Japan, and that entity would be able to be marketed to all generations with a consistent name.

The Japanese people have a great love for national teams. They're very popular not only in baseball but also in soccer and in all Olympic sports. Since there's a strong attachment to national teams and the mass media in Japan has a strong interest in baseball, there was no concern about whether or not the media would cover the team. But we wanted to build up our digital content and our presence. We decided that we should create our own media content. Looking at the digital market, we saw that Yahoo was very successful, but rather than rely on the mass media to put news up on Yahoo about us, one of our aims was to post our own digital media content.

We have tried live streaming games. We started with the MLB tours of Japan, or Nichibei baseball. This was the first attempt to have games broadcast on television and streamed on the internet at the same time, and the TV stations didn't like that because they might lose viewership. So instead of doing the same thing they were doing and just doing it on the internet, we thought that we should do something different. So, we had a play-by-play person, but instead of a color man, we got an MLB analyst as well as an NPB analyst. Rather than doing color explanations in the standard way, they used stats and figures and explained the numbers during the broadcast.

It's hard to turn Samurai Japan into a big business because we're not creating and hosting tournaments, but of course it is part of the aim to become a year-long operation and to increase merchandise sales. Samurai Japan as a team has been very successful both on the field and in marketing. Forty-plus percent of the Japanese people watched the final game of the 2023 WBC final where Japan beat the USA team. Our aim is to build on the momentum of WBC to make Samurai Japan have the strongest presence possible, create the strongest content, and build an even better product. But making money is not our only goal. Through Samurai Japan, we are able to provide kids with a dream, something big to aim for.

21 / Tomoki Negishi, Marketing and Business Development

Tomoki "Tom" Negishi was the senior director of business development for the Rakuten Eagles before moving to Pacific League Marketing. He served as the CEO of PLM from 2017 to 2024.

◆

I think Japanese baseball has a unique, fun style that Americans would enjoy. I worked for Pacific League Marketing for eleven years and was the CEO from 2017 until 2024, and I think there are many opportunities for Japanese baseball to improve its popularity in the global market.

I grew up in Saitama, about thirty minutes by train north of the center of Tokyo. Even though the Seibu Lions played in Saitama Prefecture, I was a Yomiuri Giants fan. The Lions played in Tokorozawa on the other side of the prefecture, and I could watch the Yomiuri Giants games on TV every night. At that time, they were the only team broadcasted on TV throughout Japan.

After I graduated from my university, I joined the travel agency named JTB and worked there for six years. I was in charge of the sports category, like J.League soccer and World Cup soccer. Half of my business focused on sports; the other half focused on large events and ordinary overseas or domestic trips. I touched the outside of sports business because one of my biggest clients was the Omiya Ardija, one of the J.League teams. I love sports, and I loved sports business as an outsider for those six years.

I then transferred to Johnson & Johnson. It was a totally different category of business, but I wanted to become a marketer, a global marketer. But after only fifteen months, I left because I was not happy with the company. Everything was done top down, and I felt that I didn't have any freedom. I wanted to dive into sports business. In Japan, baseball is the No. 1 sport, so I thought that I should join the baseball business and that my experience from other sports like soccer would help me. So, I joined the Rakuten Eagles.

I came to the Eagles in 2007, the beginning of their third season, as the director of the ticketing department. My role was the planning, marketing, and overseeing of ticket sales. At that time, Marty Kuehnert was a senior advisor for the Eagles, and he was also my English teacher. Together, we planned tours of the United States so that Eagles employees could learn from U.S. sports businesses. We arranged appointments with individual MLB clubs and related companies and organizations. Specifically, I learned that the most important value proposition for the baseball business isn't just to showcase the game of baseball for fans but to provide entertainment. Fans at MLB ballparks enjoy the games in different ways: some just watch baseball, others do not watch much of the game but spend their time socializing, and so forth. There are definitely various ways of enjoying baseball games.

The team's official name is the Tohoku Rakuten Eagles, but the Tohoku region (which contains six prefectures) is huge, and the population is not that large, so we decided to focus our marketing locally, not just on the city of Sendai but on Miyagi Prefecture. Miyagi Prefecture has just over two million people. I thought that was large enough to support a team, so we developed strategies for expanding the popularity of the club.

Our first goal was to get the people of Miyagi Prefecture interested in the Rakuten Eagles. We did this by collaborating with the local newspapers and the local mass media. Both produced their own original content. Once people became interested in the Eagles, we wanted them to come to the ballpark, so we made plans to improve the ballpark's menu and the ballpark's attractions and so forth. For example, we increased the number of seat categories. In 2007, we only had fifteen to twenty different seat categories, but when I left the Eagles in 2012, we had thirty-five or forty. So fans can choose their favorite type of seat or favorite view.

We also started focusing on special box seats where four people can sit around a table, or even one table for eight people. That was a unique type of seating at that time in Japan. It allows fans to watch baseball as if they were in an *izakaya* restaurant. Our rival in Sendai is not a local soccer club, but our competition is izakaya restaurants. So, on weeknights, we want people to go to the ballpark, not to the restaurants. Typically in Japan, businesspeople work really hard until 6:00 or 7:00 p.m., but then they say, "Let's go to drink or do something somewhere." So, to attract the businesspeople as they leave their offices, we sell a special discount ticket, named the *oban-desu* ticket, which is around 50 percent off after 7:30 p.m.

Our ballpark is not just a place for focusing on a ball game; it is also a place for socializing, and it's an attraction. That is a key point because Miyagi Prefecture is not a traditional baseball region where everybody knows the rules of baseball in detail. So, we wanted to make something for people who are not that interested in baseball. Instead of just focusing on the ball game, we focused on entertainment. We wanted to get all the categories of people who lived in Miyagi Prefecture to come and watch the games. We had a strategy for every type of fan. For families with small kids, we created something like a theme park. We put in a carousel and a Ferris wheel. We also put in a cotton-candy stand, and we have games for kids outside of the ballpark. It's like Tokyo Disneyland! So, the kids want to come to the ballpark even if they're not interested in baseball. Also, inside of the ballpark, we have a grass area that has no seats. As three hours is a long time for small kids, they want to move around during the game. So, the kids can run around in the grass area. That's okay. Since kids go places with their parents or their grandparents, attracting the kids is a very important strategic point.

Many of our fans are female. Nowadays, over 50 percent of our merchandising sales come from women because they focus on their favorite players. They purchase all the goods with their favorite player's name: Masahiro Tanaka towels, Masahiro Tanaka T-shirts, Masahiro Tanaka hats, or things like that. It's a very good business. The Orix Buffaloes have had huge sales from the merchandising of Yoshinobu Yamamoto gear in recent years.

My personal opinion is that some of our merchandizing patterns came from the culture of live music concerts. At the music-idol group concerts, thousands of people come to the venue wearing the same merchandising goods, and during the concerts everybody does the same actions. That's Japanese live culture. I think that culture transferred to baseball. At the Japanese games, almost all the home fans participate in the cheers and the songs. You don't see the same thing in Major League Baseball because America depends on personal culture, so not everybody sings the same song, and not everybody does the same action. So, I think the live-music culture in Japan has had a huge influence on baseball fan culture. And the live-music culture demographic is over half women. Women like kawaii (the

Japanese phrase for "super cute and loveable"). So, the music industry sold kawaii goods. Kawaii goods are also very popular in baseball.

After six years, the CEO of the Rakuten Eagles ordered me to be transferred to another section of the business, like fan-club operations. But I rejected the transfer because I wanted to keep working with promotions, media rights, and global events. At that time, I was the senior director of business development. Also, I was head of the PR and the promotions department. I was responsible for all the branding, promotions, and media rights. While working at the Eagles, I read an article about how Major League Baseball grew its business from broadcasting rights, marketing rights, and things like that. Marty Kuehnert also gave me a lot of information about what was successful in Major League Baseball and why you should focus on MLB to learn how to expand. So, I became very interested in bigger markets. I decided that I wanted to move to Pacific League Marketing. Rakuten approved my move to PLM, so I started there in 2013.

Pacific League Marketing was created in 2007. A couple guys who were watching how MLB's business was rapidly growing wanted to create a similar marketing company for the twelve professional clubs in Japan. But the structure of NPB is very different from MLB. An individual Major League Baseball club is owned by an individual owner, but in NPB the clubs are owned by parent companies. For example, the Rakuten Eagles are owned by Rakuten, a technology company. This is a very important point. The individual clubs' way of recruiting players and their business strategies are affected by their parent companies' culture and owners. There is a huge difference in culture between some of the parent companies. The Seibu Lions are owned by a railway company. Railway companies are conservative because if there is a train accident it's a huge problem, so that makes them have very conservative ways, which affects the Seibu Lions. On the other hand, the Rakuten Eagles are owned by an IT company, which is more aggressive, so the Rakuten Eagles culture is more aggressive. The Eagles, the Lions—the name of the team does not identify the team's culture; only once we've identified their parent company can I know the team's culture. The baseball team is one of the marketing tools of the parent company. For example, the Hokkaido Nippon Ham Fighters want to sell meat, so they tie baseball with their meat and food products. The Yomiuri Giants is one of the marketing and the promotional tools of the Yomiuri media group to help expand their businesses.

Tomoki Negishi. Courtesy of Tomoki Negishi.

The marketing structures of NPB and MLB are also very different. In MLB individual baseball clubs are all considered under the MLB marketing umbrella. On the other hand, in NPB each of the twelve individual clubs controls its own marketing and business rights. So, the individual clubs have huge power—100 percent control over their home-game media rights. NPB does not have any commercial rights for the regular season games. NPB only controls the rights to the All-Star Game and the Nippon Series. As a result, NPB does not have a lot of business power. That's a huge difference between the leagues.

So, in 2007 the founders of PLM wanted to create a marketing company for the entire NPB—all twelve clubs. But the Central League teams were only interested in marketing individually. The Yomiuri Giants and the Hanshin Tigers are the two top-positioned teams, like the Yankees and Dodgers in the United States. They have huge business power just by themselves, so they didn't want to lose their advantages. Also, the parent companies of the Central League teams own them for different reasons. The Chunichi Dragons and Yomiuri Giants are owned by newspaper companies, and the clubs are one of their marketing tools for the newspaper business. The Yakult Swallows are owned by a global company that sells drinks. The Hanshin Tigers are owned by a local railway company, so they don't want to focus on global business. The Hiroshima Carp are just unique, and they're just local. So, I don't think that a single marketing strategy or any policy would get them together. Instead, the founders decided to focus just on the Pacific League, which is the reason why the company is called Pacific League Marketing.

When I joined PLM, there was nothing in the business policy like a mission statement or vision or philosophy, so I created these things. PLM's mission is to increase the fan base around the world and to create new baseball fans. It's very simple. The individual clubs have huge power in their franchise's local markets. For example, the SoftBank Hawks have huge marketing power in Kyushu, and the Eagles have huge power in Miyagi Prefecture. But from a national perspective, they don't have much marketing power. So, PLM's mission is to increase the number of new baseball fans across Japan and the world.

Pacific League Marketing is focusing on three points. Internet business is growing rapidly in Japan, so we are focusing on digital marketing, including media. The second one is international business. So far, it's small, but I think that we can become better positioned in the global market, and I think it will work twenty years in the future. The third one is corporate sales—that is, corporate sales with promotional events with the six clubs. So, we are focusing on only three categories. These three categories did not even exist twenty or thirty years ago, so that makes these a new value or new position for the Pacific League.

At first, it was not easy to increase revenue, but we could help the clubs reduce costs. One way was to manage all six clubs' official websites. That was a very efficient way to reduce costs because we went from six servers to only one big server. I think for the American baseball fans, it is common sense to have a Major League Baseball site, but when I joined PLM, there was no Pacific League website. So, we made a Pacific League official site. We followed the Major League Baseball site and named ours pacificleague.com. Once someone is interested in the Pacific League, or in a specific

Pacific League team, we will be the primary touchpoint for potential fans or casual fans. We have not only player data but also game videos. If our fans want to know more, they can go to the players' social media sites or the individual club's site.

We manage the Pacific League clubs' media rights, just like MLB Advanced Media, so we have an original private channel named Pacific League TV, and also, we have a channel named Pacific League TV Official on YouTube. That is a huge success for us. The live channel (Pacific League TV) is not free. It's a subscription model, so if people want to watch the live games, they are charged. It also has archived games.

But Pacific League on YouTube is free to watch everywhere, any time, so it's hugely successful, especially for YouTube. We upload twenty to thirty videos every day and have more than twenty thousand on the site. We have about 1.44 million subscribers. YouTube has two strong points for us. The first is that everybody in Japan can watch the YouTube channel because it's free, so it's a great marketing tool. The other one is that YouTube has a younger audience. In Major League Baseball and here in Japan, the main age category of fans is around forty-five years old. Since YouTube is most popular among twenty-to-thirty-year-olds, we can more easily connect with a younger age group through it. So, it helps the mission of our company to increase the number of new baseball fans.

We have had some success bringing people from the digital site to the ballparks. We send Pacific League TV subscribers an invitation to come to the ballparks with a unique ID so we can follow their activities. Some stay only in the digital world, but others also go to the ballparks. But we are little bit slower getting people to transfer from the website to the ballparks in recent years because COVID-19 has had a huge effect on the ballpark business. On the other hand, our company grew during COVID-19 because we don't have ballparks and we don't have players and we are focusing on only digital.

In 2013 the number of baseball fans following the Pacific League was around fifteen million, and nowadays (after the 2023 season) it's sixteen million, so it's grown a little bit. But the number of all baseball fans is decreasing because in the Central League the number of fans is decreasing. So, in the ten-year perspective, the Pacific League is increasing, but the Central League is decreasing, but totally it is decreasing because the Central League's fan base is twice the size of the Pacific League's. The individual baseball clubs in the Pacific League are also making a profit. Around thirty years ago, all six clubs had huge red figures each fiscal year, but nowadays most of the six clubs are in the black. So, I think PLM has been successful.

I feel that there are so many opportunities to grow our content in the global market, but we are going step by step. I've been focusing on international business since 2014. Our marketing in Taiwan is hugely successful for us because there are so many fans and also Taiwan is very close to Japan, so many travelers from Taiwan come to our ballparks.

But in North America, the United States and Canada, we have a small presence. I feel that there are so many opportunities, so much potential. Shohei Ohtani, Yoshinobu Yamamoto, Yu Darvish, now great players in MLB, have graduated from the Pacific League. So, I think that there are many white spaces—like English voiceover for videos and games and international merchandising business in America and Canada where everybody is interested in Shohei Ohtani and other Japanese players and teams.

Hopefully, NPB will increase their content touchpoints in America. Not only should they have a website with the rosters and stats, but they should also export every type of content, including video, Shohei Ohtani's history, and things like that. A three-hour NPB baseball game might be boring for an audience from the United States, right? Just my idea here—maybe collaborate with Netflix or Amazon and make a documentary showing Ohtani's history with Japanese baseball culture, like the cheering styles or the beer girls or things like that. I think that we have a unique, fun style of baseball that we can show best to the audience in the United States with a documentary or through a story-behind-the-story program. I feel that NPB baseball culture is from Koshien culture, that of the National Baseball High School Championship. So, I think that they should show Shohei Ohtani at Koshien. People from the United States would think it strange: "Why do they shave their heads? Why are they wearing white uniforms? Why are they all silent before the start of the Koshien games?" I think that viewers would have so many questions, and I think questions attract people. So, I believe that not only baseball but also NPB culture, combined with Koshien culture, would be interesting for North American audiences because it's a unique and different baseball culture.

I want to invest more and more in international business, but some of the six individual clubs are not behind PLM's investment in the North

American market. They are more focused on the near future, two or three years from now, when ten to twenty years is needed to really expand our global business.

On the other hand, MLB and the Dodgers have already expanded into the global and Asian markets. The Dodgers are a great brand here in Japan, and after investing all that money for Shohei Ohtani and Yoshinobu Yamamoto, the Dodger brand is just stronger. Ohtani has definite market power and market value in both the United States and Japan. My parents are not baseball fans, but even they follow Ohtani. They ask me, "What is he doing today? What is today's batting order?" They ask me this! I think it's incredible that everywhere in Japanese common culture, not just baseball culture, Japanese are interested in Shohei Ohtani. Almost all Japanese guys will visit Dodgers content during the next seasons, and the people will probably be able to see every Dodgers game, either on NHK for free or through a subscription model or on the internet.

From the Pacific League and NPB perspectives, Major League Baseball and the Dodgers are not competitors. I think there are good opportunities for developing some sort of business plans. For example, since Ohtani played on the Nippon Ham Fighters, we have videos of all of his games in Japan. I feel that there are opportunities to sell jerseys or T-shirts with Shohei Ohtani and the Nippon Ham Fighters in the United States if the Fighters could get the IP [intellectual property] rights for the overseas categories. We should communicate more and more with Major League Baseball and the Dodgers. I think it's a great opportunity for exchanging ideas and moving the Pacific League and Japanese baseball forward.

22 / Naomichi Yokota, Marketing and Merchandising

A graduate of the University of Tsukuba, Naomichi Yokota spent thirteen years in marketing and merchandising for the Yomiuri Giants. He also helped develop the team's community outreach and charity programs.

◆

Solving social issues through sports is the theme of my life.

I grew up in Yokohama and went to the University of Tsukuba because I wanted to find a job connected to sports and it had courses in sports management. In my first and second years, I played on the university baseball team. I realized I didn't have the talent to enter professional baseball, so I decided to become a teacher and perhaps coach baseball.

Part of being a teacher is giving students guidance about life and about their futures. But every student comes into the classroom with his or her own personal background. When I thought about my own background, I realized that I had a pretty good life. I had good upbringing. I had two parents. I went to a decent school. I ate well. But I felt like I had lived in a small world. I hadn't really gone out and seen the world or experienced very much. So, I didn't think that I would be able to provide the proper guidance for students, given the lack of variety in my own background.

I realized that before I got into teaching, it might be a good idea to see the world and gain some life experience, to experience some hardship or at least know what it means to struggle a little bit. Also, I wanted to learn about the different value systems in the world. One of my upperclassmen told me about the Japan Overseas Cooperation Volunteers (currently called JICA Overseas Cooperation Volunteers). I learned that there might be an opportunity to teach baseball to children in developing countries. Since I wanted to become a baseball coach as well as a teacher, I thought this would be a good place for me to gain some valuable experience, learn a lot about myself, and learn about coaching as well.

After I graduated in 2005, I went to the Republic of South Africa for two years through the Japan International Cooperation Agency (JICA) program to teach baseball to children. Some of the children had to walk for two hours to come to practice, and many were poor and did not have enough money for equipment. Apartheid had only officially ended ten years before, so there were issues with racism. Whites and Blacks did not live together or socialize. Sports venues were one of the few places where whites and Blacks could mix and spend time together.

Through playing the game and through competitions, I saw the students grow. I saw them gain skills. I actually saw whites and Blacks spending time together and some racial barriers being broken down. I could see that sports had the power to do that. I realized that if a proper environment is set up for the sport to be played, it can have a huge impact on those involved.

But the reality in South Africa was that the environment was not very good. There were the remnants of apartheid, and unemployment was a problem. My students loved the game so much, and it was wonderful that they found this new love of baseball, but many had to quit for reasons that were out of their control. I realized just how hard it is to set up an environment in which the game can be played so that the benefits could be obtained. It also made me think about the huge gap between their environment and the very blessed environment that I grew up in. That got me thinking about how I could bridge that gap.

So, I went out to South Africa with the intention of gaining experience to prepare myself for my career. But as I spent more time there, I started to realize that it wasn't about me. I started asking myself, *What can I do to make positive contributions to society?* From my experience, I came to believe that it is possible to improve society through sports. So, I decided to make creating a better society through sports the major theme in my life.

While I was in South Africa, I blogged about my experiences. An upperclassman from my university who was working in the human resources department for the Yomiuri Giants read it, and he talked to people there about it. When I came back to Japan, the Giants asked me to come in and talk to them, and they hired me.

My first job was in marketing. It was mostly about gathering data from fans and trying to increase attendance at the games at Tokyo Dome. When fans came to games at the Dome, they could receive a member's card. Every time they came to Tokyo Dome, we would scan it, and they would receive points for coming to games. They could trade those points for merchandise or tickets. The card also enabled us to collect data about who was coming and how often they were coming.

From this data, we found that roughly 65 percent of the attendees were male and 35 percent were female. Also, we found a large number of fans were in their forties and fifties, but there were not many in their thirties. There were also a lot of fans in their teens and twenties. What we determined from that data was that many fans came to the games as families. Parents brought their kids, and that's why people in their fifties and the people in their teens and twenties were regular attendees. We also realized that the people who were in their thirties in 2008 were kids when J.League professional soccer made its entry into Japan and gained popularity. So, this demographic became soccer fans, and that's why we didn't have as many fans who were in their thirties.

We also were able to pull data on how often fans were coming to the games. We found a sample of people who used to come to games but had not come in a while. So, we focused our marketing on bringing these people back. We sent out postcards to these people's home addresses with an offer that if they brought the postcard back the next time they came to the game, they would receive some kind of limited-edition merchandise. It was a fairly successful way to get people to come back.

Although I centered on marketing, I still had the desire to create a better future through the power of sports. So, I helped launch the social-contribution project G Hands and helped create a partnership between the Giants and JICA.

Athletes can influence people and spread the word about certain things more quickly and in a more powerful way than others can. Although the players were already involved in various charitable activities on their own, like donating to kids in need, visiting hospitals, those types of things, I felt we could do something as an organization to support them officially and consolidate their efforts. That was the motivation behind setting up G Hands in 2015.

Through G Hands, the Giants organized and supported a variety of social programs and relief efforts. For example, we helped in a campaign about bone marrow donations. With professional athletes helping spread the word,

Noamichi Yokota. Courtesy of Noamichi Yokota.

charities were able to get more donors because of the players' influence. We collected clothes and towels that we no longer needed, and instead of just throwing them out, gave them to people who truly needed them.

G Hands also supports sports for people with handicaps. We not only donated equipment but also held events—not just baseball events but also soccer for the blind or soccer for people who have only one leg, various things like that. We would invite players to these events, and this would help to raise awareness. We invited people with no physical challenges to come to these events and try to play these sports with a simulated handicap. So, it wasn't just about the money. Of course, the financial donations were very important, but it was not only about that. It was also about raising awareness, about breaking down the walls between the people with handicaps and the people that came to these events.

When Tokyo received the right to host the Olympics, Prime Minister Shinzo Abe made a public commitment that these Olympics would be about the growth and development of sports in the world. In South Africa the kids I got to work with became obsessed with baseball. They really loved it. Based on that experience, I was pretty confident that it could become a popular sport in other countries. With my connection with the Giants and my past association with JICA, I thought that I could help grow the appreciation for baseball worldwide. So, I talked to the team about my vision and my hopes.

As part of the program we set up, Giants coaches have traveled and conducted baseball clinics in about ten countries. These included Costa Rica, Argentina, the Philippines, Malaysia, Fiji, and Tanzania. And then, with the help of JICA, representatives from some of these countries came to Japan to learn more about baseball through the Giants organization.

Major League Baseball is also going to different countries to try to grow the game. When I was in South Africa, I had an opportunity to work alongside people from MLB, and I came to realize the different approaches between MLB and Japan. The MLB approach was to find talent and to bring that talent to the United States. For example, if there were one hundred players in a league, they would look for the one or two that might be capable of playing in Major League Baseball. On the other hand, Japanese baseball culture is more focused on education through baseball. Rather than pulling the top two and trying to get them over to Japan, it's more about teaching the entire group and giving them skills that they can use, whether they continue in baseball or not. The Japanese approach focuses on establishing baseball in those countries themselves, and not just pulling the talent out of those countries.

I actually got to work in Major League Baseball for a year. The Yankees and the Yomiuri Giants have a partnership. They have a program in which the Giants dispatch somebody to the Yankees for one year, and I was chosen to be that person. I helped in the Yankees marketing department. Specifically, I was looking at how to bring the Japanese residents of New York, of which there were some sixty thousand, to the stadium and how to target them. Also, because New York has a Japanese-language newspaper, I was translating things into Japanese to be put in that newspaper.

I was impressed with the level of professionalism that goes into the sports business world in New York. In all aspects of operations, whether it was marketing, tickets, or broadcasting, employees did the job very professionally and worked very hard. That's something that I really respected about the team, and I noticed the gap between how they did things versus how things are done in Japan. In the case of the Giants, the parent company is the *Yomiuri Newspaper*, and the Giants are just a piece of it. So, when it comes to filling jobs, people from the parent company would come down to the Giants to become part of the Giants staff, even if they were not trained in the world of sports. Whereas in America, they're very professional. They have the specific skills to do that exact job. So, I really respected how they ran their team as a business.

Of course, America is a land of diversity, but I was impressed with the way the Yankees as an organization and as a business embraced it. They were able to give the appropriate attention and respect and acceptance to groups such as LGBTQ, minority races, women, people with handicaps, and so forth. One example of that would be the way that the stadium is built and designed. Yankee Stadium has about forty-seven thousand seats, but they have places for between seven hundred to one thousand wheelchair users to attend their games. On the other hand, Tokyo Dome seats 45,600 for a baseball game, and they've got space for thirty wheelchairs. So, there's a big gap there. I was really impressed with how the Yankees have their eye on the community as a whole and the well-being of that community when those people attend games. I think that's really important when it comes to growing business.

I was surprised that within American society a lot of people grow up playing multiple sports. They might have played football, baseball, and basketball growing up. So, among the fan base there's this multisport mindset. People who grow up playing more than one sport later watch more than one sport. What does that mean for growing your market? Well, it means that one fan can contribute to multiple sports markets. That helps the ability to grow those markets, because you have a larger fan base. In Japan, people who play baseball typically play nothing but baseball. People who play soccer play nothing but soccer. It's a one-sport commitment. You choose your sport, and that's what you play from morning until night, year-round. And when you grow out of the sport of your youth, that's the only sport that you will attend as a fan. That makes it more difficult to grow the market, as the number of potential fans is limited.

When I returned to the Yomiuri Giants, I managed ecommerce and merchandising. The Giants play in Tokyo Dome, and they are blessed to always play to a full house. If the stadium has reached its capacity, you can't grow ticket sales, but what you can grow is the sale of merchandise. That has an unlimited ceiling. That was where the Giants wanted to focus more energy to build up that market. Up until then, the Giants were more into licensing. They would license their products and would receive a return on the sales of those products. The Giants were also not really into ecommerce at the time, even though the world was becoming more digitalized. So, I was responsible for setting up an ecommerce system. This required risk on the part of the Giants, as there was an investment that had to be made, but there would be better returns on this than they were getting on licensing products.

Our top seller was jersey uniforms of individual players. We used to order the uniforms from the manufacturers at the beginning of the season. But that was not ideal because some players' jerseys would sell out immediately and others would not sell nearly enough. But now we have an on-demand system. We have a rough idea of what the demand might be, but then we also have an unlimited supply of the ones that the fans really want. That system increased sales significantly.

Another big seller is what we call "hot market" items. This means creating merchandise that will sell immediately, while it's hot. An example of that might be when a player sets a record or reaches a milestone or makes an epic play that fans are going to want to remember. I was able to set up a built-to-order manufacturing system. Back in the day, it was not possible to make things that quickly, but now, almost immediately after these events occur, we have products that can be sold while that event is still hot.

Even though our fan-base demographics are 65 percent male to 35 percent female, when it comes to merchandise, women tend to buy a little bit more than men. So we target that audience a little bit more. There definitely is a market for kawaii items, especially among female buyers. We take advantage of that by trying to create different products that will fit into that category. One example that was rather successful was turning the players into cute animals, giving them an animal motif. Hayato Sakamoto became a kawaii, or cute, lion. That was a really big hit. We put the players' animal faces on various merchandise products, like furry tote bags, key chains, hair bands, and plushy hand puppets.

The players receive payment for the merchandise that has their name or their image on it. For that reason, almost all of our merchandise features current players. Even though the Giants have a storied history, we rarely sell merchandise featuring former players because there are no contracts in place with them. Therefore, that type of merchandise is not made available. From time to time, however, if there's a special event, the team will contact a former player and make an agreement to produce a certain amount of merchandise that they'll be able to sell. But that's not a regular occurrence.

In recent years, we've been thinking more about sustainability and the environment when it comes to producing merchandise. For example, if we make uniforms of certain player and then that player gets injured right away or if that player retires, then we have all these extra uniforms on hand. We can't keep them on the shelves, so we would throw them away. Now, we try harder to find the balance between supply and demand to make sure that we are in line with sustainability and care of the environment. That has become a big challenge in recent years.

Of course, I'm of the belief that sports have the power to make society better. From my way of thinking, sports play seven important roles in the world. The first one is the most basic one, and that would be health. Second—and this one is especially true in Japan—is the power to educate people. The third one is leisure. The fourth one is sports as a business, which provides employment. The fifth one is that it creates community, it encourages interaction between people, it crosses borders, and it results in new relationships. A perfect example of that is between you and me. The relationship we have formed here is through sports. The sixth one is to make improvements to society. This comes in the form of teams', or players', campaigns for social causes—for example, raising awareness of AIDS or helping to reduce poverty, things like this. And the seventh way sports benefit society—and this is especially true in more recent years—is the technology that is coming out of sports that is then able to help people in other ways. You put those seven together, and sports as an infrastructure has an extremely powerful role in the world. So, you could very simply say that better sports make a better society.

23 / Ryozo Kato, NPB Commissioner

After graduating from Tokyo University, Ryozo Kato worked in the Ministry of Foreign Affairs from 1965 to 2008. He served as Japan's ambassador to the United States from 2001 to 2008 and as the commissioner of Nippon Professional Baseball from 2008 to 2013.

◆

From its very beginning in 1872, baseball has been the heartstrings of the Japanese summer. It's a good game. Even the translation of *baseball*, "yakyu," is beautiful. *Yakyu* means "field ball." Field of Dreams and the green extends in all directions. *Yakyu* sounds very beautiful. Baseball fits very well with the psyche of the Japanese, the Japanese mentality. It's a good mix of fair play, but at the same time you can steal!

I hadn't seriously thought of becoming a baseball commissioner, but shortly before I resigned from being the ambassador to the United States, one of the owners inquired whether I was interested. Since I'm a great fan, a baseball nut, I thought this was a terrific idea, but at the same time I wanted second opinions. The second opinions were very much in favor of me becoming the commissioner. I won't say it's a mean occupation, but it's kind of a difficult occupation. So, I hesitated. Actually, I declined two times. Then, while I was in Washington DC in late 2008, there was a leak here in Japan that the next commissioner would be Kato. That made the situation difficult for me to say no. I was sort of trapped.

The history of the NPB commissioner is very different from that of the MLB commissioner. Professional baseball in Japan started as one league, then in 1950 separated into two, the Central and Pacific Leagues. During the one-league era, the owners didn't feel any need for a commissioner. They managed to deal with all sorts of problems and issues by themselves. But once they had two leagues, there were interleague legal problems, differences in rules, and other things, and a commissioner became a necessary evil.

The commissioner in Nippon Professional Baseball has no legal status. He is just one of the members of the board of NPB. He's called the commissioner because the "chairman of the board of NPB" doesn't sound great. The "commissioner of Japanese Baseball" sounds more effective and authentic. Unlike the commissioner of MLB, the NPB commissioner does not control broadcasting rights and has very little power. Naturally, the Japanese owners try to minimize the power of the commissioner, so, to the best extent possible, they can be on their own. The salary of the NPB commissioner is about one fifteenth of the MLB's commissioner.

Being the commissioner of NPB is not a very popular job. It's a headache and a pleasure: a pleasure meeting with the players; the headaches—No. 1, the owners; No. 2, the union. The commissioner's office deals with lots of complaints from teams that the umpires are not so good, and scandals, because the NPB owners don't want to get involved, such as the yakuza and drugs. Dealing with the yakuza was one of the few things that was successfully accomplished, mainly with the help of the Yomiuri Giants. There used to be many yakuza at baseball games. They would buy up all the tickets before the games and resell them at higher prices. This was really a bad thing for children. The kids would stand in the line for tickets, but they would be all sold out. With the help of the police, we could easily identify who these guys were, so the girls selling tickets behind the glass could recognize them and not sell to them. These days you don't see many yakuza around—way less compared to twenty years ago—and they are reduced to almost nothing at Tokyo Dome and Koshien Stadium.

When teams go to other cities, the players are often entertained by guys associated with the yakuza. It's very difficult to prevent that from taking place. Therefore, each year in the month of February or March, we have a two-day session for the players in Tokyo, where we tell them to be careful about the yakuza and corruption, as well as honey traps and tax evasion. Every player has to attend, and they get a certificate to show that they completed it.

Steroids are not as big a problem in NPB as in the United States—much less. Most of the players are Japanese, and they tend to abide by the rules. But unintentionally they may take medicines that contain banned drugs, including eye drops. Drugs for capacity enhancement are illegal, but what is for medical use is okay under the Japanese rules. Hirokazu Ibata once became caught up in that kind of situation. I talked in-depth with him, and I found it was genuinely for the cure of his eyesight. After collecting all sorts of evidence, I said, "He's innocent."

There were other very dubious cases involving steroids and supplements. These were kept quiet, but there were lots of rumors inside the baseball world: "He's a drug guy." But some players, foreign and Latin players, used steroids beyond the limit. It's such a tempting thing, you know. There's such severe competition. So, it's tempting to take them. I understand that, but a rule is a rule, and they are hazardous to your life. Steroids are dangerous. These players were called into the office and suspended for fifty games. But that hurts the players, yes? They have to be in there consistently, otherwise their skills decline very quickly. That kind of penalty is not productive, but you must do it.

The commissioner's office also deals with labor relations. Japanese people don't like a real fight. We always try to be benign, so by and large dealing with the players union was not so difficult. But at the same time when it came to the philosophical level, I had difficulty persuading the union. For example, after the big Tohoku Earthquake on March 11, 2011, the players union said, "We'd like to have a period of mourning, when we don't do anything—no games, nothing." I thought it should be the other way around at that difficult time. People impacted by the earthquake might wish to know what's going on in baseball. Just reading a newspaper article, that someone had an exceptional game and hit two home runs and he's a big prospect this year, kind of helps. But the union thought, "Now is not the time to play baseball. It's insulting to the suffering people. We should just suspend play." Some of the players said, "I'm ready to go there to help dig up things."

And I told them, "I appreciate your enthusiasm to help people by yourself, but you're useless this soon after the earthquake devastation. There's nothing much that you can do."

But they didn't listen. They're straightforward and single-minded, but not knowledgeable. That was a headache.

The work stoppage spilled over into the end of March, and the season opening was delayed. I think it was stupid. Also, I told them—which they couldn't understand at all—that baseball is a very important part of Japan, and if baseball resumed in Japan, it would send a very important message to the world, that Japan was all right. Look at the United States after 9/11.

They restarted games just six days later, and it encouraged people go back to everyday life. Resuming baseball in Japan would send a similar message, that Japan was not beaten by the natural disaster. We are back, healthy. See, that's very important, But they couldn't understand that kind of message.

I also had trouble with the players union over the WBC in 2013. Takahiro Arai of the Hanshin Tigers, who was the president of the players union, said, "We don't want to participate in the World Baseball Classic under the current conditions. For us to participate, the conditions toward Japan need to be improved." I told them that I shared their feeling, but they must understand that the WBC games are hosted by Major League Baseball. They pay all the expenses for the teams, and they even offered to pay for the Japanese team. We declined to receive it, and we send people on our own. Only Japan is doing that because we are a member of the G7, and therefore we should be a little bit different from the others. It's a sense of pride. But with the expense that Major League Baseball is shouldering, there's a limit in a realistic sense what Japan can require as a share. But they were still ready to boycott the games. But you see, that's not the way to treat the Japanese baseball fans who are anxious to see our best baseball team. Finally, the players agreed to participate. Arai didn't know much about the facts, but for the Japanese baseball fans Arai is a hero; the commissioner is not.

The WBC is very popular in Japan. The fans are always anxious to see the WBC games. Most of the Central League owners are supportive, but the Pacific League owners, if not negative, are indifferent. They're more concerned about the condition of their players. There have been many individual complaints: bad shoulders, hurt arms, backaches.

Shortly after the 2009 World Baseball Classic, the players complained that the baseballs in Japan were very different from the MLB balls. They said, "Let's try to unify the Major League baseball and the Japanese traditional baseball." I thought that was a very good idea because each time the Japanese team participated in the World Baseball Classic, several players became injured, and one of the reasons seems to be a difference in the baseballs. I think that Japanese baseballs are better quality. They are more expensive. Their stitches are well made, and the leather is softer and dry, not slippery. We use the best part of the cow for the leather. In America they just don't care, so some balls are very good, and some balls are not so good.

Ryozo Kato with Robert Fitts. Courtesy of Robert K. Fitts.

At that time, there were four or five different types of baseballs approved for use in NPB. The was a rumor that one team in Kansai used two different kinds of baseballs in the same game: dead balls when they were on the defensive and lively balls when they were on the offensive. That's unfair. But there was nothing in the rule book against it. Many players noticed it, but most of the players are not that brave, and nobody made an official complaint. But some whispered, and it came to my ears. Tsuneo Horiuchi, the former Giants 200-game winner, is a very extroverted guy, and he said that before you talk about the unification of Major League baseballs and

Japanese baseballs, first let's deal with Japanese baseballs. Four or five different balls is a shame.

In 2011 we introduced the new official NPB ball made by Mizuno through a transparent process. The commissioner's office made it clear that the new baseball would carry less than previous ones, and when the new season started, home run output was significantly down. The majority of the fans and owners were not happy about the new baseballs because home runs are a popular thing. Everybody welcomes home runs, right? The secretary general of NPB and I started to discuss the need to make the baseballs a little bit livelier. We agreed that the balls should be slightly modified, but the exact specs should be further discussed and that the rules should not be changed too soon or too quickly. But without my knowledge, the Japanese balls were quietly juiced up. During the 2013 season, home run output seemed to be up. In June the secretary general, in response to a question from the press, said that the baseballs had already been modified to become livelier. The press immediately started to accuse me that I, as commissioner knowing that the baseball being changed, had been hiding the fact. I told them that I had not okayed the change and was unaware that the baseballs had already been modified and that telling a lie is against my principles. Nonetheless, the players union called for my resignation. Even though a third-party commission report said that there was no evidence that I had known about the modification of the baseball, I decided to leave the office because the issue had been blown out of proportion and was becoming a distraction to baseball. But even now, the Japanese ball still carries further than the Major League baseballs. So therefore, we will continue to see the Japanese players who go to the Major Leagues have their home run output go down significantly.

When I became commissioner, I had two goals, but I was unable to achieve either. I would have liked to see the barriers between amateur baseball and professional baseball in Japan lowered. Baseball developed in Japan in a very different way compared to the United States, which started in the community. But here in Japan it was started by academics. Horace Wilson came to Japan in 1871–72 shortly after he fought in the Civil War. He became an English teacher for high schoolers. It started from that and expanded to other high schools and colleges. These amateurs looked down upon professional baseball as a mean occupation. Playing baseball for money was considered immoral. Amateur baseball, and especially the Waseda and Keio games, were far more popular than professional baseball up to the middle of the 1950s. It was only after Shigeo Nagashima joined the Giants and Sadaharu Oh joined him the next year that professional baseball became more popular. These days, amateur baseball and university baseball are no longer very popular. But the amateur baseball people continue to look down upon the professional baseball league as a kind of indecent occupation. As a result, professionals are not allowed to coach amateurs. Mr. Nagashima, for example, was not allowed to coach his son, even at home. I wanted to take out this barrier between amateurs and the professional baseball completely, but I could not.

I also wanted to see the expansion of Japanese baseball, like Major League Baseball, to other parts of the world and the realization of a United States—Japan real World Series. The World Series is not really a World Series. It's a U.S. series. The WBC is there, but it's a neither-fish-nor-fowl kind of thing. It's before the season. Wouldn't you like to have a champion-to-champion tournament after the postseason? It's the very simple and natural extension of the desire of Japanese baseball fans. Bud Selig was genuinely interested to a significant extent, but I didn't have much backing from the Japanese owners. The Giants, Hiroshima, and the Seibu Lions were the only three among the twelve that were interested. The others thought that it was a burden on the players—too long of a season. They don't try to pursue their dreams because, you see, the biggest difference between Major League Baseball and Japanese professional baseball is the owners. American owners really love baseball. They're baseball nuts. In Japan, the teams are owned by companies and corporations, and the professional baseball teams are the propaganda arm of these companies.

Now, I think the most fundamental challenge to Japanese baseball is the declining population. Ten years ago, at least four thousand high schools in Japan had baseball clubs, and they competed for Koshien, but now it's decreased by a third or something like that. It's still the largest number in Asia and in the Pacific, but it's a clear decline. Baseball is also becoming a relatively expensive game: the uniforms, the bats, the gloves. It's much too commercialized. When I was a kid, I used to play bare-handed. In addition, the atmosphere in Japan is not so baseball friendly. For example, they prohibit baseball being played at school grounds because they are afraid that if the ball is hit too far it might break the windows. They say that it's a dangerous game. That is a fundamental difficulty.

But headache No. 1 for baseball is population decline and how to deal with it. Maybe extend baseball in Asia—not just in Korea, Taiwan, and China but also to East Asia and Southeast Asia and even India and eventually, this is sort of a dream, Africa. You see, if we're talking declining population, it's only in North Asia and advanced countries. In Africa the population is 1.2 billion. They need enjoyment, and baseball can play some role. I recently talked with Sadaharu Oh about the possibility of inviting African kids to participate in the World Children's Baseball Games. We don't have enough funds to invite an African team, but we can invite individual players. He thought it was good idea. It's a matter of the strength of the wish and the willpower.

If Major League Baseball wants to increase its presence in Asia, it is more than welcome. The United States is a superpower, the No. 1 country on the face of the earth because the United States always tries to solve problems. See, many people can identify problems. They can make some comments, but they can't solve the problems. The United States does all these things in different ways of life. I hope they can persuade China and India to be a bigger part of world baseball.

NPB can overcome our declining population by expanding into Asia. The owners should have a commitment to baseball as such, not just as part of their businesses, and they should figure out how to increase the size of the pie instead of trying to get a bigger share of the pie. We need more pie bakers, not just eaters. One way to do that would be to make Taiwanese and Korean teams part of Japanese baseball and part of the pennant race. Think of an Asian baseball league with the winner playing in the World Series against the United States. That is my dream. It's not impossible.

24 / Edwin Dominguez Alvarez, Agent

After working in the Dominican Republic's diplomatic corps, Edwin Dominguez founded DTO Sports & Entertainment in 2015. He works as a player agent specializing in bringing Latin players to Asia.

◆

My firm, DTO Sports & Entertainment, focuses on placing young Latin American ballplayers in the Japanese and other Asian professional leagues. At first, we were solely in Japan, but last year we were able to place a client in the CPBL with the Chinatrust Brothers. And this year we have a client in the Korean Baseball Organization (KBO) with the Samsung Lions, so it's expanding beyond Japan. My agency is very player-centered. It's about understanding a player's needs and being able to customize the service toward each individual player's needs. Being based in Japan, I'm able to follow up with my clients and give them as much 360 servicing as possible. I go beyond the contract negotiation; I help with client-management services and even the cultural adaptation and the process of companionship, which I think is very important. That's what has really given me the opportunity to establish myself in the market, because this industry has a lot of big fishes and a lot of big corporations, and I have to compete with all of them. But players see the value in having someone right next to them who understands the country specifics. That's how I've been able to keep the business growing.

Many of the Asian teams are interested in Latin players because they often have an easier time adapting to Japanese baseball. They've already done it once when they made the cultural adaptation to the United States. I was in Okinawa for spring camp earlier this year, and a club executive brought this up. His team went all-Latino this year. They brought in five Latin players. In many cases when Latin players come to Japan, they are more open-minded and hungrier to keep accomplishing their career goals or financial goals. There are different expectations in terms of what Latin players want to earn throughout their playing career, because usually after they're done they rely on what they made as a player. American players with a higher level of education, more financial resources, and other types of exposure can walk out of the game at an earlier age and bump into other productive endeavors. Also, many Latin players come from more challenging conditions, like having to move overseas younger, and sometimes that translates into adjusting better in Japan.

I'm originally from the Dominican Republic, born and raised. In the DR, the process of trying to turn somebody into a future pro player starts at a very early age. My baseball career started when I was seven years old. All through my high school years, I had tryouts with MLB teams and a lot of back and forth. That gave me inside information on how the system works from the grassroots level. I wasn't able to sign a pro contract, but I did get a scholarship to go to a junior college in Iowa. I transferred to Hannibal-LaGrange University, a four-year private school in Missouri, and was an all-conference DH. But once I graduated with my bachelor's degree, it was kind of over for me as a player. After college, I entered the foreign service and became the assistant to the Dominican ambassador in Japan. While I was doing that, I had the opportunity to go to school in Japan and get an international business and economics master's degree.

Soon after I arrived in Japan, I saw my first game. I was invited as a guest because I was part of the embassy. They gave me a field pass, enabling me to go down and really soak it in. There was this Ohtani dude whom you are probably familiar with. I remember all the fuss about the guy. After the game started, I just enjoyed the whole experience: the crowd, the constant entertainment. I felt it was like coming out to a concert. It's constant, and it's fun. You don't get a dull moment. You're immersed in the experience. Even after all the games I've been to since then, it never ceases to amaze.

I like the tradition, the way the baseball still feels historical. It goes back to the roots. Some people observe it in terms of playing small ball and playing the fundamentals and so on, but I'll say as a person who goes to the stadium both for work but also just to enjoy the overall experience, it's the consistency of the traditions of the game: the way they practice, the way spring training starts each year on February 1, the way some of cheering songs from the stands go back decades—they just change the players' names. These things keep it very consistent. When you see footage from NPB thirty to forty years ago, there are still many similarities in terms of the essence of the game. I think being able to maintain that is a reflection of Japanese society. It blends well with what Japan does, which is maintaining its traditions and values as it embraces modernity. Living in Tokyo—that's something I experience every day. You are walking through high rises, lots of buildings, lots of corporations, and then you bump into a temple and a park. There's always that blend of the traditional and the modern. In Japan, I like the fact that traditions and the values of the game are more protected. MLB has turned into a much bigger industry, but I feel it goes a little bit too quick in terms of adjusting to new trends, and then the identity of the traditional sport gets lost.

When I got to Japan in 2016 after I finished school in the States, some of my acquaintances in the DR started sending me messages like, "Hey man, you're in Japan, and I have this player. Can you get him a job?" I was like, "I haven't thought about that, but why not give it a try?" I just started cold-calling NPB teams. I got some assistance with the language barrier, and I could tell that pretty much all the twelve teams were open to hearing me out. I was a twenty-two-year-old from the Dominican Republic, freshly graduated from school, but I had some baseball-related background. I was able to visit the Yomiuri Giants, the Yokohama BayStars, and the Nippon Ham Fighters. I gave them good intel, but it wasn't good enough to make a deal at that point. It was a learning process.

After that point, I did my research, and I bumped into the independent league teams, which I wasn't familiar with before. I got connected with the Toyama Thunderbirds. It was already 2017 at that point. I took the bullet train, gave them a sales pitch about the players I was representing. (It was not even that formal; it was me promoting a friend of a friend.) They decided to make an offer, and I signed two players with the Thunderbirds that year. After making those deals, I got connected with the Tokushima Indigo Socks, which is another independent league team, and we did two contracts that year as well. Francisco Peguero, one of the guys who signed with the Thunderbirds, had a big year. He hit .380 and broke the single-season hits record. So, he got a contract with the Chiba Lotte Marines for the next season. He was my first NPB player. Subsequently, I was hired by Bryan Rodriguez during the 2019–20 off-season to be his agent while he was preparing to negotiate a contract renewal with the Nippon Ham Fighters, and I have been his agent ever since. (The year 2024 is my fifth season representing him.) Everything kind of came in together. I wasn't looking to become an agent, but it excited me because it gave me the opportunity to get back to baseball. I finished my diplomatic duty in 2021. At that point, I made DTO my official, full-time job and business. That's how it started. I didn't go to school for it, and I wasn't planning to do it. It just came to be.

In the States, you have to be a certified agent with the players union to represent big league and Minor League players or players who are coming from overseas as free agents. But in Japan and NPB that works differently. As a foreign agent, I have never been required by any NPB team to be part of the NPB players union. As long as you build the trust, you build a relationship and the credibility, and you have some documentation that you're representing the player who teams want, then there's a chance they will talk to you.

I am fortunate that all the NPB teams I have been interacting with have been very respectful. The communication lines have always been open, and that helps a lot. It's not like, "Okay, you don't have anything now; we don't want to hear back from you." They give me the chance to keep coming, and I always try to keep coming back better. Even if I don't talk to a team for months, when I come to them, I want to have something of value. I think that keeps the relationship alive and healthy.

So far, I've only had two Japanese-born clients. There's not really a database where you can verify information, but I think that only about 10 percent of the Japanese NPB players have agents. There's a strong relationship between Japanese-born players and their clubs. Having an agent is frowned upon unless you become a big star and it becomes a necessity. They'll understand at that point, but if you haven't reached that level, it's frowned upon, and there's a lot of peer pressure about how to do things and when to do them in Japan.

Once a player gets drafted by an NPB club, the team has seven years of domestic rights over the player. (Players can become international free agents after their ninth year.) After that, the player has the opportunity to test out domestic free agency, although many players do not, because either they don't have an agent or just the peer pressure to stay with the organization that drafted them. They think twice before even deciding to test out free agency.

Edwin Dominguez Alvarez. Courtesy of Edwin Dominguez Alvarez.

In terms of salary, there is a yearly assessment, and how much a team pays a player depends on performance. It's pretty much set by the team. It can even go down. Based on the NPB uniform contract, it can go down as much as 40 percent from the previous year. Each team has a salary assessor. These days, they run a lot of data and use analytics to define the value of a player. But also, the player's brand popularity factors into what he is paid. So, stars get paid for what they do on the field, but they also get remuneration because of what they represent for the whole brand as a business. Guys get compensated well at an early age if they are already contributing at a very high level. That doesn't happen necessarily in the MLB ecosystem because they are under the prearbitration and then the arbitration system, and then they're able to hit free agency. So, even though NPB teams have a lot of control over contracts whenever a player reaches stardom quickly, his salary goes up quickly as well.

If a player rejects the team's offer, he can go to arbitration. Arbitration is handled by the commissioner's office, and the ruling is final. You don't get to see many arbitration cases because of the ongoing dynamics within the industry. Players are highly remunerated, and there is an expectation for players to follow what their predecessors did. If player XYZ didn't ask for that amount, why would you ask for that if you're not at his level? So, there's a lot of cautiousness there.

There are several avenues for a foreign player to come to Japan. Heading into the offseason, the players who are at the top of the NPB teams' lists are guys who had a very solid AAA year and will become free agents after the season is done. They have to decide, *Should I take another Minor League deal with a spring training invitation, or should I take the opportunity and test out Japan?* The NPB teams structure their rosters around these players.

To fill out their rosters, NPB scouts will go to the winter leagues, mostly the Dominican Winter League, which has the one of the most competitive levels, but also Venezuela, to look for talent. During the season, the NPB teams will look again at AAA players who have opt-outs or buyouts in their contracts in case they need to bring them over to replace an injured or underperforming player. Another group of foreigners is already playing in the Japanese independent leagues. They already have work visas. If they are playing well and an NPB team suffers a midseason injury, they are sometimes signed. Younger players also can be signed and brought over to Japan on a development player contract, which is basically a nonroster player, a trainee player. A few times a year, NPB teams host tryouts in the DR to look for these players, or they might come out of the Carp Academy in the DR. Those are the main ways in which foreign players can end up in NPB.

As an agent, you need a clear vision of your goals. If I try to go over all available players without having a strategic outlook, then it's difficult to have some level of success. There are many different personalities. There are different markets, and there are many different situations you need to understand as an agent to find the right fit. For example, one of my clients, Geronimo Franzua, played several years with the Hiroshima Toyo Carp, and now he's with the Pittsburgh Pirates. He's set to begin the year with the Triple-A club in Indianapolis, but we are expecting him to get the call up in 2025. For me, that's a way to see some of my clients going into the big leagues—having a guy come to Japan, have some success, and if we get the opportunity to go back to the States, we do that. That's a better business model for me than trying to sign a kid in rookie ball in the States, wait five to seven years, hoping he makes it to the big leagues, and then go through prearbitration and arbitration.

A big part of the recruitment process for me as an agent is being able to identify which player is going to gather interest from NPB clubs. I then want to see if that player is available and if we are willing to make a deal. Other times, I already represent a player, and I do the promotion and the shopping around, and I put the player on a team's mind. Then I need to be strategic in terms of understanding what a team needs at a given point and what's their budget.

Occasionally, one player can gather interest from two or three clubs, but that's not the standard. Usually, when a player gets approached by an NPB team, that team is very serious about him. As an agent, you need to understand that to carry out the negotiations, you don't want to overplay your hand because the way of negotiating in Japan is more of trying to find a mutually beneficial agreement. You need to understand that they do a lot of work before coming to a player and making him an offer. It's a process that may take an entire season. You may well say, "Why all the fuss if you're only giving him $800K or $1 million per year," but that's their priority project for that off-season, and as an agent you have to be respectful of that process. You also have to understand that even though they speak English and some even have lived in the States, they are still Japanese and have their own way of doing things. As long as you can respect that throughout the negotiation, there's a better chance that it's going to go smoothly.

As I mentioned before, because I'm in Japan I am able to support my clients when they come here. Each player is different, and they are grown, mature men, but I'm here by their sides as much as I can be. I think a baseball player needs to get enough support to be able to concentrate and actually play baseball, which is very hard. Living in Japan as a foreign person, there's a lot of stuff that is going to create noise just because it's different. I came to the conclusion that it's not good or bad; it's just different. And you need to understand that it's different. You've got to adjust to it, and it helps having someone who can give you that perspective. So, I do as much as I can do for the player so that he can focus on baseball.

Usually, the players just have minor problems. One that's common is that when a player signs a contract, he will want to post it on social media. But Japanese teams like to be the ones to make the official announcement. Sometimes, the players forget and post it themselves, or they put something on social media, and the teams don't like that. The teams usually kindly ask, "Please take it down until we formally announce it." Luckily it hasn't gone further than that.

In terms of NPB teams, you rarely see big problems because they have international departments, and the players have interpreters, and there's more support. But I can tell you with the independent teams, since there are limited budgets and a wider gap in terms of the cultures, I've had different experiences. I brought in a player to an industrial league team, and they prepared him a room in a dorm. They prepared him a Japanese-style bed on the floor. And he calls me like, "Hey, man, I'm going back home. Like I can't do this. I can't sleep on the floor." I was able to go in the next day and figure it out. I got the team to buy him a Western-style bed and a TV and get Wi-Fi and all that minor stuff. But if you don't have someone who is able to fix those situations, things can go south very quickly.

But all the cultural support and adaptation doesn't mean much unless I can get a deal for the player. I've got to get him a deal and get him the best deal I possibly can. To do that, I need to understand my client and the market and have a strong understanding of negotiation skills. The player relationship really forms itself once there's a deal done.

As a baseball agent, it's also important to understand the game. By understanding the game, you're able to understand the players. I always say that the heart of the show, the center of the industry, are the players, and we are all around the players in some way or form, as an agent, as a coach, as a team executive, as a writer. But it all comes back to the players. They are the protagonists and we're just supporting them. And at that point, just enjoy the show.

25 / Tatsuo Shinke, Sport Cards

Tatsuo Shinke has worked in the sports-card industry since 2000. He worked for BBM and Upper Deck before joining Mint in 2010.

◆

My first sports card was an Upper Deck NBA card from the 1993–94 season. I've been a fan since then. I remember a small NBA apparel shop called Buzzer Beater in the area of Shinsaibashi in Osaka, known for its many Western clothing stores in Amerikamura. Although the store no longer exists, it used to sell a few cards, along with jerseys and T-shirts. I bought an Upper Deck pack for 300 yen and found a wonderfully cool regular Michael Jordan card in it, which made us cheer. Then, the shop owner showed us a Beckett magazine and pointed to the section where that card was listed. Seeing the number 3.00, I thought it meant $300, which was roughly 30,000 yen at the time's exchange rate, and we cheered even louder. We were first-year high school students and didn't know that a decimal is placed between dollars and cents. The shop owner quickly explained it to us, but the fact that a card worth 300 yen came out of a 300-yen pack, and that it was listed in the price guide, was a very exciting experience for me. Above all, that Michael Jordan card was very beautiful and cool.

I immediately started looking for other card shops in the area. I found that there were two or three more specialized shops nearby. However, all of them were located in very narrow spaces inside mixed-use buildings, which, for me, required courage to enter. The prospect of talking to unfamiliar adults was all the more daunting, as I wasn't accustomed to such interactions.

By the time I graduated from university, I wanted to turn this hobby into a career and dreamed of owning my own shop. I started looking for work in card shops. By then, there were chain card shops with several stores across Japan. I directly approached the owner of a card shop in my local Kansai region and sent my resume to shops in Tokyo and made phone calls in search of a job. However, none of them hired me. Reluctantly, I applied for a part-time job at World Sports Plaza, a chain store with about twenty outlets nationwide dealing in sports apparel and goods.

The store was owned by a company called Japan Sports Vision, which was founded in 1989 for importing and selling videotapes of sports from around the world. By the time I joined in 2000, it had become a dream company for sports enthusiasts, extensively dealing in apparel and goods related to the four major American sports, as well as domestic and international soccer and martial arts. This included trading cards and memorabilia. The company held sales licenses for the four major American sports and was also capable of manufacturing and selling original merchandise.

The manager at the time told me during the interview, "Our store used to have a large portion of its sales from trading cards, but now we have shifted to a mainly apparel-based product lineup and have grown significantly. However, if you love cards, you can engage in that area." That was the beginning of my career in this industry.

I started working on the sales floor in 2000 and, after a year and a half, was recognized for my sales achievements and became a buyer for trading cards and memorabilia at the company's headquarters. By that time, my interests had expanded well beyond the NBA to include MLB, World Wrestling Entertainment (WWE), soccer, and more. I was able to gain a variety of experiences over about two-and-a-half years. My days were long, starting at 9:00 a.m. and often not returning home until after 10:00 p.m., but they were enjoyable and fulfilling. I also spent weekends doing work-related activities, but I didn't mind at all. I feel fortunate to have been surrounded by many supportive seniors, colleagues, and business partners, both domestic and international, who helped me transition into a buyer role.

As a buyer, I worked as part of a team of four. We handled everything from deciding the order quantities for all trading-card products, memorabilia, magazines, and books to arranging distribution to our retail stores, creating point-of-purchase (POP) displays to enhance sales, developing sales staff manuals, and conducting store visits. Of course, discovering new products to add to our lineup or developing them was the most enjoyable part of this department. Since the awareness of trading cards was still quite low in Japan, creating POP displays to explain them and training sales staff were significant roles for me. It wasn't easy to get people who joined the company with an interest in apparel to take an interest in cards, and similarly, it was crucial to get customers who came in for apparel to take an interest in cards and continue purchasing them. By this time, my focus had completely shifted from collecting cards myself to getting more people to enjoy this hobby.

I was also delighted to attend card shows regularly in the United States. I fondly remember purchasing single cards of Japanese Major Leaguers and other star players at these shows and then spending nights in the hotel, sparing no time for sleep, as I priced each card. It would be incredibly satisfying to know that the Ichiro, Ken Griffey Jr., and Derek Jeter rookie cards, which passed through our hands to Japan, later scored high in grading services and increased in value. We were also able to expand the scale of our trading-card products to rival our apparel division. In 2004, however, the company went bankrupt.

After leaving Japan Sports Vision, I spent a few months helping an acquaintance who was running an online memorabilia shop. During that time, Baseball Magazine Company contacted me to see if I was interested in working for them. They are an established sports publishing house with a history of fifty years at that point. In 1991 they started producing baseball cards under the brand name BBM. Soon, BBM cards dominated the industry in Japan. At first, I declined the offer because I wanted to continue the partnership with my friends. But then I started thinking that there were no memorabilia brands in Japan like Upper Deck or Steiner. I realized that I could create something similar if I worked with Baseball Magazine. So, when they approached me again, I explained my idea, and they agreed. I joined Baseball Magazine Company in January 2005.

After a few months of preparation following my joining the company, I was able to launch the memorabilia brand BBM Authentic Collection. The smooth progress of this initiative was thanks to the support of Mr. Ikeda, the president of the company; the senior management; and the editorial staff of historic and traditional magazines like *Weekly Baseball*. The brand is similar to Upper Deck Authenticated, featuring a system that verifies the authenticity of athlete autographs through signature witnessing and anticounterfeit holograms. The plan could not have been realized without the backing of Baseball Magazine Company. In the United States the MLB players union controls the rights to the players' images on sports cards, but in Japan the teams control those rights. Baseball Magazine Company, due to its long-standing contributions to the professional baseball world, had strong contacts with the baseball teams and various sports organizations. Once the company contacted the teams, I explained the concept of the project and engaged in negotiations.

The first product of this line was memorabilia commemorating Daisuke Matsuzaka's 1,000th strikeout. This was followed by products associated with big-name players like Tomonori Maeda and Kenjiro Nomura. The BBM Authentic Collection became very popular, and the company is still running the brand, almost twenty years later.

There was a reason I wanted to realize this project. Ever since I was a primary school student, I had a fascination with autographs and always wanted one from Tatsunori Hara, whom I supported at the time, but I never had the chance to obtain it. However, I knew someone of the same age who got Hara's autograph through their parent's work connections. The idea of an opportunity to obtain an autograph stayed in my mind.

Later, when I became an NBA fan, I learned about the existence of autographed products with certificates of authenticity. However, in the early days, I think there were many such certificates whose authenticity was not certain. Amid this, Upper Deck Company introduced fully authentic products with Michael Jordan's autograph to the market. This was revolutionary for me, as I always had the idea of an opportunity to obtain an autograph in my mind.

During my time at Japan Sports Vision, there was a brand called JSV World Premium, inspired by Upper Deck, which commercialized autographed products mainly from European soccer players. The vague idea I had as a child of an opportunity to obtain an autograph without special connections or chances to meet players had come around to me, giving me the chance to create such opportunities in Japanese sports, including professional baseball.

While advancing the BBM Authentic Collection project, I also took on the role of a salesperson in the Ikebukuro district bookstores as part of the sales department. I followed the path that every newcomer in a publishing company's sales department must take. Even in this environment, there was ample opportunity for me to work in my area of expertise, trading cards. I engaged in marketing activities to help the trading-card production department create better products and significantly contributed to product development by adding my experience and knowledge from my previous job. This period was incredibly stimulating and enjoyable for me.

At that time, there was still significant resistance to including cards with serial numbers less than thirty. When gathering feedback from collectors, there were strong opinions like, "If cards with such limited serial numbers are issued, completing sets becomes impossible; I will stop collecting BBM cards." However, I strongly advocated not only for cards with less-than-thirty serial numbers but also for the inclusion of one-of-a-kind, one-of-one, cards. This was already the norm in American cards, and I wanted to bring BBM cards up to global standards.

Additionally, I was in charge of a project to include Hideki Matsui's autographed cards in BBM sets like Home Run Chronicle and Historic Collection, even though he was an active Major Leaguer. It was thought impossible to use images from his professional baseball days and get his current autograph. Hearing that President Ikeda's annual New Year interview with Mr. Matsui had become a tradition, I suggested he discuss this with Mr. Matsui. I then finalized approval with Mr. Matsui's father's office. This led to the realization of the project, and since then, cards of star players who went to the Majors have been issued in Japan.

I also conceived and worked hard to commercialize the BBM Rookie Edition Premium set that was first released in 2007. Rookie Edition Premium was a groundbreaking brand concept at the time. While products focusing on rookies, like Rookie Edition, had existed before, there was significant skepticism about products composed solely of rookies, like the Rookie Edition Premium. However, considering that rookie autograph cards are among the most popular collectibles in the trading-card industry, I conceived this project and was determined to realize it. With the cooperation of the company's team representatives and Mr. Sato, who had just joined the production department, we were able to bring this idea to fruition. For me, the fact that this concept was not even present in Major League cards was a crucial element.

The players featured in the Rookie Edition Premium were exclusively rookies of that year. The centerpiece autograph cards included both a limited vertical version and a standard horizontal version. A unique concept emerged, specific to Japan, where the vertical cards were produced in smaller

Tatsuo Shinke. Courtesy of Tatsuo Shinke.

quantities within a single product. The design, based on a simple and luxurious white theme, is still carried on in the same brand today.

When Upper Deck set up a branch in Japan in 2006, they approached me, and when the offer became serious, I decided to make the move in 2009. It was a very difficult decision to leave Baseball Magazine Company, where I had wonderful seniors and colleagues and the work was fascinating, but Upper Deck had captivated me ever since I bought that first Michael Jordan card as a teenager. I worked in the sports division. My primary role involved wholesaling NBA, MLB, NFL, and NHL cards to retail shops. We had plans to create a card game in Japan and manufacture products for Japanese professional baseball. But the Japanese office was closed before we could start. The company had lost their licenses for the NBA, MLB, and NFL. Additionally, the development of a unique card game for the Japanese market did not progress well. My career at Upper Deck was short, lasting only a year and a half, and felt somewhat unfulfilled. However, even there, I was able to meet new colleagues and business partners who were highly skilled and inspiring.

When Upper Deck decided to close its Japanese office, I went to inform the people of Mint, which was one of our wholesalers at the time, about this unfortunate news. Immediately, members of Mint approached me with the offer, "Would you like to join Mint?" In fact, I had gained experience in the sports-card industry as a store clerk and buyer, and in sales and planning and manufacturing roles for both Japanese and American manufacturers. I was contemplating looking for a different job and had already started my job search. However, Mr. Mitsutake, who was the representative of Mint at the time, passionately persuaded me by saying, "It would be a significant loss for the trading-card industry if someone with your extensive experience were to leave." His earnest invitation led me to decide to join Mint. I am still deeply grateful to him for that moment.

Mint was one of the oldest sports-card shops in Japan. It was established in April 1995, and the first store was located in Tsudanuma, a not-so-large town in Chiba Prefecture. At that time, BBM had started manufacturing professional baseball cards in full swing, and cards for the J.League, which began in 1993, were also starting to be produced. Furthermore, the debut of Hideo Nomo in MLB had created a significant buzz. Mint expanded quickly and, when I joined in 2010, had become a chain with eleven directly operated stores and nine franchise stores. The company contributed to creating the culture of sports cards in Japan.

Initially, I was placed in the sales department. Since the job wasn't particularly new to me, I was able to transition smoothly into it. Later, a senior colleague from Japan Sports Vision introduced me to a good store location in Shinjuku, leading to the opening of a new store there. I was chosen as the manager of this store. There, I implemented what are now standard practices, such as creating uniforms for the staff and setting up an individual online sales site and social-network accounts. One of the things I enjoyed most was conversing with customers while they opened packs and boxes across the counter.

At that time, Mint primarily focused on NPB baseball cards and Japanese soccer cards, with the selection of American cards being quite small. There were no graded cards then. Honestly, the appeal of the showcases was limited, and there was a noticeable decline in sales momentum.

During this challenging period for Mint, the toy company Bandai launched a card game called Pro Baseball Owners League, an internet-based game that was gradually gaining popularity. We focused significantly on this game and focused on selling single cards for the Owner's League and developed an impressive assortment. The sales of Owner's League singles were surprisingly good for us, and they managed to cover the shortcomings in other genres. The game was incredibly fun, and I thoroughly enjoyed playing it myself. I approached my former company BBM to propose the publication of a specialty magazine for this game, and once it started, I supported the editorial team. Panini's Prizm World Cup cards were released in 2014. Given the high popularity of soccer in Japan, we extensively handled this product and managed to sell volumes beyond our imagination. These products allowed Mint to continue.

I believe that sports cards in Japan have undergone significant changes since then. In the 1990s and 2000s, they were not widely known, and many stores were located in mixed-use buildings, making it intimidating for beginners to enter alone. Now, some of our stores are located in large commercial facilities within close proximity to major train stations. We also pay strong attention to the design and fixtures of our stores. Our goal is to create spaces where more people naturally enter, discover trading cards and memorabilia, engage in conversations, and deepen their affection for this hobby. This store design is our first major promotion. In addition, we continue to utilize social media, appear on TV, and advertise in various sports specialty newspapers. We also do *pack breaks*, which is when you open up packs for viewers to watch on YouTube. It's a great promotion, but in Japan pack breaks are not as popular as they are in the United States.

In 2012 we launched Mint Mall. To briefly explain Mint Mall, it's a platform where each direct store has its own individual online shop, all integrated into one. As mentioned earlier, around 2010, direct stores were not very active in buying and selling single cards. The reason for the current increase in activity can also be attributed to this. By enabling sales of single cards not only in physical stores but also online, we were able to create a more dynamic card market.

Our sales, however, are still overwhelmingly driven by in-store purchases, especially for packs and boxes. Chase cards are the main focus of pack openings, I believe. While collecting complete sets is the foundation of the hobby, it can be challenging to sustain, especially when considering the need to purchase many boxes over the years. In Japan, where living spaces are often limited, this challenge becomes even more significant. We place a strong emphasis on communication with our customers, and the habit of customers opening products in-store is quite strong. When I used to work in the store myself, I found interacting with customers to be the most enjoyable aspect. Even now, when I occasionally visit the store, I engage in conversations with customers who remember me.

Thanks to the effect of winning the World Baseball Classic, both NPB and MLB cards are very popular now. Although NBA and soccer cards are also popular, more customers are purchasing baseball cards. Graded cards have also become popular in Japan, significantly influenced by the expansion of Professional Sports Authenticator (PSA) into the country. We fully committed to PSA because I had been interested in grading services since my university days when I collected NBA cards and owned several PSA cards.

As I mentioned before, 2010 to 2014 was a difficult time to sell American cards, partly due to Mint's poor inventory. I made it a goal to increase the sales of NBA and MLB cards. Initially, our handling volume was insignificant, but through repeated promotional campaigns, we gradually increased the number of team members who shared our enthusiasm. Now, the market for American sports cards in Japan has grown significantly, and I believe Mint has become a central figure in this arena. Of course, there is still considerable room for growth.

Collectors interested in Japanese vintage cards are extremely rare, and these cards' value has not been recognized. I think we may need to focus more on Japanese vintage cards, but now they are difficult to find. The dealer who handles these cards works out of America. But modern cards of historic NPB stars sell well. Shigeo Nagashima and Sadaharu Oh are the first names that come up. Their autographed cards, which started being issued around 2010, are considered the pinnacle cards of collections. Despite these nostalgic cards, many younger fans are not well informed about the history of baseball. We need to do more to propagate the kind of card culture that revives some of that history and brings fans closer to it.

It's interesting to note that the culture of valuing rookie cards is weaker in Japan compared to the United States, and many collectors find significant value in autographed cards. Autographed cards are wonderful for fans, but it's not always healthy to be overly fixated on them. There are plenty of amazing cards without autographs. After all, the most expensive card in the world (the T-206 Honus Wagner) is one without a signature.

Two other things are different in Japan. We do not have large sports-card shows. Before the pandemic, Mint organized card shows twice a year, but only nine hundred to one thousand people would come. That is so small, nowhere near the scale of the shows you would see in America. We also no longer have a price guide in Japan. Baseball Magazine Company used to publish one, but they stopped issuing them. Now, people just check the online auction prices or even the prices in online stores to find a card's value. That's kind of the price guide now, so there are not really any plans to resuscitate a printed price guide or even create a specialized website.

Our customer base is over 90 percent male, mostly in the twenty-to-forty-year-old range, but we have many young customers under twenty. In the 1990s, if a grown man collected sport cards in Japan, the term *otaku* was commonly used. However, nowadays, you rarely hear that term. Back then, even adults who watched anime were considered otaku, but now, everyone watches Japanese anime, and most of the blockbuster movies are anime works. Hobbies, including collecting trading cards, have gained full acceptance, and I believe it has become one of Japan's important industries. In 2022 the retail market for trading cards in Japan was reported to be ¥230 billion (about $155 million) according to the Japan Toy Association. While this is a significant market, the share occupied by Japanese sports cards is still relatively small. But it is growing; Mint now has nineteen directly operated stores and seven franchise stores. New stores have been added in areas such as Shinjuku, Shibuya, Kichijoji, Kasumigaseki in Tokyo; Shinsaibashi in Osaka; Sannomiya in Kobe; and Hiroshima.

The investment aspect of trading cards is more pronounced when it comes to Pokémon cards. They are considered global assets. Japanese sports cards—while some cards like those of Shohei Ohtani have dramatically increased in value and gained international recognition—still have a relatively small investment-minded community. I remember Ohtani's 2013 BBM 1st version rookie card selling for ¥300 (about $2) each. Now, it's around ¥60,000 (about $400), and if it's graded PSA 10, it can reach ¥350,000 (about $2,350). The most valuable Japanese baseball card right now is the 2013 Rookie Edition Premium Shohei Ohtani autograph rookie insert. In 2020 during the pandemic and before Shohei's breakout season, it sold on Yahoo Japan auction site for ¥500,000 (about $3,380). That's so cheap; now I wish I had bought it. It's worth over ¥5 million (about $34,000) now—if it's a PSA 10, maybe $100,000. Seeing this, I believe it's only a matter of time before the investment mindset grows.

So, I feel that there is significant potential for growth in the Japanese sports-card market, and the future looks very promising. Starting in 2021 Topps began releasing NPB cards. They have placed their products in convenience stores, expanding the collector base, which is a positive for hobby shops like ours. MLB cards, including Shohei Ohtani's autographed cards, continue to be popular among Japanese fans. Furthermore, in April 2024 the Japanese game maker Bushiroad released an NPB card game. They have grown significantly by producing their own anime programs, promoting them, and selling card games based on them. We expect significant promotion for this NPB product, which will likely become an opportunity for many baseball fans to get closer to trading cards. This will not only benefit their card game but also existing manufacturers' trading cards.

Moreover, the presence of Japanese athletes performing at the top level in the world's sports, such as Shohei Ohtani, who is considered one of the greatest baseball players in history, adds to the bright future of this industry. In boxing, Naoya Inoue has become a top level player in discussions about pound-for-pound best. While his cards have not been released yet, figure skater Yuzuru Hanyu is also in the same category. Additionally, golfer Hideki Matsuyama won the Masters. Players like Rui Hachimura and Yuta Watanabe playing in the NBA make the NBA more accessible to Japanese fans. In soccer, numerous players are excelling in European leagues. As mentioned earlier, the trading-card market in Japan, pioneered by card games like Pokémon, is well prepared to make a leap in the sports-card genre as well. We want to continue pouring our passion into shaping this industry, working together with all companies, individuals, and customers, to achieve the hobby's leap and stable continuation.

Part 7 / **Conclusion**

26 / Bobby Valentine, Manager

Former Major League player Bobby Valentine managed the Texas Rangers, New York Mets, and Boston Red Sox as well as the Chiba Lotte Marines in 1995 and 2005–2009. He led the Marines to the championship in 2005.

◆

I went to Japan for the first time in the early 1980s. I was invited by Mizuno Sporting Goods because at that time I was thought to be the first player to use a Mizuno glove in the Major Leagues. In 1978 Mizuno's master glove maker, Nobuyoshi Tsubota, came to spring training in Florida and set up a little workshop in a Winnebago he parked on the street right outside the players' parking lot. I was riding by on my bike, and I stopped in, and Tsubota-san made me a glove. I used it from that day on. Later that season, I was going to be in the starting lineup for some reason and the game was going to be on national television. Joe Torre was our manager, and his brother Frank was the vice president of Rawlings. The game was on a Saturday, and Frank came to the stadium on Friday night. When I arrived on Saturday morning to get ready for the game, the Mizuno label was ripped off my glove! But I used it, and it was the first time a Mizuno glove was used in the Majors—or so I thought. Later, we found out that Lou Gehrig had his glove stolen during the 1934 tour, and Mizuno made him a replacement that he used when he returned to the States.

Then in 1986 I went over as a coach on the postseason All-Star tour. My first impression was that the players looked better than I thought they would. Then in 1989 I went over as part of the Japan-U.S. baseball summit that Tatsuro Hirooka put together. I got to meet a lot of the baseball hierarchy, including Shigeo Nagashima, Katsuya Nomura, and Hirooka-san. Once again, I was impressed, especially by a young player named Hiromitsu Ochiai. So, by the time I got there in 1995 to manage the Chiba Lotte Marines, I already had a good impression of Japanese baseball. Then in that first year,

I got to work with Hirooka-san. I was amazed at his knowledge and his understanding of the game. He was as spectacular a baseball man as I had ever been around. And I had been around a lot of the older baseball guys in America. I had played baseball and been a young coach on the same staff as Frank Howard and George Bamberger, and I was really close to Tommy Lasorda and Al Campanis and then later Bobby Bragan.

In the early 1990s most Americans' understanding of Japanese baseball was totally misconceived. It was based on Tom Selleck and *Mr. Baseball*—almost totally based on that and the stories that guys told from their experiences. Most of the guys were bad storytellers, and most of them had an ugly American's perspective. I think that some of the guys who could have told the story properly were never asked, or it never got into the mainstream media, which was presenting a very opinionated and uneducated view of Japanese baseball, in my opinion.

There was a lot of resistance to acknowledging the baseball culture of Japan. There was still prejudice, probably hangover effects from the war. I knew some Americans who had actually experienced World War II and had a preconceived prejudice of the Japanese being the enemy. It wasn't acceptable by my standards, but I thought it to be natural. They were very comfortable having a predetermined opinion of what the culture was and what the baseball culture was in Japan. When I went over with the Major League All-Star team in 1986, to a man they played and respected the Japanese players. They said, "Hey man, that pitcher is pretty good. Hey, this guy can hit. Hey, they're throwing from the outfield just like we are." There was a reckoning from those who were seeing without blinders on.

When I got there in '95, Japanese baseball culture had an inferiority complex. Nearly everyone believed that it was a lesser league, a lesser brand of baseball. A lot of that was based on a size and speed comparison. There wasn't that really fast guy, and there wasn't that really big guy who was born from Japanese parents. So, there was that physical inferiority, but there was also just the idea of watching a championship game from the United States on TV and having it called the World Championship and then watching your championship on TV and having it called the Japan Championship that lends itself to an inherent inferiority situation.

The same year that I first managed the Marines, Hideo Nomo came over to the States. I always thought of that as an exchange, basically the first player coming over here and the first manager going over there.[1] We did a crossover. What I was expecting when I got to Japan was an enthusiastic fandom for Nomo, a superhero trying to do something that no one had ever done before. But instead, he was treated like an outsider, and the fans and the baseball community, mainly the older baseball community, were pulling against him at the beginning and saying he would fail. I remember having conversations with Hirooka-san and others, and they thought he was going to fall on his face, and they weren't really rooting for him, which I found really amazing. Or maybe, in their hearts they were pulling for him, but they were embarrassed to come out and say it in case he failed. So, I'm not sure what the true mentality of the baseball hierarchy in Japan was at the beginning of Nomomania. I know what I heard, and I know what they said, but it's such a different culture that sometimes you have to get an interpreter to understand what's really meant.

After managing in Japan, I had an even greater appreciation of the Japanese game. I always thought it was real baseball, and then I got to experience it and I was like, "Holy cow!" When I brought the Marines to Arizona to practice in the spring of 1995, I had Nolan Ryan and Tom House come out to watch Hideki Irabu throw. He wasn't like Nomo with the whirlwind windup and the split finger that confused everyone. He was actually someone who stood out there and had a fastball better than everyone else. And he was from Japan!

When I was the Mets manager in 1997, I went to Shigeo Nagashima's spring camp, which started two weeks before we did, and I asked him if he could give me a pitcher who was not going to make the Yomiuri Giants ichi-gun (main team) so that I could take him to spring training and have him pitch for the Mets. He was like, "Why would you want to do that?" And I said because I want to show the Japanese community, as well as the U.S. community, that a guy who can't pitch for your team can pitch for mine. So, I brought over Takashi Kashiwada, and he actually pitched for the Mets and did a decent job.

Measuring change is one of the hardest things in the world to do. You look back twenty years, and you realize that things have really changed, right? When I came back to manage the Marines in the mid-2000s, it seemed that the decade between my two stints was like the 1975 to 1985 decade in the States when times were changing. There had been a kind of cultural swing. I think that Nomo going to the States allowed a freedom of spirit to be attached to baseball in Japan.

In 1995 I misunderstood why I was there. I thought I was there to teach the Japanese how to play the game, because that's what I was told when I was being interviewed for the job. They said that Hirooka knew how to play the game, but the Japanese players really didn't. As it turned out, they knew how to play the game. They just needed someone to let them know that they knew how to play the game. Ten years later when I went back, that was my mission, not teaching them how to play the game, but letting them understand that they knew it well enough to compete at any level. But by that time, Ichiro was doing his thing, and Matsui was on the Yankees, and that inferiority complex that I thought they had was no longer there.

There have been several noticeable changes since 1995, both on and off the field. One of the most challenging times of my life was getting the Japanese hierarchy to understand one thing that I thought they needed to change. They thought that a hitter should always swing down on the ball and hit ground balls because they weren't big enough and strong enough to hit home runs. I argued, "How could you say that when the guy who hit more home runs than anybody on earth was a Japanese and my size?" You don't have to be a big guy to hit it over the fence. What you need is a good swing.

But even Sadaharu Oh thought you should swing down at the ball. In 1995 I had weekly debates with Hirooka-san, who was on the same team with Oh and saw how Oh developed the swing that made him hit more home runs than anybody else who ever lived. And it was a downswing. So one time, after showing me videos in slow motion and stop action, Hirooka-san brought in a wonderfully fine-tuned samurai sword and a bundle of sticks bounded by a rope. In one of the great training exercises that Oh did with the sword, they hang this bundle of sticks, and you swing the sword, and if you swing properly, at the right angle with the right velocity, you go through that bundle as though it was a piece of paper. And if you don't, then the sword ricochets back and it might hit you in the forehead and cut your head open! They had me try it. And they were right. If you went in at the right angle, and it was a bit of a downswing with the sword, it would go through. It went through on my first attempt. Then they had me swing up at it, and it bounced off, and the ricochet almost stabbed me in my backside!

Bobby Valentine with former MLB pitcher Masato Yoshii. Courtesy of Jim Allen.

That was all cool, but then I needed another two months to explain to Hirooka how a sword has no weight at the end of it, and a bat has a weight at the end of it. These interpretive conversations were multiple and always the same. I said the same thing, and he would always agree that he understood what I was saying, but that he didn't agree with what I was saying. Then finally at the end of the year, and it was one of the most satisfying moments, he said to me, "I understand what you're saying, and I understand that you are right, but I just don't want the players to know that." There was so much time and effort invested into this philosophy of hitting in Japan that they didn't want to reverse it, so they just let it be. Luckily, some of the players kind of got the message. Today, many of the hitters in Japan, and in Korea for that matter, definitely have an upswing.

The other major change is on the field. The Japanese now have incorporated the backhand as a standard way of fielding. In 1995 there was a rite of passage for those who entered the professional ranks of baseball in Japan. You had to field one thousand ground balls at one time without leaving the field, and while fielding them if you went to your right, you had to go so hard that you got in front of the ball. That was the way you fielded. When you went to your right, you always got in front of the ball, so the ball hit you in the chest if it didn't go into the glove. But from about 1995, some of the infielders started to incorporate the backhand, and that made a big difference in their range factor and in their ability to throw the ball across the diamond more efficiently.

Those are the two technical things that changed from the first time I got there. The hitting one is rather large and the fielding one is a little more subtle. By incorporating those two changes, the players now look very similar to the professional players in the States.

Another thing that's changed—Japanese baseball now leans toward recovery, not only toward effort. The idea that doing more, and more was better, has changed just a little. When I got to Japan in 1995, to miss a minute of practice while your teammates were practicing, even if you had to go to the bathroom, would be frowned upon. Everyone played all the time, and there was no pitch limit. I instituted a 15 pitch-per-inning goal and a 135-per-game maximum. You would have thought that I was asking families to give away their first-born child! Suggesting that a pitcher should have a limitation on his pitches per inning and per game was unheard of in Japan.

While I was managing there, Masahiro Tanaka pitched twelve innings in the 2006 Koshien final that ended in a tie and then came back the next day and pitched seven innings. I mean, are you kidding me? It was some of the greatest stuff I've ever seen in my life. It was a badge of honor to leave it all out on the field. The idea that you had to come back and do it again the next day wasn't necessarily part of the equation.

A crazy example of this happened in my first year. After a game we lost, I got showered and dressed and then came out, and Hirooka, the general manager, was standing behind the batting cage, and my third baseman was taking batting practice. It's about 11:30 at night. Sweat is pouring off of his chin, and he had just played nine innings. And the pitcher is throwing curveballs. I watched for a while because I figured, well, he needed practice hitting curveballs. And I watched for a little longer. I guess he needed a little *more* practice hitting curveballs. Then, I went over to Hirooka-san and asked, "So how long is he going to be hitting here tonight?"

And he said, "Until he can hit the curveball."

Of course! I thought. There was no consideration that the next day was a day game, and it was going to be 93 degrees, and this guy had to go home, come back, and then play nine more innings.

That has changed. The players are not wearing themselves down as much, and that's why I think the athletes now are bigger and stronger. They have time to recover and build rather than just breaking their bodies down through constant work.

I have to touch on this. Somewhere it should be said, or maybe it shouldn't be said, but it took Japan about twenty years to discourage players from smoking cigarettes. In traditional Japanese baseball culture, that was what you were supposed to do. If you looked at the back of a magazine, all the stars in the ads were smoking. And if they were smoking, you had to smoke. When I first got there in 1995, right behind the dugout there was something like a table with a grid on the top where you put your cigarette out and then just dropped it into this long ashtray. The guys would come in from the field and line up like it was buffet line, eight or nine of them smoking cigarettes. It was crazy! But that has changed as well.

You know that doing the same thing over and over again and expecting different results is insanity, but businesswise the Japanese teams had a way of doing the same thing over and over again and being very satisfied with the same result. So, when I came back in 2005, I was hired to do more than the managing. I was also there to help them transition into more of a Major League–type business, to help them run the club as a standalone business instead of an advertising vehicle for the international company that lends its name to the team.

Akio Shigemitsu, who ran the club, was the son of the owner of Lotte, and he was only part Japanese, so he was seen as an outsider. I think that's what gave him the idea to give Hirooka-san the go ahead to find a foreign manager. Shigemitsu-san wasn't getting the weekly memo from Watanabe-san (the president of the Yomiuri Giants) that everything in Japanese baseball is great and don't try to change a thing until I call and give you the go-ahead. He didn't totally follow the marching orders. All of the interaction we ever had was at these very formal geisha dinners: private room, sitting on the floor, geisha gals pouring your sake, talking about the weather and all the other really important things that we could definitely agree on to make sure there wasn't going to be any confrontation at this social event. But we would also talk about doing things a little differently to make the Marines a better team and business.

When Shigemitsu-san gave me the go-ahead to talk with people about marketing, it was marketing the mascot and the team brand. It was never marketing the players. Japanese baseball, just like Japanese culture, in my opinion, is such a closed culture. They treated baseball as an entertainment vehicle that was closed to the public. There was an idea that players should not interact with the fans. It was as if it would lower your image if you didn't keep a barrier between the players and those who paid to see them play. I think what they wanted was the secretive, aloof, no-contact kind of superstar, the Joe DiMaggio type. But, marketing the player and promoting the player and letting the fans have contact with the player have changed for the better over the years. It's now part of the business side that they're trying to sell, not only the brand but also the talent.

Between-inning entertainment has also become part of the business. The teams always had the mascots, but now there are mascots, cheerleaders, plus other events between innings to entertain fans. Japanese teams have become more cognizant that they need the fans to have the game. At one time, the fans needed the game, so they provided the game. The mentality changed a little so that now the game needs the fans. I think they're getting it now. It's a different ownership situation.

But it was tough to change the marketing. Marketing is one of those weird concepts in Japan. People are supposed to want to buy your product, right? Having to persuade consumers is a newer concept, and baseball is one of the older and more conservative businesses there. For example, I almost needed an act of Congress to allow kids to come on the field after Sunday games and run around the bases.

I'm concerned that NPB will become like the Negro Leagues. I tried to tell players that the good players should stay there and that the medium players should go to the States and make more money. But don't take the stars away from their teams because that's what MLB did to the Negro Leagues. The Negro Leagues were great leagues for their fans. The last Negro World Series was in 1949, two years after Jackie Robinson came to the Dodgers. That's a whole story for another day, right? But that's always my fear, that MLB is going to do that to another great league.

I think a lot has been taken away from NPB because the players want to go where the grass is greener. They need to plant a few new lawns, and the beginning is to get new venues. You can then charge more money for suites and generate revenue from within the business itself rather than from the parent company. Then that money can be reinvested in R&D (research and development) and the minor leagues and in major league salaries and talent.

It looks like NPB is actually moving to do it with the Hokkaido new dome and the plans to renovate Jingu and make that into a spectacular downtown venue. The Giants are going to be forced to do something. Chiba, I hear, is going to spend over a billion dollars to build a new stadium along with Lotte and ZOZO in partnership.

One solution for NPB would be to increase their minor league system and their R&D. The problem with their system has been that they have eighty players in each organization. Thirty of them are basically on the ichi-gun (top team), and fifty of them are in the single ni-gun (minor league) team. The ni-gun manager has to keep sharp the guys who might come up to the big leagues as temporary replacements. Since there's only one team, there is no room to develop young players. Sometimes, players are in the minor leagues for years without playing in a game. But they go to practice every day, five and six hours a day of practice. That's the mentality: keep practicing, and you'll get better. Well, I kept trying to tell them that they need to play to get better. It's a game of playing, not just a game of hitting and throwing. Three of the organizations now have more than one minor league team, so that's a start.

NPB also has to improve their feeder system. When you have four thousand high schools and eighty colleges playing baseball and then you draft only seventy or eighty kids a year, that is not forward thinking. They've got to spend more on developing players because there are a lot of players who fall through the cracks. Japanese kids develop physically later, and basically when they're seventeen, they're being judged whether or not they're going to be a professional player. The feeder system has changed a little bit. It used to be Koshien to contract. Star in high school Koshien, and you get a contract. You're one of the eighty players selected by a team. But now, teams are giving more opportunities for college and even industrial and independent league players to play professionally.

Still, Japan needs to embrace the independent leagues. We have Minor League teams in the States that allow fans who aren't close to a Major League franchise to go out and watch a professional baseball game. In Japan, there are independent league teams in all these little country towns. As in America, these should be seen as the place to go in the community. One could go to a baseball game with your kid and enjoy it and then go home without worrying about catching the last train out of Tokyo to get home. But the independent leagues haven't built up a strong fan base. I was trying to expand the independent leagues when I was there because a stronger independent league system would produce more players for NPB. In 2006 when I was managing the Marines, I scouted independent teams, and I took a kid named Katsuya Kakunaka from an independent team in the draft. After I left, he wound up leading the league in hitting in 2012.

So anyway, that's what I think NPB needs to do. They need to improve their facilities, create more minor league teams and more independent teams, and then they need to get together on what they're doing. I think what they need to do eventually is change the baseball hierarchy. And I think that's already starting to change.

And I think they should at least explore the possibility of having a division of Major League Baseball in Asia—not where teams are traveling back and forth between Asia and the United States, but where the winner of an Asian division enters the playoffs for a true world championship. Now, of course, that would change the model in Japan, and I don't know that change is what they would really like to do. But I think that if baseball wants to expand and continue to grow worldwide, it would be better to merge and grow rather than just have MLB handpick talent and eliminate the competition.

Of course, we have the WBC. But it interrupts the season. I don't think that you're ever going to get the best brand of baseball being played before the season. If it's a true all-star situation, then I think it should be played midseason with everyone taking a break. Or it should be an Olympic sport played during the Winter Olympics. I always thought that would be the sensible thing to do, play the tournament in a dome during the Winter Olympics because it's the off-season.

But you know, after winning the first one, and winning it often, I feel that Japan should get a bigger cut of the pie. I thought that they should have negotiated that from day one, but they didn't. I felt and feel that it could be a big boost economically for the players. Also with the WBC, people will continue to say, "Oh, yeah, Japan only won because they take it more seriously. Japan only won because they practiced more before it started." Well, if they're going to practice more and use better players and be better prepared, which makes it a better event, then they should be rewarded economically for that.

My advice to American fans seeing their first Japanese game? Well, they should understand that the food is going to be better than they've ever had at a baseball park, so order properly: that the kegs are on legs and you're going to get a very cold and foam-filled glass of beer that you absolutely have to have, and that you should pay attention to the game just like everyone else around you, because they won't miss a pitch or an inning regardless of the score or who's at the plate. The Japanese give the game that respect when they're in the stands. There's a better understanding of the game from the fans. It's not necessarily vocalized or transmitted through action. If someone thinks something is good here in the States, they stand up in front of the person behind them and start yelling and waving their hands, regardless of whether the guy behind them can see. It's a little different in Japan. But if you turn to the seventy-year-old woman to your left and ask what the count is, she'll probably know. That should be appreciated.

The Japanese players will look and act in a very similar way, and they do that out of respect for the game. They feel that there's a certain way to dress, a certain way to act when they're on the field, a certain way to swing and miss in a very dramatic fashion. There are little moments of drama in a Japanese game that are kind of unique, but you have to know what you're looking at to actually see them. There's a little bit of Kabuki theater when they have a collision or get hit by a pitch or swing violently and miss or dive for a ball. Also, the idea of the count going full is respected a little more in Japan, that the battle has taken place and now it comes to this crescendo and the outcome will be on the next pitch. That's Japanese baseball in its truest, purest form. The game is built around those moments. That's why they love it.

Appendix A: Tips on Following NPB from Outside of Japan

Before 2020, following Nippon Professional Baseball from outside of Japan was difficult. There were very few opportunities to watch games or even get daily scores and league standings. Thankfully, that has changed. To help readers who live outside of Japan and do not read Japanese keep up with NPB, I have put together this list of resources. Because individually run blogs and podcasts come and go quickly, I am focusing on the more established resources, many of which contain links to blogs, podcasts, and YouTube channels that may not be mentioned in this section.

Watching Games

Currently, the best online venue for watching NPB games is Pacific League TV, a subscription service run by Pacific League Marketing that provides live games and archived games dating back to 2012. As the name suggests, the service only contains games from the Pacific League, along with interleague games held in Pacific League ballparks. Besides the games, the Pacificleague.com website contains thousands of videos, including game highlights, player profiles, news, and feature stories and league and player stats. The website and the games are in Japanese only, but there is an English-language page providing directions on how to join and navigate the site. As discussed below, Pacficleague.com also runs two YouTube channels, one in Japanese and one in English.

Another way to watch NPB games is through subscription services that allow you to stream Japanese cable television. A number of these services are available. One is Nozomi, which provides over eighty Japanese channels, allowing one to watch many Central League games both live and archived for two weeks after the initial broadcast. Programs can also be recorded. If the subscription service offers Fuji TV1, I recommend the nightly television show *Pro Yakyu News*, which airs Tuesday through Sunday at 11:00 p.m.

Japan time. Although the show is in Japanese, it shows game highlights, provides news and commentary, and announces the starting pitchers for the following day.

YouTube

One of the easiest ways to follow NPB is by subscribing to select YouTube channels. There are a number of very good channels focusing on Japanese baseball. One of the best is run by Pacific League Marketing. Pacific League TV Official is a Japanese-language channel that contains over twenty-two thousand videos, including game highlights, player profiles, and much more. Pacific League Marketing also has an English-language channel called Pacific League TV, with nearly two thousand videos. The channel contains highlights, features on top Japanese and foreign players, archived games with English commentary, a podcast, and my favorite: the top-ten plays of the week.

There are two other can't-miss YouTube channels for English-speaking fans. The Gaijin Baseball channel is one of my favorites. It contains about one hundred videos on the history of Japanese baseball. The stories are well researched and often contain compelling narratives with great graphics. This is the best place on the web for a beginner to learn about the history of the game in Japan.

Another great channel is Yakyu Cosmopolitan, which contains close to three hundred English-language videos covering NPB. Video topics include preseason predictions, postseason roundups, This Week in Japanese Baseball news, player profiles, and discussions of hot topics, such as who will be the next NPB player to be posted. There is also a companion Patreon site that contains the videos plus exclusive interviews.

Podcasts

The best place for following NPB in English is the podcast *Japan Baseball Weekly*. Hosts John E. Gibson and Jim Allen have been providing commentary since 2011. These hour-long programs recap the previous week in NPB, contain exclusive interviews with players, and tackle broader topics. Special episodes provide preseason, midseason, and postseason reviews. The episodes are a great way to learn about current star players and provide insight into the Japanese game. Archived episodes are available at Japanesebaseball.com.

Social Media

There are many social-media pages focusing on Japanese baseball on Facebook, Instagram, X, Reddit, Pinterest, and others. As the lifespan of these pages is often fleeting, I will not review specific pages here, with one exception. The r/NPB on Reddit is the most active social media site in English dedicated to NPB, with thirty-one thousand members in 2024. Members post game scores, standings, video highlights, and links to stories on other platforms. It is also a great place to ask questions about the game, learn how to buy tickets, find memorabilia, and read about other topics.

Websites

Japanball.com, the home for the baseball tourism company JapanBall, is packed with information about Japanese baseball. Included are pages featuring each NPB team and stadium, articles on the history of the game and current players, exclusive interviews, current NPB news, game schedules and statistics, and information on their organized tours of Japan. You can also sign up for weekly updates on NPB via email.

Jballallen.com, the personal website of sportswriter and podcaster Jim Allen, contains a blog featuring NPB news and scores, articles on the rules and practices in NPB, and more. Jim also provides a weekly newsletter via email.

The subscription site Robertwhiting.substack.com features weekly articles by the journalist and author of *You Gotta Have Wa*, Robert Whiting.

The official website of Nippon Professional Baseball (npb.jp) currently contains no news or multimedia content but provides useful information, such as schedules, scores, statistics, standings, and links to individual team sites. As of 2024, most of the NPB team sites do not have English-language content, but some have instructions in English on how to purchase tickets.

Japan-baseball.jp, the home page to Japan's national teams, known as Samurai Japan, contains schedules, rosters, scores, and information on all the national baseball teams.

Both npbstats.com and Delta Graphs (1point02.jp) are incredible databases of traditional and sabermetric stats covering the entire history of Japanese professional baseball.

The large English-language baseball site Baseball-Reference.com includes stats from past and current baseball leagues around the world. It is one of the easiest ways to check out current NPB standings and stats.

I cannot resist putting in a link to yakyu-ouen.net; although entirely in Japanese, the fun site contains links to the oendan fight songs for each team's players.

Appendix B: Tips on Collecting Japanese Baseball Cards and Memorabilia

The first Japanese baseball cards date to the late nineteenth century. Whereas early trading cards in the United States were either advertisements or inserted into tobacco products, the first Japanese cards are from a children's game known as *menko*. Menko are cardboard disks with a picture on one side that are used in a flipping game similar to the American practice of flipping baseball cards. These early menko depict generic players and baseball scenes.

The first cards depicting actual named players were postcards. From 1901 to the early 1920s, Japan went through a postcard craze. Thousands of commemorative postcards were produced to mark all sorts of events, including baseball games. Small sets of about a half dozen were issued to commemorate college and high school matches and games with visiting American teams. These sets usually included both action shots and team pictures. This is the only medium in which one can obtain cards of many early Japanese Hall of Famers.

Starting in the mid-1920s, menko and bromides, collectible photographs printed on paper, started to depict star collegiate and even high school players. Several bromide sets feature Americans players, such as Babe Ruth and Lou Gehrig, who came to Japan on postseason barnstorming tours. These menko and bromide sets usually contained fewer than a dozen cards. All such Japanese cards are rare due to the destruction of the country during World War II.

No known baseball card sets were issued in Japan between 1936 to 1946, so there are no known cards of prewar or wartime Japanese professional ball players. The Holy Grail of Japanese baseball cards would be a card of pitcher Eiji Sawamura, who dominated the early years of professional baseball before being killed in the war. Production restarted in late 1946. Despite Japan's postwar economic turmoil, the late 1940s became the heyday of the vintage Japanese baseball card. The period contains the greatest variety of cards and some of the most attractive cards produced on either side of the Pacific. Menko and bromides still dominated the card industry, with about two hundred different menko sets and about one hundred bromide sets having been identified from this period.

In the early 1950s the production of menko dwindled, but bromides remained popular and candy and gum and game issues became widespread. As candy and gum cards were inserted into wrapped sweets, most of these cards were printed on thin paper, making them fragile. As a result, the cards are now uncommon and rarely found in high-grade condition. Two types of game cards became popular during the late 1940s and early 1950s. The first were statistics-based simulation dice games. These game cards usually came in boxed sets that included the rules and playing field but sometimes came in uncut sheets inserted into magazines. The second was a card-matching game called *karuta*. Sets usually came in boxes and were often printed on high quality cardboard. They are among the most attractive Japanese cards.

In 1956 a new type of menko emerged. Often called "tobacco-sized menko" by American collectors, these cards are rectangular, measuring about 1.75 by 3.0 inches, with player photos on the front and various symbols and numbers on the backs. This style dominated the Japanese card industry from 1957 until the cards abruptly stopped after the 1964 season. The earliest tobacco-sized menko were black and white, but soon colorized photos predominated.

To date, over eighty-five tobacco-sized menko sets have been cataloged, and at least a dozen more sets are known to exist. Many of these sets contain approximately forty cards, but some are much larger. These cards were usually packaged in envelopes made of newspaper (one card per pack), and these envelopes would be strung together by running a string through a hole punched through the top of the envelope. These bundles are known as *taba*. About a half dozen cards in each taba would be stamped with the number 1, 2, or 3 on the back. These are known as prize cards. The finder of a prize card could choose an item from a poster-sized display sheet. Third prize was usually a pair of cards, second prize an uncut group of four cards, and first prize an uncut sheet of sixteen or twenty cards. These prizes were often cut into individual cards by children, so hand-cut cards with uneven boarders are common.

Candy and gum cards continued to be produced in the early 1960s. Unlike the candy cards of the early 1950s, these later cards were mostly produced on thick stock.

In 1965 the Yomiuri Giants, under the direction of former batting star Tetsuharu Kawakami, won the first of nine straight Japan Series championships. Although this streak is one of the most famous accomplishments in Japanese baseball history, few baseball cards were issued during this period. The only major set produced during this time was the Kabaya Leaf set issued in 1967. This set of 105 cards was imported to the United States by Mel Bailey and sold through baseball-card newsletters. As a result, although the set is rare, it is more common in the States than in Japan. Because Bailey was not able to purchase equal amounts of each card in the set, there are four very rare and an additional five rare cards.

Baseball cards proliferated from the mid-1970s to the late 1980s. Numerous companies produced sets ranging from 8 to 1,436 cards. Menko were still produced in small quantities but were printed on heavy stock and are thus known as *thick menko*. None, however, dominated the market like Calbee Potato Chip cards. In 1973 Calbee produced its first set of ninety-one cards. A single card was included in each package of Calbee snack food. Since 1973 Calbee has produced at least one baseball set each year. Besides Calbee, other major manufacturers of baseball cards during this period include Yamakatsu, NST, Nippon Ham, Takara, Pino, and IST.

BBM transformed the Japanese baseball card industry in 1991 with their first set of 399 cards. Modeled after modern American cards, the set included most of the active players, along with cards of league leaders and a special subset of all-time great players. Like American cards, BBM cards came in packs of ten and in factory sets. Over the years, BBM has added more annual sets. By 2010 they usually produced a preseason set, a regular set, a premium set, individual sets for each team, sets featuring retired players (known as nostalgic sets), and special-issue sets. Sets now include inserts such as parallel, autographed, and game-used cards. BBM cards are widely collected in both Japan and the United States, and the company is responsible for transforming card collecting in Japan into a large business.

In 2000 Epoch made its debut with a set of NPB stickers, and in 2009 the company started issuing sets featuring retired players. It began producing sets of current NPB players in 2015. Packed with autograph and game-used inserts, Epoch now rivals BBM as the most popular Japanese card manufacturer. In 2021 Topps entered the Japanese market with their first NPB set. Unlike BBM and Epoch, which are available at card shops and bookstores, Topps distributes their packs through convenience stores. NPB Topps sets follow the same design as their MLB sets but so far have not been very popular among Japanese collectors.

Collectors may also be interested in game-used memorabilia and autographs. Vintage game-used items from Japanese professional baseball are rare. Historically, teams owned players' uniforms and would collect them at the end of the season. As a result, few game-worn uniforms made it into collectors' hands. Many of the uniforms on the market today belonged to foreign players who brought them home as souvenirs rather than returning them to the team.

Luckily for collectors, vintage autographs are more common. Japan has a long history of autograph collecting, making it possible to obtain signatures of early-twentieth-century stars. Many autographs come on white cardboard rectangles called *shikishi* that measure about 10.5 by 9.5 inches. Autographs from the late 1940s and early 1950s are also commonly found on bromide cards. Japanese autographs are often difficult to decipher, as many players develop stylized signatures that bear only passing resemblance to printed kanji characters. As printed versions of autograph shikishi and balls have been sold at stadium souvenir shops since the mid-1970s, collectors need to be careful when purchasing these items. As of the date of this publication, no company authenticates vintage Japanese signatures.

There are four important resources for collecting Japanese baseball cards. Gary Engel's *Japanese Baseball Card Checklist and Price Guide: Vintage Edition* is a must for all collectors. This 280-page publication contains checklists for over one thousand sets, as well as useful information such as a list of Japan Hall of Famers, a guide to how to read Japanese names, and a short history of Japanese cards. The current version is available as a fully searchable PDF with color pictures. Dave McNeely's blog, *Japanese Baseball Cards* (http://japanesebaseballcards.blogspot.com), is the best resource for post-1980 Japanese cards. Updated several times a week since 2007, McNeely reviews recent releases, writes features on individual players and their cards, and provides general information about collecting Japanese cards. Two illustrated books cover the history of Japanese cards. The first is my own *An Illustrated Introduction to Japanese Baseball Cards*, with seventy-eight glossy pages featuring pictures of over two hundred cards. The second is the out-of-print *Sayonara Home Run!* by John Gall and Gary Engel. This beautiful 190-page paperback features color photographs of hundreds of vintage cards.

Unlike in the United States where sports-card shops sell both vintage and modern cards, in Japan the vintage and modern card markets are separate. Although many Japanese collect Calbee cards from the 1970s, few people in Japan collect earlier vintage cards. Visitors to Japan are unlikely to find vintage cards, although they can sometimes be found at flea markets and at Biblio, a bookshop in the Jimbocho section of Tokyo. As the primary market for vintage cards is in the United States, the best place to purchase them is eBay. In addition to the many items offered at auction, several sellers specialize in Japanese cards. The most established eBay stores are Prestige Collectibles Auction and my own store Robs Japanese Cards. Prestige Collectibles also holds private auctions several times a year that feature only Japanese cards and memorabilia. More information is available at https://prestigecollectiblesauction.com.

Modern (post-1991) cards are readily available in Japan at sports-card shops and large bookstores, such as Kinokuniya. The sports-card franchise Mint currently has more than twenty-five locations across Japan. Their stores sell graded and ungraded singles, along with sets and unopened boxes and packs. Most stores, however, do not carry older BBM singles or unopened material, as they do not have the space to stock older cards due to the high price of commercial real estate. Modern cards are also readily available on eBay and Amazon.co.jp.

Appendix C: Tips on Attending Games in Japan

If you would like to immerse yourself in Japanese baseball but are hesitant about heading to Japan on your own, the JapanBall tours are the perfect solution. JapanBall currently runs two group tours to Japan, a spring camp tour in February—March and an NPB tour in August—September.[1] The spring tour goes to Okinawa and Miyazaki to visit the training camps and watch preseason games. The NPB tour is broken into several options. One can sign up for just games in Tokyo, games in western Japan, or games in northern Japan, or one can attend all the games and visit all twelve NPB stadiums.

There are several advantages to taking the tours. First and foremost, JapanBall creates a logical itinerary and takes care of the hotels, transportation within Japan, and game tickets. In addition, they usually get better ballpark seats than you can purchase on your own. The tours are led by JapanBall owners and bilingual local guides, so there are people who can answer your questions about Japan, Japanese baseball, and the concessions and help you navigate situations by using their Japanese. Finally, there is the pleasure of traveling and attending games with others who are also fascinated by Japanese baseball. Enduring friendships are often created on the tours, with many participants returning in following years.

If you are going to Japan on your own and want to attend a game, there are several ways of getting tickets. To purchase tickets before your trip, you need to buy them online. Unfortunately, there is not a single site to purchase tickets from all the teams; instead, one needs to visit the teams' individual websites. These are all in Japanese, but with translation tools, one can switch the display into English to see ticket availability and prices. One needs to be aware that some teams release their tickets for the entire season in February, while others release their tickets in six-week blocks throughout the season. Many of the sites will require a Japanese mailing address, but because the tickets will be sent to your email address, you can use any valid Japanese address, such as a hotel you may be planning to stay at.

Once you are in Japan, there are other ways of buying tickets. Some convenience stores contain ATM-like machines where you can buy tickets. Of course, the directions are in Japanese, but store employees might be able to help. At some hotels, the concierge might be able to get you tickets to upcoming games. There are also ticket booths at the stadiums. The availability of tickets on the day of the game depends on the team and the day of the week. The more popular teams, such as the Yomiuri Giants, Hanshin Tigers, and, to a lesser extent, the Hiroshima Carp, rarely have walk-up tickets available, and weekend games tend to sell out across the league; however, tickets for weeknight games for the less-popular teams are often available.

When attending a game, there are a few differences in etiquette compared to American baseball. First, the home team's cheering section is located in the right-field stands, while the visiting-team's cheering section is located in the left-field stands. Fans should avoid wearing the opposing team's gear or cheering for the opposing team when sitting in these areas. In some cases, fans violating this convention might be asked to leave by security. There is also no American-style booing in Japanese baseball. Generally speaking, fans are sympathetic toward the players when they are struggling and respectful of the opposing players. There's even no booing the umpires. Cheering takes the form of group chanting and singing. Individual spontaneous cheering or shouting is rare and often frowned upon.

Fans are welcome to take photographs of the players and performers from their seats or on the concourse, but standing in the aisles is not allowed, nor is going down to the front row to take pictures. If you are obstructing somebody's view by standing or if your equipment is blocking somebody's view, you will probably be asked to put it away. People in Japan can be sensitive about being photographed by strangers. So, taking a picture of somebody without their knowledge is sometimes considered a breach of privacy. If you wish to photograph particular fans, beer girls, or concession sellers, please ask their permission.

Trevor Raichura notes, "Generally speaking, Japanese fans are really happy to have non-Japanese people in the stands. If they speak English, they might want to take a picture with you or talk with you. Interact as much as you can. It's a great experience. I've had nothing but good experiences talking with the Japanese fans."

Information of the farm team's (ni-gun) games can also be found on the teams' websites. These games rarely sell out, so tickets are often available on the day of the game from the stadium box office or online. The atmosphere at the farm games is quite subdued. There's not a lot of singing or organized cheering, so it is often quiet with polite applause when the players do well. The players are more accessible at the farm team games and will occasionally sign autographs.

Some fans may want to attend NPB's spring camps. The camps start on February 1 and usually continue until early March. Seven of the twelve teams hold their camps in Okinawa, while three train in Miyazaki. Two teams split their time between the two locations. During the first week or two, there are no games, as teams focus on training. Fans are welcome to watch the workouts for free. Games start around the second week of February. Many of the games have free admission, but toward the end of spring training some teams charge admission. Tickets are available online, at convenience stores, and at the stadiums' box offices.

If you are in Japan and want to purchase NPB jerseys, hats, or other souvenirs, the best places are the team shops located at the stadiums. At this point, there are no NPB merchandise shops where one can buy items from all teams. Raichura explains, "In Japan, team jerseys and hats are not fashion items like they are in the United States. Instead, they are almost like a costume that you wear to the stadium when you're going to watch a game. You wouldn't wear gear if you were not going to a game. So, if people only buy this stuff to wear it at a game, why would they sell it in a store that's nowhere near a stadium?" These team shops have a vast array of souvenirs from uniforms to towels, to keychains, to prepackaged food with team logos. Most of the team shops, however, carry little to no merchandise from opposing teams. At games, visiting teams will usually sell merchandise just outside stadium entrances. Many teams also have small shops at major department stores in their hometowns, and all the teams have online shops but usually will not ship overseas.

There are a number of baseball-themed museums in Japan that fans might enjoy. The best known is the Japan Hall of Fame and Museum located at Tokyo Dome. The museum contains the Hall of Fame with plaques for all members, an exhibit area, an interactive area, and a library. The permanent exhibits include rooms on the history of Japanese amateur and professional baseball, as well as uniforms and equipment from the current teams. The museum's collection contains about forty thousand items with around two thousand on display. There is also a special exhibition room that hosts four to five different themed exhibitions annually. The institution also sponsors public events.

If you go to the Osaka area, the Museum of Hanshin Koshien Stadium, located next to the stadium, should not be missed. This fabulous museum has two sections, each fascinating. One centers on the history of the Hanshin Tigers and the stadium, while the other focuses on the national high school tournaments held at Koshien Stadium. Both sections have been renovated recently and are packed with artifacts and interesting displays.

There are also player specific museums in Japan. The Sadaharu Oh Baseball Museum is located next to the Fukuoka Dome. This spacious museum depicts the life of Japan's great slugger from his childhood to the present. The beautiful exhibits are full of artifacts, statistical graphics, and multimedia displays. The Hideki Matsui Baseball Museum, a large museum chronicling the life of the great hitter, is located in Nomi, Ishikawa Prefecture, on the western coast of Japan. Walls are packed with awards, equipment, and photos from Matsui's career. The Ichiro Exhibit Room is a more modest museum but does contain over three thousand items covering two stories in a small building near Nagoya Airport. Located in the Yamamoto-dori section of Kobe, the Yu Darvish Museum is full of memorabilia from the pitcher's Japanese and MLB career. Notable are the lifelike statues of the pitcher in various poses and the interactive Yu versus You game, where fans try to hit virtual pitches thrown by the star.

Appendix D: Recommended English-Language Books on NPB

Overviews of Japanese Professional Baseball

Fitts, Robert K. *Remembering Japanese Baseball: An Oral History of the Game.* Carbondale IL: Southern Illinois University Press, 2005.

Kelly, William W. *The Sportsworld of the Hanshin Tigers: Professional Baseball in Modern Japan.* Oakland CA: University of California Press, 2019.

Whiting, Robert. *Chrysanthemum and the Bat: Baseball Samurai Style.* New York: Avon, 1983.

———. *The Samurai Way of Baseball.* New York: Warner Books, 2005.

———. *You Gotta Have Wa.* New York: Macmillan, 1989.

Historical Topics

Fitts, Robert K. *Banzai Babe Ruth: Baseball, Espionage, and Assassination during the 1934 Tour of Japan.* Lincoln: University of Nebraska Press, 2012.

Fitts, Robert K., Bill Nowlin, and James Forr, eds. *Nichibei Yakyu: U.S. Tours of Japan.* Vol. 1, 1907–1958. Phoenix AZ: Society of American Baseball Research, 2022.

———, eds. *Nichibei Yakyu: U.S. Tours of Japan.* Vol. 2, 1960–2019. Phoenix AZ: Society of American Baseball Research, 2023.

Sayama, Kazuo, and Bill Staples Jr. *Gentle Black Giants: A History of Negro Leaguers in Japan.* Fresno CA: Nisei Baseball Research Project, 2019.

Biographies

Altman, George, and Lew Freedman. *George Altman: My Baseball Journey from the Negro League to the Majors and Beyond.* Jefferson NC: McFarland, 2013.

Cromartie, Warren, and Robert Whiting. *Slugging It Out in Japan.* New York: Kodansha, 1991.

Fischman, Aaron. *A Baseball Gaijin: Chasing a Dream to Japan and Back.* New York: Sports Publishing, 2024.

Fitts, Robert K. *Mashi: The Unfulfilled Baseball Dreams of Masanori Murakami, the First Japanese Major Leaguer.* Lincoln: University of Nebraska Press, 2015.

———. *Wally Yonamine: The Man Who Changed Japanese Baseball*. Lincoln: University of Nebraska Press, 2008.

Fletcher, Jeff. *Sho-Time: The Inside Story of Shohei Ohtani and the Greatest Baseball Season Ever Played*. New York: Diversion Books, 2022.

Ijuin, Shizuka. *Hideki Matsui: Sportsmanship, Modesty, and the Art of the Home Run*. New York: Ballatine Books, 2007.

Oh, Sadaharu, and David Falkner. *Sadaharu Oh: A Zen Way of Baseball*. New York: Vintage, 1984.

Snelling, Dennis. *Lefty O'Doul: Baseball's Forgotten Ambassador*. Lincoln: University of Nebraska Press, 2017.

Stanka, Jean, and Joe Stanka. *Coping with Clouters, Culture, and Crisis*. Wilmington DE: Dawn Press, 1987.

Staples, Bill, Jr. *Kenichi Zenimura: Japanese American Baseball Pioneer*. Jefferson NC: McFarland, 2011.

Valentine, Bobby, and Peter Golenback. *Valentine's Way: My Adventurous Life and Times*. Brentwood TN: Permuted Press, 2021.

Baseball Cards

Engel, Gary. *Japanese Baseball Card Checklist and Price Guide: Vintage Edition 3.0*. Santa Clarita CA: Prestige Collectibles, 2022.

Fitts, Robert K. *An Illustrated Introduction to Japanese Baseball Cards*. New York: RobsJapaneseCards.com, 2020.

Gall, John, and Gary Engel. *Sayonara Home Run! The Art of the Japanese Baseball Card*. San Francisco: Chronicle Books, 2006.

Notes

1. Robert Whiting

1. Earlier games had been played in Kobe in 1869, between the crew of the USS Colorado and the Japanese garrison of Osaka Castle in 1871, between the Yeddo Royal Japanese Troupe of acrobats and the Olympic nine in Washington DC in 1871, and between a team of American expats and Imperial College in 1876.

4. Natsuo Yamazaki

1. Seventeen ejections in a single MLB season would be high in the modern era. For example, Mike Estabrook led all MLB umpires with 13 ejections in 2019. But Yamazaki's 17 NPB-leading career ejections are a far cry from Bill Klem's MLB-leading 288 career ejections.

5. Trey Hillman

1. Players had to remain at a particular level for ten days.

14. Ichiro Kitano

1. During the same ten-year period, 2014–2023, sixty-one MLB pitchers underwent Tommy John surgeries. In both 2014 and 2021, eleven pitchers underwent the procedure. Mark Graban, "Analyzing MLB Tommy John Surgeries: Data Insights and Trends from 2000–2024," *Lean Blog*, April 16, 2024, https://www.leanblog.org/2024/04/theres-no-special-cause-of-common-cause-variation-tommy-john-surgeries/#:~:text=Surgeries%20are%20up%20in%20mlb,also%20also%20getting%20better%20milb.

26. Bobby Valentine

1. Masanori Murakami played in the Major Leagues in 1964–65, but his tenure did not lead to other Japanese players coming to the big leagues. Joe Lutz managed the Hiroshima Carp in 1975, and Don Blasingame managed in NPB from 1979 to 1982, but neither had previously managed in the Major Leagues.

Appendix C: Tips on Attending Games in Japan

1. I would like to thank Trevor Raichura for providing much of the information for this section.

Acknowledgments

The idea for this book came in September 2023 while I was on a tour of all twelve Nippon Professional Baseball ballparks run by JapanBall. Since that time, JapanBall's president Shane Barclay has provided invaluable support by introducing me to potential interviewees and resources. During the JapanBall tour, I also met Trevor Raichura, the author of the blog *Hanshin Tigers English News*. Trevor has helped at every stage of the project, acting as my interpreter during interviews, handling correspondence in Japanese, and providing invaluable insight on Japanese baseball. This book could not have been completed without his help. A special thank you goes out to Yoichi Nagata for his continued support. Yoichi was always willing to answer my numerous questions, put me in contact with umpire Natsuo Yamazaki, and accompanied me to the interview with Tomoko Namba.

Many others have offered their support, help, and guidance. George Gmelch, coauthor of *In the Ballpark: The Working Lives of Baseball People*; William Kelly, author of *The Sportsworld of the Hanshin Tigers: Professional Baseball in Modern Japan*; and Marty Kuehnert provided tips on approaching and interviewing club employees. Brad Lefton, Masanori "Max" Ninomiya, Jennie Roloff Rothman, and Robert Whiting answered my numerous questions about Japanese baseball and culture. Jim Allen, Jonathan Greenberg, Roberto Gamoneda, Robert Garratt, Yuri Karasawa, Saya Nomura, Deanna Rubin, R. J. Lara, and Tom Shieber provided insight along the way.

I would also like to thank William Brooks, Jerald Halvorsen, Hiroshi Kitamura, Robert Klevens, Kenju Murakami, and Kaoru Tatsumi for providing introductions to interviewees. I also appreciate the help of Shinya Aoki and Joshua Ryu Bosley of the DeNA BayStars; Kento Fujiwara, Yusuke Morishita, and Maxwell Ratsch of the Hiroshima Carp; and Chen Liang of Mint.

I interviewed twenty-nine people for this book. For a variety of reasons, not all of the interviews were included in the final draft, but I would like to thank all who consented to be interviewed: Jim Allen, Shigeo Araki, Edwin

Dominguez Alvarez, Jonathan Fine, Taylor Foote, Shungo Fukunaga, Trey Hillman, Ken Iwamoto, Kenji Kajita, Shun Kakazu, Yasuro Karibe, Ryozo Kato, Marty Kuehnert, Ichiro Kitano, Matt Murton, Toshihiro Nagata, Tomoko Namba, Tomoki Negishi, Saori Ogure, Takao Ohashi, Jennie Roloff Rothman, Tatsuo Shinke, Masanobu Shoji, Bobby Valentine, Robert Whiting, Natsuo Yamazaki, Noamichi Yokota, and Hiroki Yoshimoto. I would especially like to thank Edwin Dominguez Alvarez, Jonathan Fine, and Ken Iwamoto for introducing me to other interviewees.

Rene Bernard, Carter Cromwell, Jennie Roloff Rothman, and Myrna Watkins read drafts of the book. Their insightful comments and critiques made the book stronger. I would like to thank the staff of the University of Nebraska Press, especially Robert Taylor, who helped me refine my approach; Taylor Martin; Katrina Vassallo; and copyeditor Joseph Webb.

And finally, a special thank you to my wonderful wife, Sarah.

Index

Abe, Shinzo, 200
Africa, 168, 198, 200–201, 212
Allen, Jim, 53–63, 239, 249
Amerikamura, Osaka, 221
analytics, 29, 53–54, 111–13, 117–24, 133, 162, 171, 176, 197, 217
Aoyagi, Koyo, 121
Arai, Takahiro, 208
Arakawa, Hiroshi, 6
Araki, Shigeo, 181–87
Arizona Diamondbacks, 122
Asahi beer, 98, 100, 101, 171
Asahi Evening News, 53
Asahi Shimbun, 4, 53
Asian baseball market, xii, 159, 167, 196, 212, 244
Attic in Kobe, 144

Bailey, Mel, 253
Bamberger, George, 236
ba no kuuki wo yomu, 69
Barclay, Shane, 265
Baseball Magazine Company, 144, 223–24, 226, 230
baseball memorabilia, 23, 222, 223–24, 249, 251–55, 258, 259
Bass, Randy, xix, 143, 147
BBM Card Company, 144, 223–26, 227, 228, 230, 253–54, 255
beer girls. See *uriko* (beer girls)
Belluna Dome, xxiii, 36
Boston Red Sox, 164, 165, 235
Bragan, Bobby, 236

Briggs Stadium, 5
Brisky Bear, 50
Brown, Marty, 150–51
Brown, Mike, 44
Bushido: The Way of the Samurai (Yamamoto), 44
Bushiroad, 231
Buzzer Beater, 221

Calbee, 144, 253, 255
Camden Yards, 172
Campanis, Al, 236
Canadian American Association (Can-Am League), 26
Carp Academy, 170–71, 218
Carp *joshi*, 173
Central League: economics, 182, 192–93, 194; history, xv, xvi, xviii, xxi, xxii, 121, 205, 208; teams, xxiii, 186; umpires, 35; watching games, 247
Charlyze, 112
cheerleaders, 89, 90–97, 107, 242
Chiba Lotte Marines: economics, 161–62, 181–86, 242; fan behavior, 64–65, 71–72; history, xx, 10–11, 20, 47–48, 161–62, 215, 235–36, 237, 244; stadium, xxiii, 182–83, 243
Chicago Cubs, xx, 15, 176
Chiitan, 88
China, 167, 212
Chinatrust Brothers, 213
Chrysanthemum and the Bat (Whiting), xix, 3, 9, 260

/ 267

chuhai, 98, 100, 101, 102
Chunichi Dragons, xxiii, 74, 126–31, 193
cigarette smoking, 16, 22, 241
Cleveland Indians, 43
Climax Series, xv, xxi
Clothing Size Strategy, 182–86
clubhouses, 8, 21, 22, 32, 56, 123–24, 133
COVID-19, xvi, xxi, 31, 35, 36–37, 83, 96, 110, 130, 167, 194
CPBL (Chinese Professional Baseball League), 32, 213
Cromartie, Warren, 44, 260
Cuba, 164–65, 166, 168
Cuban Baseball Federation, 165
Cuban Sports Ministry, 164

daihyo, 146
Daily Yomiuri, 54
Darvish, Yu, xxi, 150, 195, 259
Denbo, Gary, 44
Descente, 143
designated manager system, 183
DiMaggio, Joe, 242
Dominguez Alvarez, Edwin, 213–20
Dominican Republic, 126, 164, 166, 170–71, 212, 214, 215, 218
DTO Sports & Entertainment, 213, 216

ecommerce, 202–4
Eldridge, Brad, 70
Enatsu, Yutaka, 9–10
Engel, Gary, 254, 255, 261
Es Con Field, xxiii, 91–92, 97

fall camp, xvi, 31, 134
fans of Japanese baseball: behavior of, 17, 26, 65–70, 73–80, 86, 87, 89, 99–100, 107–8, 110; demographics of, 71, 190, 198–99
Fighters Girls, 90–96
Fine, Jonathan, 169–77

First Higher School of Tokyo (Ichiko), 3–4
Foote, Taylor, 81–89
foreign players, scouting and signing in Japanese baseball, 163–64, 166, 174–76, 218, 220
Forsyth, Logan, 23
"The Fox (What Does the Fox Say?)," 96
Franzua, Geronimo, 218
Frep, 96
Fukumoto, Yutaka, xix, 144–45
Fukunaga, Shungo, xxi, 25–32
Fukuoka Dome, 259
Fukuoka SoftBank Hawks, xx, xxiii, 11, 63, 110–11, 161, 165–67, 193
Fukuoka Zoo, 142
Fukura, Junichi, 53

gaiya, xxv, 67–68, 69, 71
Gall, John, 255, 261
Gehrig, Lou, xvii, 4, 235, 251
general manager's role in Japan, 145–48, 162, 171
Gerónimo, César, 171
G Hands, 199–200
Gibson, John E., 53, 55, 248
Griffey, Ken Jr., 223
Grinnell College, 105, 110
Gurriel, Yulieski, 164

Hachimura, Rui, 231
Hamamoto, Eisu, 181
hanseikai, 8–9
Hanshin Tigers: economics, 192–93; fans, 99–100, 102, 108; history, xix, xx, xxi, 9, 62, 149, 150; marketing, 23; ni-gun, 27–29; organization, 15–17, 118; stadium, xxiii, 99–100, 259; tickets, 257; use of analytics, 120–21
Hanyu, Yuzuru, 231

INDEX / 269

Harada, Cappy, 141
Hara, Tatsunori, 224
Harper, Bryce, 130
Harry Wendelstedt Umpire School, 35
Haruta, Makoto, 154
Hawk-Eye technology, 121–23, 124
Headley, Chase, 23
Heiwadai Stadium, 142
Hello Kitty, 88
Hideki Matsui Baseball Museum, 259
Hillman, Trey, xx, xxi, 43–50, 134–36, 137
Hirooka, Tatsuro, xix, 235–36, 237, 238–39, 241, 242
Hiroshima Toyo Carp: economics, 172–73, 193; fans, 80, 87, 173; history, xix, xx, 81–82, 119, 127, 169–70, 218, 263n1 (chap. 26); mascot, 82–88, 173–74; oendan, 73–75; organization, 170–71, 173–76; stadium, xxiii, 89, 171–72
Hokkaido, xx, 43, 49–50, 74, 90, 92, 134, 243
Hokkaido University, 33
Hong Kong, 167
Horiuchi, Tsuneo, 209
Hoshino, Senichi, 150–51
House, Tom, 237
Houston Astros, 132, 168
Howard, Frank, 236

Ibata, Hirokazu, 206–7
Ichiba, Yasuhiro, 150
ichi-gun, xvi, xxv, 237, 243
Ichiro Exhibit Room, 259
Ikeda, Ikuo "Ike," 144, 223, 225
An Illustrated Introduction to Japanese Baseball Cards (Fitts), 255
India, 212
Inoue, Naoya, 231
Irabu, Hideki, 237

Ishikawa Prefecture, Japan, 259
Isobe, Koichi, 148
Ito, Tomohito, 122
Iwakuma, Hisashi, 148
Iwamoto, Ken, 132–38
Iwate Prefecture, 137
izakaya, 189

Jackson, Michael, 84
James, Bill, 53
JapanBall, 249, 256, 265
Japan Baseball Weekly, 53, 55, 248
Japanese baseball: baseballs, 18, 36, 208–10; commissioner, 152, 205–11; cultural and national significance of, x, 22, 50; differences in style of play from MLB, 18–20, 26; financial structure, 62–63, 181, 191–93; future of, 50, 62–63, 152, 159–60, 167, 176, 195–96, 211–12, 243–44; labor relations, 207–8, 216–17, 223–24; managers, 20, 31–32, 45–46; merchandise, 155, 171, 173, 190–91, 195, 202–4, 258; pitching strategies, 18–19; small ball concept in, x, 48–49, 68, 214
Japanesebaseball.com, 248
Japanese Baseball League, xv
Japanese media, 22–23, 48, 49, 55–62, 92–93, 97, 133–35, 142–43, 183–84, 187, 189, 192, 194, 236
Japan Hall of Fame and Museum, xviii, 61–62, 251, 254, 258–59
Japan Series, xv, xvii, xix, xx, xxi, 11, 35, 59, 66, 144, 152, 192, 253
Japan Sports Vision, 222–23, 224, 227
Japan Times, 54
Jballallen.com, 55, 249
JET (Japan Exchange and Teaching), 64
Jeter, Derek, 105, 223

JICA (Overseas Cooperation Volunteers), 197–98, 199, 201
Jim Evans Umpire School, 35
J.League, 188, 199, 227
Jobe, Frank, 10
Johnson, Kris, 119
jokamachi, 185
Jordan, Michael, 221, 224, 226
JSV World Premium, 224
Judge, Aaron, 130

Kabaya Leaf set, 253
Kajita, Kenji, 105–13
Kakazu, Shun, 110–11, 161–68
Kako, Junji, 117
Kakunaka, Katsuya, 244
kamizumo, 86
Kaneda, Masaichi, 41
Kaneko, Makoto, 45
Kannai Station, 159
Kansai Independent Baseball League, 25
Karibe, Yasuro, 73–80
karuta, 252
Kashiwada, Takashi, 237
Kato, Ryozo, xxi, 205–12
katsudon, 21, 23
kattobase, 6
kawaii, xxv, 83, 88–89, 173, 190–91, 203
Kawakami, Tetsuharu, xviii, xix, 12, 253
Kawasaki, Munenori, 163
kayui, 4
KBO (Korean Baseball Organization), 213
Keio University xvii, 211
Kimura, Yota, 156
Kinokuniya, 255
Kintetsu Buffaloes, xx, 145, 148
Kirin Beer, 101
kisha club, 61
Kishi, Nobusuke, 142

Kitahiroshima, xxiii, 91
Kitano, Ichiro, 125–31
kitsune, 96
Kobe, xxiii, 16, 17, 144, 145, 230, 259
Komiyama, Satoru, 134
Korakuen Stadium, 5–6
Korea, 43, 50, 133, 159, 167, 168, 212, 213, 240
Koshien Stadium, xvii, xxiii, 4, 17, 22–23, 27, 29, 36, 74, 98–102
Kuehnert, Marty, xx, 140–52, 189, 191
Kumamon, 88
Kuriyama, Hideki, 137–38
Kuroda, Hiroki, 176
Kuroiwa, Akira, 143
kuroko, 86, 87
Kyocera Dome, xxiii
Kyodo News, 52, 54, 60–61
kyujo, 185

Lasorda, Tommy, 236
The Last Samurai (Zwick), 44
Leo, 83
Lewis, Colby, 162
Los Angeles Dodgers, xviii, xix, xx, xxii, 166, 192, 196, 243
Lotte Orions, 41, 75, 153
Lucky 7, 87, 88

madogiwazoku, 146
Maeda, Kenta, 176
Maeda, Tomonori, 224
Mainichi Shimbun, 60
Manuel, Charlie, 125
Marantz, Ken, 54
marketing in Japanese baseball, xi, 23, 49–50, 141–42, 152, 155–56, 171, 173, 181–87, 188–96, 197, 198–99, 202–4, 224–25, 242–43
mascots, xx, 50, 65, 81–89, 96, 107, 141–42, 173–74, 242

Matsuda, Hajime, 81, 170, 173
Matsui, Hideki, xix, xx, 12, 105, 225, 238, 259, 261
Matsunaka, Nobuhiko, 62
Matsuyama, Hideki, 231
Matsuzaka, Daisuke, 12, 143, 224
Mazda Zoom-Zoom Stadium, xxiii, 73, 82–87, 89
McGough, Scott, 122
Meiji Gakuin, 3
Meiji Jingu Stadium, xvii, xxiii, 36, 69, 105, 107–10, 243
menko, 251–53
Mexico, 25, 26, 31–32, 166
Mikitani, Hiroshi, 145, 148, 150
Mint, 221, 226–30, 255
Miyagi Prefecture, 189–90, 193
Mizuno Sporting Goods, 210, 235
Moneyball (Lewis), 117, 161
Mr. Baseball (Schepisi), xix, 16, 44, 236
Mukahari Bay Town, 185
Murakami, Munetaka, xxii, 122, 123
Murakami, Shoki, 102
Murata, Choji, 10
Murton, Matt, xxi, 15–24
Museum of Hanshin Koshien Stadium, 259

Nagashima, Shigeo, xviii, xix, xx, 5, 6, 7, 12, 61–62, 211, 229, 235, 237
Nagata, Toshihiro, 117–24
naiya, xxv, 67
Nakahata, Kiyoshi, 155
Nakajima, Hiroyuki, 163
Nakamura, Nagayoshi, 141, 142, 143
Nakamura, Shogo, 72
Nakanishi, Futoshi, 144
Namba, Tomoko, 70, 153–60
Nankai Hawks, 153
National High School Baseball Championship (Koshien), xv, xvii, 4, 25, 259

National Hiroshima Toyo Carp Private Cheering Federation, 73–74
National Red Carp Union (Higoikai), 74
NBA (National Basketball Association), 88, 97, 174, 221, 222, 224, 226, 229, 231
Negishi, Tom, 188–96
Negro Leagues, xviii, xx, 45, 105, 192, 201–2, 238
New York Mets, xx, 10, 64, 132–34, 136, 234, 237
New York Yankees, xviii, xx, 45, 105, 192, 201–2, 238
Neyer, Rob, 55
NFL (National Football League), 97, 226
NHK (Japanese Broadcasting Corporation), 151, 196
Nichibei, 187, 260
ni-gun (farm team, Japanese minor league team), xvi, xxv, 25, 27–29, 31, 34, 35, 44, 47–48, 70, 111–13, 122, 129, 131, 151, 162, 163, 165–66, 243, 244, 258
Niigata, 153
Nikkan Sports, 33, 34, 54
1934 American League All-Stars tour of Japan, xv, xvii, 4, 235, 260
Nippon Ham Fighters, xx, xxiii, 43–44, 47, 49–50, 90–97, 134–38, 191
Nippon Ham Fighters Dance Academy, 91
Nippon Television, 60
Nishioka, Tsuyoshi, 20, 163
Nishinomiya, xxiii, 20, 163
Nomi, 259
Nomo, Hideo, xix, xx, 10, 12, 227, 236–37, 238
Nomura, Katsuya, 61, 150–51, 235
Nomura, Kenjiro, 171, 224
NPB Amateur Draft, xix, 25, 27, 55, 137, 149–50, 216, 243–44

NPB vs. MLB World Series, 11, 152, 159–60, 166–67, 211, 212, 244

oban-desu, 190
Ochiai, Hiromitsu, 235
oendan, xxii, xxv, 6, 65, 67, 68–69, 71, 73–80, 96, 99–100, 250, 257
Ogure, Saori, 90–97
Oh, Sadaharu, xviii, xix, xx, 5, 6–7, 61, 211, 212, 229, 238, 259, 261
Ohtani, Shohei, xxi, xxii, 11–12, 130, 137–38, 167, 176, 195, 196, 214, 230, 231, 261
Oishi, Daijiro, 53
Okinawa, 15–16, 213, 256, 258
Okoso, Hiroji, 136
Okubo, Hiromoto "Dave," 151
Orix BlueWave, xx, 145, 148
Orix Buffaloes, xx, xxiii, 148, 190
Osuna, José, 123

Pacific League: economics, 63, 146–47, 152, 167, 182, 185–86, 191–96; history, xv, xvi, xviii, xix, xx, xxi, xxii, 53; teams, xxiii; umpires, 35; watching games in, 247, 248
Pacific League Marketing, 152, 181, 185–86, 188, 191–96, 247–48
Pacific League TV, 194, 247–48
Park, Chan Ho, 133–34
Peguero, Francisco, 215
Petagine, Roberto, 149
Pettitte, Andy, 105
Philadelphia Phillies, 125–26
Phillie Phanatic, 82, 107, 173–74
Pikachu, 88
Pittsburgh Pirates, 218
players union, 207–8, 210, 216, 224
Pokémon, 230, 231
Posada, Jorge, 105
Powell, Alonzo, 151

Powerful Professional Baseball (Power Pros), 78
Pro Baseball Owners League, 227
Pro Yakyu News, 247
PSA (Professional Sports Authenticator), 229, 230

Raichura, Trevor, xiii, 147, 257, 258, 263n1 (appendix C)
Rakuten, 145, 150, 191
Rakuten Mobile Park Miyagi, 189–90
Rakuten Monkeys, 31
Rapsodo, 112
Rara-chan, 141–42
Rawlings Sporting Goods, 235
Reddit, 249
Rhodes, Tuffy, xx, 62
Rivera, Mariano, 105
Robinson, Jackie, 243
Rodriguez, Bryan, 215
Rothman, Jennie Roloff, 64–72
Ruth, Babe, xv, xvii, 4, 251, 260
Ryan, Nolan, 237

sabermetrics, 117–19, 249
sacrifice bunting, x, 7, 18, 48–49
Sadaharu Oh Baseball Museum, 259
Saitama, xxiii, xxv, 188
Saitama Seibu Lions, xix, xxiii, 63, 83, 143, 188, 191, 211
Sakamoto, Hayato, 203
Samsung Lions, 213
Samurai Japan, 11, 181, 186–87, 249
San Diego Chicken, 173
San Francisco Giants, 134, 162
Sankei Shimbun, 60
Santana, Domingo, 122
Sapporo Dome, 91
Sasaki, Roki, 10–11
satei tantou, 117–18
Sawamura, Eiji, 251

Sawamura Award, xviii, xix, xxi, xxv, 119
Sayonara Home Run! (Gall and Engel), 255, 261
Scherzer, Max, 11
scouts, 24, 27, 60–61, 111, 117, 118–19, 122, 137, 162–64, 174, 175, 218, 244
Seibu Dome, 43
Selleck, Tom, xix, 236
Sheets, Andy, 149
Shigemitsu, Akio, 242
shikishi, 254
Shikoku Independent Baseball League, 25–26
Shimada, Toshi, 133–34
Shinjo, Tsuyoshi, 133–34
Shinkansen, 87, 89
Shinke, Tatsuo, 221–31
shi no renshu, 5
Shirai, Kazuyuki, 48, 49, 53
shochu, xxv, 100
Shoriki, Matsutaro, xv, 11
Shukan Bunshun, 56
Slugger, 54, 60
Slugging It Out in Japan (Cromartie), 44, 260
Slyly, xx, 81–88, 173–74
South Africa, 198, 200, 201
sports cards, 144–45, 221–31, 251–55
Sports Hochi, 60
Sports Marketing Laboratory, 181, 186
spring camp (Japanese spring training), xv–xvi, 7, 9, 15–17, 36, 44–45, 126–27, 130–31, 175, 214, 256, 258
Stars and Stripes, 53
steroids, 206–7
Suntory Malts, 144
Suzuki, Ichiro, xx, xxi, 12, 16, 163, 223, 238, 259
Suzuki, Keishi, 10
Suzuki, Seiya, 176

taba, 252
taibatsu, 151
Taiheiyo Club Lions, 141–43
Taiwan, 25, 26, 31, 32, 159, 167, 168, 195, 212
Takahashi, Yoshinobu, 149
Takara, 253
Takatsu, Shingo, 123
Tanaka, Kensuke, 49
Tanaka, Masahiro, xxi, 56, 190, 240
Tao, Yasushi, 148, 150
TBS (Tokyo Broadcasting System), 60, 117
team dormitories, 4, 27–28, 90, 170–71
Texas Rangers, 43, 162
Thorn, John, 55
thousand ground ball drill, 7, 9, 130–31, 240
Tobita, Suishu, 5
Tohoku Earthquake, xxi, 207
Tohoku Rakuten Golden Eagles, xx, xxi, xxii, 142, 147–51, 188–91
Tokorozawa, xxiii, 188
Tokushima Indigo Socks, 26, 27, 215
Tokyo Dome, xxiii, 5, 56–57, 62, 123, 198–99, 202, 206, 258–59
Tokyo University, 156, 181, 205
Tokyo Yakult Swallows, xxiii, 60, 65, 89, 106, 107, 108, 117, 121–24, 193
Tommy John surgery, 10, 129–30, 263n1 (chap. 14)
Topps, 231, 254
Torre, Frank, 235
Torre, Joe, 235
Toyama Thunderbirds, 215
Trackman, 29, 111–12, 120–22
trainers, 21, 28, 71, 125–31, 132–33
Trout, Mike, 130
Tsubakuro, 89, 107
Tsubota, Nobuyoshi, 235
Tsuiji, Hatsuhiko, 53

Tsutsugo, Yoshitomo, 65
Tsutsumi, Yoshiaki, 143

Umpires, 20–21, 33–42, 206, 257, 263n1 (chap. 4)
University of Tsukuba, 197
Upper Deck, 221, 223, 224, 226
uriko (beer girls), xi, xxv, 6, 98–104

Valentine, Bobby, xx, 44, 47, 65, 133, 161–62, 181–82, 185, 235–46, 261
Vantelin Dome, xxiii
Venezuela, 218
Verlander, Justin, 11
Vogelsong, Ryan, 162

Wagner, Honus, 144, 239
Waseda University, xvii, 5, 134, 145, 211
Watanabe, Tsuneo, 242
Watanabe, Yuta, 231
WBC (World Baseball Classic), xxi, xxii, 11, 12, 50, 59, 79, 137, 159, 186–87, 208, 211, 229, 245
Weekly Baseball, 223
weight training, 11, 21, 29, 111, 129, 131
Whiting, Robert, xix, 3–12, 44, 249, 260
Williams, Jeff, 118
Wilson, Horace, xv, xvii, 3, 210

yakuza, 206
yakyu, xxv, 68, 205
Yakyu Cosmopolitan, 248
Yamaguchi, Shun, 61
Yamaguchi Zoo, 142
Yamakatsu, 253

Yamamoto, Yoshinobu, xxii, 167, 190, 195
Yamata, Masao, 138
Yamato, Kyushi, 4
Yamazaki, Natsuo, xix, xxi, 33–42, 263n1 (chap. 4)
Ylvis, 96
Yokohama Country and Athletic Club, xv, xvii, 3–4
Yokohama Chinatown, 159
Yokohama DeNA BayStars, xxi, xxiii, 60, 70, 147, 153–60, 163
Yokohama Stadium, xi, xxiii, 70, 72, 155–57, 158–59
Yokohama Stadium Company, 156
Yokota, Noamichi, 197–204
Yomiuri Giants: amateur draft, 149, 150; charity work, 199–202; control of yakuza, 206; control over media, 59–61; economics, 146, 191, 192–93; history, xv, xviii, xix, xx, 5–7, 11, 75, 211, 237, 253; influence over NPB 149, 242; location, xxiii; marketing, 198–99, 202–4; ni-gun, 111–13; and Taiwan, 167; television, 75, 153, 188; tickets, 257; use of analytics, 111–13
Yomiuri Shimbun, 53, 60, 202
Yoshii, Masato, 10–11, 239
Yoshimura, Hiroshi, 54, 136, 138
You Gotta Have Wa (Whiting), xix, 3, 16, 44, 249, 260
Yu Darvish Museum, 259

Zobrist, Ben, 23
ZOZO Marine Stadium, xxiii, 68, 71, 181–83, 185, 243